WITHDRAWN

MELVILLE

AS LECTURER

MELVILLE

AS LECTURER

By

Merton M. Sealts, Jr.

Harvard University Press

Cambridge, Massachusetts

1957

Distributed in Great Britain by
Oxford University Press
London

Publication of this book has been aided by a grant from the
Ford Foundation

Library of Congress Catalog Card Number *58–5542*

Printed in the United States of America

For
Eleanor Melville Metcalf
and
Henry K. Metcalf

PREFACE

Since Willard Thorp's pioneering article on "Herman Melville's Silent Years" appeared in 1937 [1] there has been a steadily growing interest in the latter half of Melville's career—a career which was far from over when *The Confidence-Man* appeared in 1857 as the last of his works of fiction to be published during his lifetime. Some of the new interest has been primarily biographical in character; some has been expressed in works of interpretation and criticism dealing chiefly with Melville's poetry and with his last novel, the posthumous *Billy Budd,* which has recently been adapted both for the drama and for the opera. Among scholarly editions of this material— Melville's literary output between 1856 and 1891—the most recent contribution has been Howard C. Horsford's scrupulous work on the prelude to all these others, the manuscript journal covering Melville's Mediterranean travels in 1856 and 1857. The present volume is concerned with the immediate sequel to this trip, Melville's three seasons as a lecturer between 1857 and 1860, and with the lectures themselves, the bridge between his fiction and his poetry.

"A lecture from the author of 'Typee,'" as the Chicago *Daily Press and Tribune* remarked in 1859, "might properly be set down as a novelty, whether sustaining the reputation of that fascinating work, or otherwise." But though Melville's lecture engagements were widely reported in the press of his day, neither the "novelty" of his lecturing nor its effect on his professional reputation and subsequent career has drawn more than the casual attention of twentieth-century students. Perhaps his biographers, guided by the reprinted texts of a few newspaper reviews, have assumed from this limited testimony

[1] *University Review,* III (Summer 1937), 254–262.

that the lectures, far from "sustaining" his reputation, were so unsuccessful with lyceum audiences that the less said of them to modern readers the better. And since manuscripts of the lectures themselves have apparently not survived, it may be an insufficient knowledge of what Melville actually said on the platform that explains the prevailing neglect of their content. Much spade-work, in short, has remained to be done in uncovering "the whole evidence on Melville as a lecturer" called for by Newton Arvin in 1942.[2] Since Melville himself chose not to print his lectures after abandoning the platform and presumably destroyed their manuscripts following his abortive third season of 1859–60, there is no hope that all the "evidence" can ever be brought together. But by locating every newspaper review that is extant—fifty-four articles in all—it has now become possible for the first time to discuss both the content of the various lectures and their relation in theme and idea to Melville's other writings both earlier and later in time.

Only one brief report of the third lecture, "Traveling," appeared in the contemporary press, but through collation of the various newspaper summaries and verbatim quotation by reviewers of its predecessors a partial reconstruction of both "Statues in Rome" and "The South Seas" has been achieved. Perhaps three-quarters, and possibly even more, of the content of these two lectures is given here in the composite texts, whose language is that of Melville himself as quoted, paraphrased, and summarized by professional reporters. These texts have made possible an examination of the sources, the organization, and something even of the literary style of the lectures. As for Melville's public reception, which is also considered in detail, the evidence of his press notices taken as a whole makes it necessary to modify and correct the tentative conclusions reached by previous scholarship in estimating his success in the lecture field. A study of these reports, incidentally, throws new light

[2] "Toward the Whole Evidence on Melville as a Lecturer," *American Notes and Queries*, II (May 1942), 21–22. Arvin's query stimulated a number of other scholars to locate and reprint additional reports by contemporary newspapers of Melville's lecture engagements.

upon the tastes of popular audiences of the late fifties in America, bringing out significant regional differences in the responses which Melville received during his various tours.

My interest in the lectures, it might be added, goes back to the summer of 1940, when I first examined and transcribed Melville's notebook of lecture engagements, among the manuscript material in the Harvard College Library presented by his granddaughter, Eleanor Melville Metcalf. For use of this and other manuscripts at Harvard authorization has been granted by the Librarian of the Houghton Library, Harvard University. Mrs. Metcalf, Miss Carolyn Jakeman of the Houghton Library, Mr. Jay Leyda, compiler of *The Melville Log*,[3] and Professor Perry Miller of Harvard University have been particularly helpful during the years since 1940 when I have intermittently worked on the lectures. I am also indebted very deeply to the librarians in both the United States and Canada who assisted in collecting information about Melville's lecture engagements; their names are individually recorded elsewhere in this volume.

For further reference by other students of Melville and his lectures, copies of the newspaper source materials assembled in the course of this study have been deposited in the Houghton Library. Introductory notes to the composite texts of the lectures as printed in this volume indicate their relation to these materials. A survey of all scholarly and critical work dealing with the lectures which has been published to date is embodied in the chapters which follow and in the annotation which accompanies the reconstructed texts.

M. M. S.

Lawrence College
Appleton, Wisconsin
September 1956

---

[3] Frequently referred to throughout this study, *The Melville Log* (2 vols., New York, 1951) is cited hereafter simply as *Log*.

CONTENTS

PART I

MELVILLE
AS LECTURER

I

"A Good, Earnest Subject"

Statues in Rome

Late in May of 1857 Herman Melville returned to the United States from a winter of travel abroad. His trip, underwritten by his father-in-law, Chief Justice Lemuel Shaw of Massachusetts, had been intended to relieve him from overtaxing literary work and thereby to restore his flagging health and depressed spirits. Going first to England, where he renewed his friendship with Nathaniel Hawthorne, Melville had continued by steamer to Constantinople and visited Egypt, Palestine, Greece, and Italy, returning to England by way of Germany and Holland and sailing from Liverpool for America. When he reached Boston, feeling better for the trip though still not perfectly well, he had decided, as he told Lemuel Shaw, Jr., that he was "not going to write any more at present." [1] *The Confidence-Man,* his latest book, had received little notice since its publication in England and at home during his absence, and its predecessor, *Piazza Tales,* in print for a year, had not sold enough copies to make its expenses. His American publishers at this period, the New York firm of Dix and Edwards, dissolved in the month before Melville's return, and their magazine, *Putnam's Monthly,* to which he had contributed, lost its identity in passing into new

[1] Lemuel Shaw, Jr., to Samuel Shaw, 2 June 1857, as quoted in Leyda, *Log,* II, 580. Unless otherwise indicated, the biographical data and the quotations from correspondence given here are documented in Leyda's assembly of day-to-day records of Melville's career.

hands. These changes during the hard times of 1857 meant the end of Melville's principal source of professional income, limited though it had been, during the past four years. While he was still abroad, meanwhile, his relatives and friends were already busy, as at earlier turning-points in his career, trying to find some government appointment that would permanently free him from the burdens of professional writing. Melville himself, who according to the younger Shaw was hopeful of "a place in the N. Y. Custom House," advertised his Pittsfield farm for sale in June of 1857, but the property remained unsold and the government job failed to materialize.

Had Melville intended to resume literary work when his health was further improved, he was by no means without further opportunities. He could again have contributed to *Harper's New Monthly Magazine,* which along with *Putnam's* had been printing some of the short stories and sketches he had turned out between 1853 and 1856. In the summer of 1857 he received and accepted an invitation to write for the *Atlantic Monthly,* then being established in Boston, but declined as he did so to "name the day when I shall have any article ready." The reason for his caution was scarcely a lack of material, since during his Mediterranean trip he had kept an extensive journal, including specific notes for such compositions as a possible sequel to *The Confidence-Man* and perhaps a series of travel sketches, either in prose or a new medium, verse. But the fate of his recent books and the condition of the literary market in 1857 made a full-length work a poor risk at that time, while the state of Melville's health, his disinclination to write, and the wishes of his family all argued against a return to the drudgery of magazine work. What then could be done with the new material gathered abroad so as to yield a profit on this accumulated literary capital?

Another possibility, one related to authorship but seemingly less taxing and wearisome than continued desk work, may have occurred to Melville either during his absence or shortly thereafter. If he were to turn lecturer and undertake a lecture tour, which would require writing only one composition that could be used throughout an entire season, he could make profitable use of his experiences in the Mediterranean, escape from another winter of confinement to Pittsfield, and possibly lay the foundation—if the experiment proved successful—for a new and financially rewarding career. But of course there were arguments against turning lecturer. Melville had rehearsed some of them in writing *Pierre* (1852), in which the hero "most conscientiously and respectfully declined all polite overtures" from the lecture committees of "Lyceums, Young Men's Associations, and other Literary and Scientific Societies" in "various quarters of the land." So Melville himself, after the success of *Typee* in 1846, had in fact refused more than one unsolicited invitation of the same kind. But then he was young and vigorous, busy with plans for his approaching marriage, and confident that his projected sequel to *Typee* would sell widely; now he was an author well past the peak of his fame, responsible for the support of a wife and four children, and in dubious health. The section of *Pierre* devoted to lecture invitations, particularly the sample letter from "Zadockprattsville," [2] leaves little doubt of his low valuation of those who managed and sustained the lyceum movement in his day, and there is not much likelihood that he had materially changed his opinion five years later. Yet the subject of lecturing was under discussion soon after his return from abroad: it arose, for example, at a dinner in Boston which he attended on 27 May 1857. The host was the younger Lemuel Shaw; among the guests were Melville's friend Richard Henry Dana, his summer neighbor Dr. Oliver Wendell Holmes, and his cousin Henry Gansevoort, who left an account of the occasion in his diary. During the conversation—at whose prompting Gansevoort did not

---

[2] See *Pierre*, ed. Henry A. Murray (New York, 1949), p. 296. Melville presumably had in mind the company town of Prattsville, New York, founded by the paternalistic Zadock Pratt (1790–1871) as the home of what was to become the world's largest tannery. On Melville's invitations to lecture in 1846, see *Log*, I, 229, 232, 233.

make clear—Holmes offered his private definition of a lecturer: "a literary strumpet subject for a greater than whore's fee to prostitute himself." Apparently none of the company contradicted Holmes, who like many of his literary contemporaries was himself adding to his audience, his fame, and especially to his bank account by just such "prostitution." By the summer of 1857 Melville too, in spite of his similar reservations but with no other employment in sight, was preparing for a lecture tour of his own.

This time, however, there were no unsolicited invitations to be counted on at the outset, nor was there a lecture bureau to take charge of advertisements, bookings, and miscellaneous arrangements. For advice and for practical assistance in securing engagements Melville turned to George William Curtis, with whom he and his brother Allan had been corresponding in regard to the affairs of Dix and Edwards.[3] Since Curtis had published his *Nile Notes of a Howadji* (1851), a travel book as popular in its day as *Typee,* he had been well received as a lecturer; Melville evidently hoped to profit by both his example and his experience on the platform. To Allan Melville in a letter of 10 September 1857 Curtis noted that Herman "thinks well of lecturing, and wants to be hung for the whole sheep, and go the entire swine"—the animal metaphors, whether originating with Curtis or with Melville, hint that the would-be lecturer viewed himself in the role of a victim awaiting slaughter. By 15 September, as Melville himself wrote to Curtis, he was actively "trying to scratch my brains for a Lecture" and seeking "a good, earnest subject." In his next letter, dated 26 September, he mentioned his receipt and acceptance of "two or three" invitations "prompted by" Curtis, probably including those from New Haven, Connecticut; Auburn, New York; and Cleveland, Ohio; where both men spoke during the season which followed. Thus by late September Melville had

---

[3] The letters cited in this paragraph are quoted in *Log,* II, 582, except for that of Melville to Curtis dated 26 September 1857 (Harvard College Library).

presumably chosen his topic and was working to prepare a manuscript for the edification of Zadockprattsville. The spirit in which he was writing is suggested by the example he offered Curtis of a subject to suit the prevailing taste of the times: *"Daily progress of man towards a state of intellectual & moral perfection, as evidenced in history of 5ᵗʰ Avenue & 5 Points."* His actual topic, surprising at first in view of these words to Curtis, was "Statues in Rome," and in the course of his discussion he did indeed manage to deal in his own way with the popular notion of man's "daily progress."

Melville's decision to lecture on Roman statuary is bound up with the fact that his visit to Rome had gratified one of his long-standing desires. A great disappointment of his previous European trip in 1849 had been that negotiations with his English publishers failed to yield enough money to take him as far as Italy. When he finally arrived in Rome during his more recent travels he at first felt an unexpected disappointment: "Whether it is having come from the East, or chafed mood, or what," he confessed in his journal, "Rome fell flat on me. Oppressively flat." But during his extended stay of nearly a month, from 25 February 1857 until 21 March, it was the "stunning" effect of Roman museums and ruins that counteracted his unfavorable first impression. Records of what he was seeing are included in the day-to-day entries in his journal, which vary in tone from bare matter-of-fact notations to full, frank expressions of his own state of mind or his pleasure in seeing some building or statue. At the end of the journal, moreover, there are several pages of notes, some of them on the city, which may have been jotted down during his visit there as the first draft of a future magazine sketch or even a lecture.[4] One item

---

[4] The journal entries which Melville drew upon for various passages of the lecture are quoted in the explanatory notes to the reconstructed text of "Statues in Rome" printed below in Part II. Unless otherwise indicated, quotation throughout the present volume is from the manuscript of the journal (Harvard College Library), although citation by date should facilitate comparison with the two printed versions: *Journal up the Straits,* ed. Raymond Weaver (New York, 1935), and *Journal of a Visit to Europe and the Levant,* ed. Howard C. Horsford (Princeton, 1955). No

calls for an elaboration of his description of the Coliseum, which he had seen on 26 February and written about under that date. A passage in the lecture is clearly the direct outgrowth of this preliminary hint to "restore" the Coliseum in imagination and "repeople it with all statues in Vatican." Whatever he may at first have intended to write about Rome, the notion of "repeopling" the Coliseum was probably the very nucleus around which "Statues in Rome" ultimately took form. The passage in the lecture describing the Coliseum is an elaborate set-piece—a "word-painting" of the imagined climax of a gladitorial combat—that comes closer to real drama than anything else in the entire composition. Its mixture of emotion and fine writing evidently had a special appeal to the lecturegoers of the time, for no other part of the lecture attracted more notice from newspaper critics.

Having decided to lecture on Rome and to discuss both the Coliseum and the statues of the Vatican, Melville hit upon a simple way of organizing material selected from various passages of the journal to round out his essay. First comes a brief introduction emphasizing the universal appeal of beauty to men of all classes, making an Emersonian distinction between the beauty of art and the beauty of nature and asserting the claims of a sincere lover of the beautiful to speak of both in his own right. Such is Melville's justification for proceeding to discuss Roman statuary despite his lack of professional training as artist or critic. Then in the body of the lecture he seeks to lead his audience through the gates of Rome into the twin worlds of art and the ancient past, thus adapting the familiar structural pattern of a journey through space that is found in most of his writing. After taking his visitors through the Vatican Museum he guides them back into the city for a panoramic view of its monuments, and finally he conducts them into the villas beyond its walls. His descriptions of statues to be seen

attempt is made here to duplicate Mr. Horsford's detailed annotation of the journal entries, since his indispensable commentary will of course be consulted directly by those interested in Melville's response to Roman art and to the Italian scene.

along the route are arranged so as to emphasize in turn the appearance of men of the ancient world, the ideals and attitudes of the Romans, and finally the quality of their lives as indicated both by their customs and by their works of sculpture and architecture. His conclusion, based on the connection between art and its social context already established, contrasts the modern attitude toward art with that of the ancients, who realized its importance to the welfare of society as the moderns do not.

Such is the general outline of the lecture. In composing it Melville probably turned for reference to one or more of the standard guidebooks on Italy, but his principal dependence was clearly upon his own journal.[5] A comparison between journal and lecture shows how he concentrated and simplified his presentation. In his discussion of portrait busts, for example, he speaks of the several which he describes as though all but that of Nero were in the Vatican; the journal, however, reveals that he had examined some of them in the Capitoline

[5] Most of Melville's journal entries were written shortly after he had visited the places which they describe, although in a few instances he was obliged to write up in one general review the events of several days past. In so doing he very likely referred to one or more contemporary guidebooks which he used during his travels. Before leaving for Europe on his previous visit of 1849, when he had vainly hoped to include Rome in his tour, Melville is known to have borrowed guidebooks for central and northern Italy from his friend George Duyckinck. These were probably current editions of the standard "Handbooks for Travellers" published by John Murray of London, who himself presented Melville with two additional guidebooks in November of 1849, after the latter had called at the publisher's office. In planning his Mediterranean excursion seven years later Melville may have again borrowed the Italian guidebooks from Duyckinck or bought later editions; his purchase in Florence of "Valery's" *Historical, Literary, and Artistical Travels in Italy, A Complete and Methodical Guide for Travellers and Artists* (Paris, 1852) suggests that until he reached that city he perhaps lacked a guidebook of his own in which he could make annotations and comments. (This volume, possibly the "hand book" mentioned in his journal entry for 26 March 1857 during his stay in Florence, is now in the Osborne Collection of the New York Public Library.) Since Melville may have used any of these compilations, as well as his own journal, to refresh and enrich his memory while writing "Statues in Rome," the notes to the reconstructed text also record passages from the various guidebooks which correspond most closely to the content or phrasing of the lecture.

Museum at Rome and others at Naples. And though he had
visited several Roman villas, it is the Villa Albani which he
singles out as representative in writing the lecture. This free
handling of materials makes one of the variant titles found in
newspaper reports, "Roman Statuary," more strictly accurate
than the form "Statues in Rome" which seems to have been
Melville's own choice.[6]

Apart from what Melville remembered directly of his visit
to Italy, the journal is thus the primary "source" of "Statues in
Rome." It should not be forgotten, however, that what he had
seen and responded to while abroad was conditioned both by
the particular circumstances and spirit of his Mediterranean
travels and also by the persistence of established attitudes and
tastes already embodied in his earlier writing. The trip itself,
a pilgrimage to the ruins of ancient civilizations, was at the
same time a flight from the evils of nineteenth-century society
pointed out again and again in his various books from the
earliest to the most recent—from *Typee* through *The Confidence-Man*. His general knowledge of the ancient world had
grown out of his wide private reading since the beginning of
his career as a professional writer rather than through his limited formal education; his interest in Rome and its art, however, can be traced back to his juvenile writings. Two of the
statues discussed in the lecture, the Apollo Belvedere and the
Venus de Medici, are mentioned in the first of his "Fragments
from a Writing Desk," published in 1839. In that early sketch
he was following a fashion popularized by one of the principal
literary begetters of the "Fragments," *Childe Harold's Pilgrimage,* the last quarter of which is largely given over to a roman-
ticized survey of Italian art and architecture as seen through
the eyes of Byron's pilgrim-hero. Throughout Melville's subsequent writing, colored as it was by his abiding fondness for
the Byronic sensibility, there are repeated allusions to these
same statues and to others also described in *Childe Harold,*

[6] And which is used in the reconstructed text. On the variant titles,
see the headnote to the lecture text in Part II.

such as the Dying Gladiator and the Laocoön, which likewise reappear in "Statues in Rome." As for the various portrait busts mentioned in the lecture, Melville's attitudes toward the historical figures whom they represent had been influenced by his familiarity with the translated writings of four of them —Demosthenes, Julius Caesar, Seneca, and Plato—and by his intimate knowledge of other classical authors, notably Plutarch, Tacitus, and Cicero. From a long discussion incorporated in *The Confidence-Man* it may be inferred that before leaving for the Mediterranean Melville had been rereading "unmatchable Tacitus," as he had called him in *Redburn* (1849), and from a later passage in *Clarel* (1876) his indebtedness to Cicero's comments on the decline of Roman religion is unmistakable.

The book that of all others may have brought to a focus the miscellaneous knowledge of Roman life and times which Melville acquired from such authors is Gibbon's *Decline and Fall of the Roman Empire,* which naturally came to his mind during his stay in Italy. When he had gone to "Gibbon's Church," Santa Maria di Aracoeli, in Rome, as his journal records for 8 March 1857, the subject of "Gibbon's meditations—Christianity" was already involved with his own impressions of Rome and its past. From "The Age of the Antonines," a later poem which Melville acknowledged to be based on Gibbon's book, it is clear that he was strongly inclined to agree with the historian's famous pronouncement that "the condition of the human race was most happy and prosperous" during the relatively stable Antonine period. Even before writing the lecture he had made disparaging remarks in various works concerning man's supposed advance toward perfection during the modern era—"Adam's alleged advance," in his own words; the proposal to lecture on man's "daily progress," as he had put it to Curtis, was merely the latest in a long series of ironic comments on the same subject. The conviction about the respective merits of ancient and modern civilizations which was to find expression in "The Age of the Antonines" underlies

"Statues in Rome" and gives it a characteristic tone linking the lecture with much of Melville's late writing, which is typically concerned with the heritage of the past rather than being descriptive of the present.

Also in "Statues in Rome" there is evidence that the reforming spirit which had animated the passages of social criticism in *Typee, Omoo, Redburn,* and *White-Jacket* was still alive in Melville, though the lecture is a less obvious example of his old penchant for lay-preaching than these earlier works. Not only had he, by 1857, become a partisan in the war between ancients and moderns but he was fighting as well an immediate battle to defend art and the artist against what he considered the encroachments of nineteenth-century science and practicality. Though he was careful to reserve a forthright statement of his fundamental position until his concluding remarks, he suggested it even at the outset of his lecture. The theme of its introduction is derived from a double allusion to Burns and Linnaeus, which sets up the contrast between artist and scientist that is resumed near its close. Burns as the artist, he affirms, can both "comprehend" and "describe" aspects of reality to which the scientific Linnaeus is blind—or in other words, as Melville implies through his image of the daisy, a scientist classifies the flower as a specimen while a poet perceives its organic relation to man. The antithesis between mechanical science and organic art suggested in Melville's figure is characteristic of his thinking. By the time he had written *Mardi* (1849) he had arrived empirically at an organic interpretation of art that is comparable to the theories of other nineteenth-century writers such as Wordsworth and Carlyle or Emerson and Whitman. Toward contemporary science, however, he was far less hospitable than were his two countrymen, and in later years his attitude was to grow increasingly hostile as science came to play an ever-larger part in the life of the time. The advancement of science as manifested in contemporary technology thus contributed in a negative way to Melville's rejection of modern "progress."

A glance at some representative Melvillian pronouncements on the subjects of science and art will serve to confirm these generalizations, to develop the point of view which the lecture itself exemplifies, and to place it in relation to the other works, both earlier and later, in which he addresses the same subjects. Melville, sharing with the romantic temperaments of his day a strong bias toward the emotions, "the heart," was appalled by such "heartlessness . . . of a purely scientific origin" as he had exposed in the naval surgeon of *White-Jacket* (1850). In *Pierre* (1852), taking to task those empirical scientists with "mere watch-maker's brains," he had implied that such men are only extraordinarily skilled mechanics, possessing no heart at all, rather than fully developed human beings. The scientist of this sort lacks not only the warmth but also the deep comprehensiveness which Melville associated with the true creative artist, in whom the heart must be at least as active as the head. Though science, as he saw it, has indeed added to the breadth of man's knowledge, its scope is nevertheless limited by the conditions inherent in a purely logical and rational methodology. This criticism Melville was to develop further in his later years. Even scientific instruments, as he wrote in a prefatory epistle to *John Marr* in 1888, are merely "inventions for sharpening and extending our natural sight, thus enabling mortals (as I once heard an eccentric put it) liberally to enlarge the field of our original and essential ignorance." In contrast to the scientist and his limitations of temper and method is the creative artist, immersed in the emotional, imaginative life of man that is foreign to the scientist as he appeared to Melville. The artist's sphere of investigation transcends the field of scientific effort just as Burns' tribute to the daisy transcends the flat description of Linnaeus. Both begin with the same basic material, provided by the world of everyday experience—"a skeleton of actual reality," Melville had called it in discussing with Hawthorne the handling of a projected story. But what the naturalist would classify as a specimen the artist will proceed "to build about with fulness and veins and beauty," developing imaginatively a new organic creation with an independent life of its own. The work he produces, infused with the imaginative vision of its creator, may exhibit to men "even . . . more reality, than real life itself can show." So Melville had affirmed in *The Confidence-Man* with particular reference to the work of the novelist, adding that the art of fiction "should present another world, and yet one to which we feel the tie."

In "Statues in Rome" the same line of reasoning is applied to the work of the sculptor, beginning with the level of purely realistic portraiture. "Here," Melville explains, "we find many deficiencies of the historian supplied by the sculptor, who has effected, in part, for the celebrities of old what the memoir-writer of the present day does for the modern ones, for to the sculptor belongs a task which was considered beneath the dignity of the historian." Since these portraits are so closely and deliberately bound to the ambiguous world of everyday experience, their appearance "is often deceptive, and a true knowledge of their character is lost unless they are closely scrutinized." Melville himself, a keen observer of the actual world and personally relishing the lifelike qualities of the portrait busts, proceeds with considerable gusto to elucidate the characters treated, using contemporary parallels to drive home his points. He then passes on to consider by contrast the idealized figure of the Apollo, an old favorite of a different order altogether, which in his words "gives a kind of visible response to that class of human aspirations of beauty and perfection that, according to Faith, cannot be truly gratified except in another world." Here are the two principal categories of representational art as he conceived them, the realistic and the idealized, though for Melville there was no polar opposition involved. For the distinctions are those not of kind but of degree, with the idealized type exhibiting, through its deeper penetration and broader comprehensiveness, still "more reality" than either "real life itself" or primarily realistic art "can show." So the Apollo, greater than the portrait busts, "gives the perfect" rather than the actual; "the Venus equally shows the beautiful"; "the Laocoön represents the tragic side of humanity and is the symbol of human misfortune." "Half its significance," he observes of the Laocoön, comes "from its symbolism—the fable that it represents; otherwise it would be no more than Paul Potter's 'Bear Hunt' at Amsterdam."

By such comparisons Melville intended no denigration of the portrait busts or "The Bear-Hunt," a huge genre painting of a type he had long enjoyed in much the same spirit—"Wonderful picture," he had in fact written of the painting in his journal after seeing it in Amsterdam. But such art treats solely of this world, and ever since *Mardi,* composed nearly a decade before the lecture, he had been increasingly drawn toward representation of that intangible other world which he had called there "the world of mind," a realm that transcends everyday reality yet is "one to which we feel the tie." In his own subsequent fiction he had sought to link the two worlds through the artistic tie of symbolism. But though from symbolism comes half its significance, as he says here of the Laocoön, the other half comes from its grounding in realistic observation of the here and now like that of the genre painter and the portrait sculptor. "Romantic as his mind in its deepest reaches was," Newton Arvin has well written of Melville, "it had always had, like most powerful minds, the other bias too, the bias toward 'facts,' toward materiality, toward the unromantic impermeability of things." [7] In the lecture as in Melville's previous writings this foundation in realism, though frequently transcended, is never abandoned; in his later prose it was in fact to reassert itself even more markedly than here.

Although Melville's pronouncements upon the merits of individual works of sculpture are in keeping with the prevailing taste of his time, what is more interesting to the student is that

[7] Newton Arvin, *Herman Melville* (New York, 1950), p. 263. Compare F. O. Matthiessen's observation in *American Renaissance* (New York, 1941), p. 353, that Melville's "lack of aesthetic sophistication, like Hawthorne's, seems to have left him distressed by most art's want of fidelity to basic nature."

the reasons which he assigns or implies for his preferences within other art forms are so directly related to his own practice in fiction: a firm grounding in realism and a strong concurrent tendency to "spiritualize" the actual world by means of symbolic representation of some ideal conception or "fable." For him it was only the artist-thinkers—the "thought-divers," he had once called them—who penetrate to that mysterious ideal world that for all men of a transcendentalist persuasion lies above, beneath, or beyond the world of appearances. Only such men, in his view, can rightfully claim either to "comprehend" reality or, through works of imagination, to depict it adequately. Among their number he had now placed those "visionaries and dreamers" among the ancients who embodied their conceptions of perfection in idealized statuary. At the conclusion of the lecture he sharply contrasts their role in the world of the past with the diminishing significance, as he saw it, of the modern artist in the life of his own times. "The ancients of the ideal description," he continues, "instead of trying to turn their impracticable chimeras, as does the modern dreamer, into social and political prodigies, deposited them in great works of art, which still live . . . bequeathing to posterity not shameful defects but triumphant successes." But in the modern world, with its uncritical, self-justifying faith in "progress," the tendency is to overvalue practical science and technology at the expense of art, to exalt the new for the sake of its very novelty regardless of its soundness or unsoundness. If the Vatican is "the index of the ancient world," that of the modern, Melville holds, is the Washington Patent Office! And as for soundness and endurance, his contrasting examples are Rome's Coliseum and London's glass-enclosed Crystal Palace.

Thus Melville, believing with Emerson that

> Things are in the saddle,
> And ride mankind,

was troubled lest "law for thing" had indeed run wild and might "the man unking." In *Clarel,* which was to be the major literary outgrowth of his Mediterranean travels, two of the characters comment on the same issues as seen from the perspective of a later decade of the century. Ungar, an embittered Southern veteran of 1861–1865, takes an extreme view of the prospect touched upon at the end of "Statues in Rome." His fear is that a "civic barbarism" will result from the modern "glut of all material arts"; he envisions

> Man disennobled—brutalized
> By popular science—atheized
> Into a smatterer. . . .

His attitude toward what he terms the "impieties of 'Progress' " is clearly reminiscent of Melville's own as voiced in 1857, though his prevailing tone in expressing it is not typical of the poem as a whole. Through other speakers, notably Rolfe, Melville takes up the theme of science and art where he had left it in concluding "Statues in Rome." There, as we have seen, he insisted that since "science is beneath art," a civilization which boasts "of our progress, of our energy, of our scientific achievements," is mistaken in thereby claiming its superiority over the ancients when it remains unable either to produce art of its own or to value properly the art of the past. In *Clarel* he recapitulates his earlier argument in pointing out that modern man, in his view, is threatened with the gradual starvation of his imaginative life. Though humanity cannot live by its reason alone, the nineteenth-century world persists in exalting the scientist, the technician, while ignoring the artist, whose work appeals to the emotions while science, which "lights but cannot warm," leaves the feelings untouched. What science offers is not a vertical sounding of the reality underlying appearances but only a purely lateral expansion of accumulated data concerning material fact. These opinions, so clearly echoing the words both of Melville's own earlier writings and also of his embattled humanist contemporaries facing what seemed the belligerent encroachments of the scientist, are expressed in the poem chiefly by Rolfe, whose outlook aptly summarizes Melville's own position:

> Canst feel elate
> While all the depths of Being moan,
> Though luminous on every hand,
> The breadths of shallow knowledge more expand?
> Much as a lightship keeper pines
> Mid shoals immense, where dreary shines
> His lamp, we toss beneath the ray
> Of Science' beacon. This to trim
> Is now man's barren office.

Such was Melville's remarkably consistent thinking, from *Mardi* to *Clarel,* on the nature of art, its relation to science, and the social implications of its neglect. By expressing his views in 1857 through the medium of a lecture on "Statues in Rome" he was risking the further disapproval of those contemporary critics who already deplored the supposedly transcendental tendencies of his more recent writing. His cousin Henry Gansevoort was one of several relatives who shared this view. Writing to his father on 23 November 1857 young Gansevoort, then a student at Harvard, set forth his reservations concerning Melville's handling of the announced subject of his new lecture: "He is able to treat this finely if he will follow 'crassa Minerva,' but if he aims at metaphysical disquisitions he will surely fail. His forte is narration or description [,] in other words a wild, bold word painting—When he essays philosophy he seeks to ascend by waxen wings from his proper sphere only to find his mind dazzled [,] his wings melted and his fall mortifying. . . ." Leon Howard, the only modern critic to consider the place of "Statues in Rome" in Melville's intellectual development, partly shares Gansevoort's reservations. Though regarding the subject as "not an altogether happy one for a man whose forte was taletelling rather than criticism," Howard nevertheless finds the lecture "a significant revelation" of Melville's attempt, at this turning-point of his career, "to order his thoughts on art."

He was still struggling with the problem of the relationship between art and myth which had excited his imagination as he wrote up his journal after his visit to the Pyramids, but he had not yet solved or wholly clarified it. Furthermore, he knew that such notions would have little appeal to a lyceum audience, and most of his manuscript was devoted to gossipy comment on his personal experiences and his impressions of what "these statues confessed, and, as it were, prattled" of matters . . . not recorded in history.

The lecture platform, in fact, was probably the worst place Melville could have found from which to develop his ideas of art. For his primary impulse was toward the sort of criticism which would develop some philosophical theory of art and its relation to the problem of knowledge and the history of mankind. But the seekers after culture who could be expected to pay to see the man who had seen the statuary of Rome wanted commentary and other prattle. His lecture wavered between his impulse to please himself and his desire to please his audiences, and it did little to satisfy his mind at a time when he needed to think deeply—and perhaps suffer some of the creative turmoil which his family dreaded—if he wanted to profit intellectually from his trip.[8]

Except that most of the lecture was in fact *not* "devoted to gossipy comment on his personal experiences"—to the regret, it will be seen, of several contemporary reviewers, Melville's approach to his new venture was very much as Howard has described it. His old conflict between what he felt most moved to write and what he thought would pay was still unresolved, and once again, as "Statues in Rome" reveals when "closely scrutinized," he was to screen his deepest thoughts behind a seemingly impersonal and yet lurkingly ironic manner. It is too much to conclude that writing the lecture failed to contribute to the growth of Melville's ideas, both on art and on society; it would be fairer to say that it assisted materially in their ordering and shaping. To what degree "Statues in Rome" satisfied his own mind it is impossible to know, but the response of his various audiences is another matter, one that can be discussed with some assurance by turning to the reviews of his first lecture season.

[8] Leon Howard, *Herman Melville: A Biography* (Berkeley and Los Angeles, 1951), pp. 257–258.

2

Melville's First Lecture Season

1857–58

THE story of Melville's reception as a lecturer begins in the autumn of 1857, before the opening of his first lecture season, with the disclosure that he was available for engagements. Since the first professional lecture bureau in the United States was not organized until 1868, the individual lecturer was still obliged, throughout the 1850's, to secure bookings as best he could, depending upon newspaper announcements, the good offices of friends, relatives, and literary colleagues, and if possible the stimulus of favorable reviews to spread the word among local lecture committees. "It is said that several of the American writers who were at that time popular in the lecture field, Mr. Curtis among them, helped to start [Melville] in his first course by referring to him in their own lectures before country audiences." So declared Arthur Stedman in 1891,[1] writing after Melville's death out of some personal knowledge of his older friend's career; his mention of George William Curtis' assistance is confirmed by the Melville-Curtis correspondence previously cited. Few of the letters which Melville himself exchanged with local committees have been preserved, but from tentative entries made in his notebook of "Lecture Engagements 1857–8–9–1860"[2] it appears that negotiations

[1] "'Marquesan' Melville . . . ," New York *World,* 11 October 1891, p. 26.

[2] See the accompanying plates. Extracts from the notebook, among the Melville papers in the Harvard College Library, have previously been given

for appearances in eighteen cities were in progress during the fall and early winter of 1857–58. Satisfactory arrangements were concluded in all but four instances, and in addition two more engagements in other cities were later arranged, so that by the end of the season Melville had made a total of sixteen appearances in all.

His initial performance, on 23 November 1857, was a benefit reading of "Statues in Rome" for the Lawrence, Massachusetts, Provident Association. It seems probable that John C. Hoadley, Melville's brother-in-law and a resident of Lawrence, was responsible for this engagement; he is known to have sought at least one later booking for Melville. Although advance publicity was meager and the crowd was not large, the proceeds were "over thirty dollars." A torrential rain on the day of the lecture "detained many from attending," according to the triweekly Lawrence *Courier* in its issue of 25 November, containing the only review of Melville's appearance in any of the local papers of which files are extant.[3] The *Courier's* article includes nearly every point of praise and blame to be found in the entire series of newspaper reviews dealing with Melville's first season of lecturing. The lecturer, "baffled" like many other visiting speakers by the poor acoustics of Lawrence's City Hall, had spoken "so low in general, as to be heard with difficulty except by those on the front seats," but his program was "a delightful entertainment" if one could hear it! Melville, described as "warm hearted and gifted," had treated

in Raymond Weaver, *Herman Melville: Mariner and Mystic* (New York, 1921), pp. 369–370; in Meade Minnigerode, *Some Personal Letters of Herman Melville and a Bibliography* (New York, 1922), pp. 189–190; and more recently in Leyda, *Log,* Vol. II, *passim.* The transcriptions by Weaver and Minnigerode are not altogether accurate, and should be used with caution.

3 Local newspaper material concerning Melville's engagements in Lawrence and in Concord, New Hampshire, is collected in Francis V. Lloyd, Jr., "Melville's First Lectures," *American Literature,* XIII (January 1942), 391–395, the basis for this portion of the present discussion. As Lloyd remarks, there are no known files of the Lawrence *Reporter* and *Sunday Sun,* and files of the *American* and *Sentinel* are incomplete for this period. Most of the Lawrence *Courier's* review is reprinted in *Log,* II, 584.

his subject with "keen insight, honest independence, bold originality, and great justness of vision." His style was "nervous
and vigorous, yet easy and flowing, and falling constantly into
the most melodious cadences; it can only be said in dispraise
that it was perhaps too highly wrought, and too uniformly excellent." The reviewer, though finding this "a fault easily par-
doned in these days of slip shod, newspaper, stump speech and
small talk writing," was constrained to hint that what Melville had written was not altogether appropriate for the occasion: it bore "the stamp of the polished essay, to be enjoyed by
the scholar in the seclusion of his study, [rather] than of the
Lyceum Lecture" intended primarily to entertain; "yet there
were many expressions eminently *lecturesque*" woven into its
content. Similar remarks, including complaints of Melville's
failure to make himself clearly heard and reservations about
the suitability of his material, are frequent in the later reviews.
It should be noticed, however, that the article, which is by no
means unfavorable, is highly complimentary to the literary
qualities of Melville's presentation.

On 24 November, the day after his appearance in Lawrence, Melville repeated his lecture in Concord, New Hampshire, but as none of the three weekly newspapers published
in Concord customarily reviewed lectures, there is no record
of his reception there. From advertisements and advance notices in two of the papers—the third carried neither—it is
learned that Melville spoke in Phenix Hall under auspices of
the Pennacook Lyceum; one of them, the *Patriot* of 18 November, had awarded him "the reputation of being an interesting
lecturer" even before he had first taken the platform.[4] The
Concord lecture, according to the complete list of his fees
which Melville kept in his notebook, yielded $30, and his next
engagement, when he appeared in Boston for the Mercantile
Library Association on 2 December, was for a fee of $40. The
Boston invitation may have been extended to him at the

4 Lloyd, "Melville's First Lectures," p. 394.

prompting of his wife's relatives, the Shaws, or possibly through Curtis, who delivered the next lecture of the same course on 9 December.

According to the Boston *Daily Evening Bee* of 3 December, Melville's appearance "last evening at Tremont Temple" was "the novelty of the lecture room this week." As "a gentleman of decided position in American literature, and the author of several unquestionably original and eccentric works" who had "recently taken to the lecture field," he had evidently attracted the curious: "his appearance in our city was looked upon as an 'event' ranging up to a 'sensation' point. Accordingly a large and distinguished character-dotted audience was present." The review in the *Bee* continues with a brief summary of the lecture identical, except for some omissions, to that in the *Daily Courier.* The *Bee's* account concludes with the observation that though the lecture was "quite able, and delivered with considerable enthusiasm," it "excited but little applause. It was, however, listened to with complimentary attention, though extended beyond the time usually devoted to these lectures." Few critical comments on Melville or his reception appear in the other Boston reviews. The *Evening Transcript* reported that "a large audience listened with evident satisfaction" to the lecture, but according to the *Evening Traveller* the attendance "was not so large as on the two previous evenings" of the course. To the *Transcript* Melville "proved himself as much at home in the lecture-room as in prosecuting his peculiar vocation" as a "pleasant bookmaker," and there was "but one defect about the evening's entertainment—the subject was too vast for an hour's consideration"; the *Traveller,* observing that "Mr. Melville spoke in a clear and distinct voice," agreed that "it was a most interesting lecture, though too long by one fifth, covering an hour and a quarter." The *Daily Journal* reported the program as "quite interesting to those of artistic tastes," but suggested that "the larger part of the audience would have preferred something more modern and personal."

Extensive summaries of Melville's remarks appeared in the *Bee, Courier, Journal, Traveller,* and *Post,*[5] and from two of these accounts, those in the *Courier* and *Traveller,* his cousin Henry Gansevoort borrowed phrases for a synopsis of his own which he transmitted to his father in a letter of 9 December devoted almost entirely to the lecture. "The audience," according to Gansevoort's independent observation, "was large and respectable. The hall however is badly planned for acoustics and consequently the speakers [*sic*] voice imperfectly reached its remoter parts." But though Melville had again, as in Lawrence, failed to make himself heard by all in the audience, he nevertheless "spoke with animation and effect." The lecture itself impressed Gansevoort as a "well conceived and executed" composition, but to him it seemed to lack "the force and beauty that characterise [Melville's] early writings." And though he had been "much pleased" with his cousin's performance, Gansevoort nevertheless concluded that in attempting to deal with ancient statuary Melville was out of his proper sphere: if he had only "treated a subject with which his name is connected and in which he would be more at home he would have done better. 'The South Seas,' 'Oceanica' or a thousand different subjects would have been preferable." [6]

From Boston Melville proceeded to Montreal, where he lectured on 10 December before the local Mercantile Library Association for a fee of $50. That his subject was a timely one for a Montreal audience is suggested by an item in the Montreal *Commercial Advertiser* of the same day calling attention to the evening's program:

[5] Clippings of five of the six Boston reviews discussed here are among the Melville papers in the Harvard College Library; the *Daily Advertiser* did not cover the lecture. The article in the *Journal* is reprinted in Weaver, *Herman Melville,* pp. 371–372, and excerpts from other accounts are given in *Log,* II, 585–586. Miss Jean Simonds of the Boston Athenaeum and Messrs. Richard G. Hensley, Frank P. Bruno, and Louis Polishook of the Boston Public Library have checked files of the Boston papers for items concerning this engagement.

[6] Gansevoort's letter was first printed in V. H. Paltsits, ed., *Family Correspondence of Herman Melville, 1830–1904, in the Gansevoort-Lansing Collection* (New York Public Library, 1929), pp. 14–16.

As a man may go over to Rome without being converted, no one need feel any compunction in going over to Rome to-night, with Mr. Herman Melville at Mechanics' Hall, when with the magnificent panorama of portions of the Ancient City passing before him, he will stand as one standing on Roman ground, and touch as it were, the very edifices which have so long been sacred to imagination. We shall see St. Peter's with its fountains and colon[n]ade, such as the Roman Catholic Bishop of Montreal proposes to erect for his cathedral. Pictures so admirably painted as those of this Panorama, and a lecture from the celebrated author of "Typee," and all for one ticket, is an entertainment, to enjoy which, ordinary engagements should be set aside.

Whether the *Advertiser* was as pleased with the lecture as with the panorama is unknown, however, as its next two issues have not been located.[7] Copies of the Montreal *Herald* for this period also are lacking, and the file of the Montreal *Gazette* for 1857 was later destroyed by fire. Although no reviews of the lecture have been brought to light, there is an interesting oblique reference to Melville and his reception in the Montreal *Witness* for 19 December, under "LECTURES":

A lady remarked, a short time since, that it was an insult to a Montreal audience to invite it to listen to the lecture on New England Humour; and so we may say, it was an insult to a Christian audience to invite to lecture before it, a man who has libelled Christian Missionaries, and shown himself to be an enemy to Christian Missions. A Society which aims to meet the wants of an intelligent people, ought to know something of the lecturers it invites, and be careful not to ask a man whose antecedents and whose teachings must make him far from acceptable to a Christian audience. The loose ideas of religion held by the denomination which is so largely represented in the present course of lectures before the Mercantile Library Association, and which ideas some of the lecturers cannot keep to themselves, make their lectures undesirable, not to say dangerous, for young men.[8]

7 A file of this paper is maintained in the Library of Congress, whose Serials Division, through Mr. Clyde S. Edwards, Chief, supplied the foregoing quotation.

8 Miss Grace Hamlyn of the Redpath Library, McGill University, located and transcribed this comment and supplied information concerning the file of the *Gazette*. Mr. L. Marchand of the Bibliothèque Saint-

This is the only newspaper item during Melville's first season which specifically recalls his sharp criticisms of some aspects of the missionary movement in *Typee* and *Omoo,* the two books almost invariably mentioned in the publicity given his local appearances. It is possible, however, that in circles strongly sympathetic to the missionary enterprise, where his name was evidently still notorious, there may have been an adverse effect upon his reception as a lecturer. During his second season, when he returned to the subject of missionaries in a passage of "The South Seas," a reviewer in Yonkers, New York, revived the issue once more, but apart from these two instances the question of Melville and the missionaries was not a factor in newspaper discussion of his public reception, however much or little it may have meant to his potential audiences.

Following his engagement in Montreal, Melville spent the Christmas holidays in Gansevoort, New York, with his mother and his sister Augusta. While at Gansevoort he was requested, evidently on very short notice, to repeat his lecture in Saratoga Springs, only eleven miles away, where he appeared without fee on 21 December. A brief but favorable account appeared in the *Daily Saratogian* three days later:

Herman Melville, the author of "Omoo," "Typee," and other popular works, delivered a lecture at St. Nicholas Hall, in this village, on Monday evening last. Only a single day's notice was given, and the audience was therefore quite small, but decidedly select in its literary appreciation. The subject "Statues in Rome" was handled by Mr. M. in a style at once graceful and instructive, and the effort was exceedingly creditable to his learning, taste, and ability as a writer.[9]

Sulpice, Montreal, has checked that library's incomplete file of the *Herald,* and Miss Margery W. Trenholme of the Fraser Institute, Montreal, has searched the files of other Montreal newspapers in the Institute's collection, but no further references to Melville's lecture have been located.

[9] *Daily Saratogian,* 24 December 1857, p. 3, col. 1. Mr. Mason Tolman of the New York State Library at Albany, who located and transcribed this notice, advises that the Library's file of the weekly *Saratoga County Press* lacks the issue immediately following the lecture, which may also have contained a review. No other file of the paper has been located.

Leaving Gansevoort on 28 December, Melville stopped in Albany to see his uncle, Peter Gansevoort, and to call at the studio of an Albany sculptor, Erastus Dow Palmer—perhaps in connection with the subject matter of his lecture. At one time he had scheduled a tentative engagement in Malden, Massachusetts, for 28 December, but this date, entered in his notebook with a question mark and later lined out, had meanwhile been canceled and a notation made to resume negotiations in January.[10]

From Albany he continued to New Haven, where he had been invited by the local Young Men's Institute to present the fifth lecture of its course in the College Street Church on 30 December (fee $50). Before his arrival in New Haven his subject was announced in the *Journal and Courier* by brief advertisements and particularly by an editorial, "Mr. Herman Melville and His Lecture," on the day of his appearance.[11] The editorial discussion was occasioned by strong public reaction to some of Melville's controversial predecessors on the local platform. But his subject, " 'Roman Statuary,' is purely artistic," the writer was at pains to point out, "and of course can arouse no jealous solicitude in regard to any possible connection between it and questions of current politics, or the vexed

[10] "Call on A. D. Lamson—70 State st. after 1st Jan—see note"; on another page, that listing his receipts for the season, Melville added "Malden" following the notation of his New Bedford engagement of 23 February 1858, but later lined out the tentative entry. Leyda, *Log*, II, 585, suggests that it was to Lamson that Melville had written in a letter lacking indication of the addressee dated Boston, 27 November 1857, saying that he would be unable to undertake a lecture in December "and must therefore regret that our negotiation must, for this season at least, fall through." (Other possible recipients may have been members of lecture committees in Wilmington, Delaware; Syracuse, New York; and Rockford, Illinois, cities also listed in tentative entries in Melville's notebook.) Attention was first called to the letter, now in the British Museum, by T. O. Mabbott in *Notes and Queries*, CLXXVI (28 January 1939), 60.

[11] Reprinted in A. S. P., "Toward the Whole Evidence on Melville as a Lecturer," *American Notes and Queries*, II (October 1942), 111–112, and quoted in part in *Log*, II, 588. As A. S. P. points out, the *Columbian Weekly Register* carried neither an announcement nor a review. Miss Doris E. Cook of the Connecticut State Library advises that the *Daily Palladium* printed brief advance notices in its issues of 28 and 30 December but did not report the lecture.

questions of theological dispute." Here if anywhere the issue of
Melville's supposed hostility toward the missionary movement
might again have been raised, but in his appearance the editorial writer evidently sensed no danger to the citizens of New
Haven or the young men of Yale College. No review of the
lecture appeared in the press, but perhaps "the New Haven
papers, as was customary in many other newspapers of the
same period, did not ordinarily report lectures." [12] Melville was
later mentioned, however, among the "principal" lecturers of
the series sponsored by the Young Men's Institute,[13] so that his
reception there would seem to have been a favorable one.

In early January of 1858, after a holiday stopover in Albany,
Melville set out on the western leg of his tour. His first appearance of the new year was in Auburn, New York, on
5 January (fee $40, plus hotel expenses), where he spoke in
Corning Hall under the auspices of the local Young Men's
Association. The Auburn *Daily Advertiser* of 2 January, identifying him as "the popular author of Typee and Omoo," observed that "this is the first winter of Mr. Melville's lectures,
and his reputation as a lecturer is not fully known.—The bril-
liancy and fascination of his published writings lead us to anticipate a splendid lecture." According to a brief notice in the
Daily American of 6 January Melville drew "a very large and
attentive audience. The production was one worthy of his tal-
ents and reputation, but not a very popular one." The *Advertiser* of that day also mentioned "a large and highly appreciative audience," evaluating the lecture as "by far the most
chaste and classic of the season," the product of "a finely cul-

---

[12] Francis V. Lloyd, Jr., "Toward the Whole Evidence on Melville as
a Lecturer," *American Notes and Queries,* III (June 1943), 40–41. This
article challenged the earlier suggestion of A. S. P. that Melville's New
Haven lecture was withdrawn.

[13] William A. Borden, *An Historical Sketch of the New Haven Young
Men's Institute* [New Haven, 1904], p. 10. Borden was Librarian of the
Institute; both Melville and G. W. Curtis are included in his "short list
of some of the principal lecturers," twenty in all. Tyrus Hillway, "A Note
on Melville's Lecture in New Haven," *Modern Language Notes,* LX (January 1945), 55–57, first called attention to Borden's reference to Melville.

tivated and highly appreciative mind." After commenting on
various passages the *Advertiser* sums up its verdict as follows:

We think that the most fastidious mind must concede that the
lecture, as a complete whole, as an appreciation of art and the
masterly productions of genius, as a racy and rich descriptive
lecture, as abounding in apt classic allusions, was an entire success. The lecture, however, did not probably please twenty in the
audience, and for this the lecturer himself is entirely to blame.

Our cotemporary, the American, was good enough to inform
us, in a little bit of reminiscence, that Mr. Melville once belonged
to a debating club, in connection with the editor [William J.
Moses], which, however, became defunct on a member's failing
to render a correct definition of the term *"philo logos*[.]" [14] It is
to be regretted that Mr. Melville's connection with this distinguished society, and his intimate terms with his equally distinguished associates, most signally failed to improve his elocution.

The lecture was completely, absolutely spoiled by his inexcusable blundering, sing-song, monotonous delivery. It was the most
complete case of infanticide we ever heard of; he literally stran-
gled his own child. The words came through his moustache about
as loud and with as much force as the creaking of a field mouse
through a thick hedge. Finely formed and well rounded sentences
were articulated so feebly that they died long before they reached
a twelfth part of his audience, and beautiful poetical quotations
fell still-born from his lips. It is inexcusable to come before an
audience with an elocution that fails to make his subject, if not

---

[14] Moses, publisher of the *American* from its founding in 1855 until
its sale in 1861, was born in Dover, New Hampshire, in 1822; he came
to Auburn in 1845 to take charge of printing a Methodist church paper
then published in the city and was active in church and civic affairs there
until the end of his life, also becoming prominent in Democratic politics.
According to an obituary notice in a paper he subsequently founded, the
Auburn *Bulletin*, 5 July 1895, p. 4, Moses "secured a good elementary
education" in the schools of Dover, but "at an early age he left school" in
order to support his widowed mother and his sister, "and was employed
in the office of the Dover Gazette, where he learned the printers' trade
which was the beginning of his career." From his "little bit of reminiscence" as given in the *Advertiser* it appears that Moses had spent some
time in or near Albany before settling in Auburn; the "debating club" referred to was the Philo Logos Society of Albany, of which Melville was
elected president in February, 1838. For details of the newspaper controversy over the club's affairs in which Melville became embroiled at the
time see William H. Gilman, *Melville's Early Life and "Redburn"* (New
York, 1951), pp. 90–96, 251–263.

interesting, at least understood. The same lecture in the hands of a Chapin, a Bethune, or Beecher, would have been considered brilliant and fascinating.—As it is, however, it must be placed among the "lost arts." [15]

Melville himself may possibly have seen this stinging comment while still in Auburn; for according to the *American* of 6 January he "visited the Prison this morning, and left town this afternoon for Ithaca, where he will lecture to-morrow evening." The next evening he spoke before "a large audience" at the town hall in Ithaca (fee $50), where a brief notice in the local *Journal and Advertiser* of 13 January—the single Ithaca review—observed that "Mr. Melville gave a very highly finished as well as critical description of the statues at Rome, Florence, etc." Although the reviewer went on to praise his "fine, quick, perceptive imagination, and . . . rare appreciation of the beauties of statuary," he also remarked that such a subject "must, from the necessity of the case, be an unattractive one to the masses, who claim, with the lecturer himself, not to be students of art and connoisseurs of beauty in its difficult departments." [16] In short, Melville had written a brilliant essay, as the Auburn critic had also acknowledged, but he had chosen a subject which he could neither treat professionally

[15] The items in the *Daily American* and *Daily Advertiser* were located by Mr. John Savage of the Cornell University Library; no notices or reviews were carried in either the *Weekly American* or the *Northern Independent*. Mr. Savage has also searched the manuscript collections in the Cornell University Library and the Cornell University Regional History Collection for possible Melville correspondence and other material relating to the two Young Men's Associations of Auburn and Ithaca, New York, but without finding additional information on the engagements there. Melville's own memoranda in his lecture engagement book include this note: "(Expences [*sic*] at Auburn hotel paid by [Young Men's] Ass[ocia]tion].)" According to local advertisements he was to be followed at Auburn by John G. Saxe, Wendell Phillips, Rev. M. B. Anderson, G. W. Curtis, and Rev. E. H. Chapin.

[16] Charles Duffy, "Toward the Whole Evidence on Melville as a Lecturer," *American Notes and Queries,* II (July 1942), 58, reprints the notice from the *Journal and Advertiser;* an excerpt appears in *Log,* II, 588. A search of the other Ithaca newspapers of the day—the *American Citizen* and the *Tompkins County Democrat*—by Mr. John Savage has disclosed no additional local notices or reviews.

nor expect a popular audience to enjoy. If he had read this de-
layed review as well as the devastating comments on his delivery given in the Auburn *Advertiser,* he might well have experienced forebodings concerning his future reception as he
continued westward to Cleveland and on to Detroit.

Melville's appearance in Cleveland on 11 January, when he
spoke in Melodeon Hall for the Cleveland Library Association
(fee $50), had occasioned very flattering advance notices in
local newspapers of that same day. The *Morning Leader,* identifying him as the "talented and distinguished author of *Omoo,
Typee, Mardi,* and *Maybe Dick* [sic]," observed that "the genius of the man, as well as the interest of the subject, justify
us [in] expecting something fine," supporting its praise of his
"graphic powers" by a three-paragraph summary of his lecture
quoted from the Boston *Daily Courier* of 3 December [17]—possibly not an inducement to a large attendance. The *Evening
Herald,* mentioning the same four works, was sure that Melville's readers "will want to see the genius who created these
singular productions. . . . The Melodeon should, and doubtless will, be crowded to hear the lecture by such a man on such
a subject." The program, however, "did not attract a large audience," according to a brief paragraph in the *Plain Dealer* of
12 January, "but those who listened to it were generally, we
believe, very well satisfied." The *Herald* agreed that "there
was not a very good house . . . partly from the effect of the
forbidding weather, and partly from the competing attractions
of the Opera" (an elaborate home-talent production of *Alessandro Stradello* by the German Glee Club), but compli-
mented the lecturer for treating his subject "in a masterly manner." The *Morning Leader,* in the longest and most favorable
of the Cleveland newspaper notices, reported that the program

was listened to with apparent interest by a very fair audience,
and was, to us at least, one of the most interesting of the season.
The fact that we, Western people, have not got sufficiently beyond the influence of the prevailing *practicality* of pioneer society,

[17] Incorrectly attributed, in the article itself, to the Boston *Advertiser.*

and are therefore, to a great extent, destitute of that cultivation of nature and taste necessary to a fine and general appreciation of Art, will undoubtedly account for the fact that the hall was not crowded to its utmost capacity, as it should have been, by the announcement of the subject . . . in connection with the name of Melville. . . .

We . . . listened to Melville's lecture with an interest equally keen, though of a different kind, to that with which we conned the criticisms of a Reynolds or Fuseli . . . for the actual significance which the triumphs of ancient Art would assume to a mind, untrammeled by the mannerisms of the schools, yet keenly alive to the beautiful . . . seemed . . . something worth becoming acquainted with. Such a nature is Melville's, and . . . we felt grateful to him for the evidence which his lecture gave us, that the divinity of Art is not a thing of education . . . but is inherent and immortal as the spirit of beauty itself. Nothing we ever read or heard said has [s]o nearly touched the fine lines with which ideality has clothed the masterpieces of the ancients . . . and we hope such lectures, upon such subjects, will become more frequent. We want something to liberate us from the iron slavery of railroad speculation, money panics, and the tyranny of the almighty dollar generally; and there is no influence more likely to accomplish that end than a cultivation of a love for true Art.[18]

Obviously colored by the sensibility of the reviewer himself, and reflecting his low opinion of contemporary "Western" culture, this article nevertheless alludes to a situation that had to be faced by any lecturer of the day in search of a popular reputation. Several critics in New England and New York had already observed that Melville's subject, however well-treated, lacked appeal to "the masses," but never before had a newspaper article so frankly deplored not the lecturer's choice of his topic but the state of public taste in a "practical" age.[19] The

[18] Excerpts from the reviews in the *Morning Leader* and *Evening Herald* are given in George Kummer, "Herman Melville and the Ohio Press," *Ohio State Archæological and Historical Quarterly*, XLV (January 1936), 34, and in *Log*, II, 589. Miss Emilia E. Wefel of the Cleveland Public Library located the advance notices in the same papers and the brief review in the *Plain Dealer*.

[19] David Mead, *Yankee Eloquence in the Middle West: The Ohio Lyceum, 1850–1870* (East Lansing, Michigan, 1951), discussing the vogue of practical and scientific lectures in the years 1857–1860, finds that in

friendly attitude of the *Leader's* critic, toward Melville himself and also toward his subject, points up his one unfavorable comment, with which the review concludes. Melville, he notes, "stands gracefully and steady, uses little gesture, and speaks well, were it not for a slight indistinctness in articulation, owing, we thought, to the mustache, spoiling the outline of the words as it does a pen-and-ink sketch to draw a camel's hair brush over it while wet." The *Herald,* which had also praised the content of Melville's lecture though in less enthusiastic language than that of the *Leader,* credited him with "a musical voice, and a very correct delivery," but felt that "a subdued tone and general want of animation prevents his being a popular lecturer." According to the Cincinnati reviews of a few weeks later, which were to include similar observations on Melville's voice and manner, "a Western audience" expected a less formal and a more animated way of speaking than was prevalent in the eastern states. Melville's difficulty, according to this line of analysis, lay not in his material so much as in its manner of delivery from the platform: "The same essay," the *Herald* continued, "read by him in a parlor as from the pages of a book, would give far greater satisfaction than . . . when delivered under the guise of a popular lecture. We repeat our axiom—good writers do not make good lecturers." But a fourth Cleveland reviewer, reporting for the *Ohio Farmer* of 23 January, found Melville's "hazy-lazy air" fascinating: the "dreamy beauty" of his utterances, "suggestive of the balmy atmosphere of the South Pacific," produced "an intoxication, as of opium or profuse odors," that " 'lapped us in Elysean pleasures.' " Stylistically the lecture, to this reporter, was "very good; superior, in that respect, to nine-tenths of the lectures usually delivered" and noteworthy for its "beautiful sentiments, felicitous diction, and exquisite choice of terms. . . . So far as the lec-

---

Ohio the "market for Eastern lecturers was considerably curtailed in the late 1850's" (p. 195), citing hard times and "increasing complaints against the inutility of the cultural lecture" (p. 198). Melville might thus have fared better in Ohio had he spoken there a few years earlier than 1858.

ture was confined to the limits of the title, it was masterly and
without offense. . . . We could have sat for hours witnessing
this skillful and appreciative master of ceremonies taking the
robes from the printed pages of Tacitus and putting them
upon the lifeless marbles of the Vatican, and there breathing into them the breath of life, till Rome became living Rome
again. . . ." [20]

Except for the *Herald's* reservations about the appropriate-
ness of Melville's subject to a popular audience and its further
comment, seconded by the *Leader,* on his manner of speaking,
the four Cleveland reviews were the most favorable notices he
had so far received. Though his first Ohio audience was comparatively small, those who attended were evidently well
enough interested in his subject to be delighted with its "masterly" treatment. It should be added, however, that the *Ohio
Farmer's* reporter, who had so easily associated Melville the
lecturer with the author of *Typee* and *Omoo,* was troubled by
certain implications of "Statues in Rome" unnoticed by most
of the newspaper critics:

It seemed to us as if the writer had never forgotten his imprisonment among the Pacific cannibals, and half regretted his extradition from that physical paradise. We would venture a bet that
Mr. Melville, with all his admiration for the Medicean Venus,
thinks Fayaway worth a score of cold unhabited marbles.

It seemed to us as if the writer had never recovered from his
captivity. His affection for heathenism is profound and sincere.
He speaks of the heathenism of Rome as if the world were little indebted to christianity; indeed, as if it had introduced in the place
of the old Roman heroism, a sort of trusting pusillanimity.

This under-current of regret, or sorrow, or malice, at the introduction of christianity, seemed to pervade the whole lecture, and
marred one's enjoyment of the fine observation and the deep sympathy manifest in every part of the performance.

This impression of Melville's underlying attitude in the lecture, reminiscent of the doubts of his religious orthodoxy previ-

---

[20] Mead, *Yankee Eloquence in the Middle West,* pp. 75, 256, first
called attention to the *Ohio Farmer's* article.

ously voiced in the Montreal *Witness,* is matched in no other review of "Statues in Rome." Although there is justification for much of what the sensitive critic has to say about Melville's "affection for heathenism" and his ambivalent attitude toward Christianity, it may be that other less orthodox listeners were not so easily shocked. What seems more likely, however, is that the restrained language of the lecture was sufficient to conceal the speaker's deeper intentions from the great majority of his casual hearers. On the whole, the more philosophical aspects of his discussion drew virtually no comment from the newspaper critics, several of whom were evidently men of some education and culture whose understanding doubtless surpassed that of the average citizen.

From Cleveland, having received "a far more favorable press than Horace Greeley was to get" after lecturing there later in the same week,[21] Melville proceeded to Detroit for his next lecture on 12 January (fee $50). The lack of an intervening day between his appearances in Cleveland and in Detroit prevented him from stopping en route at Sandusky to renew acquaintance with Richard Tobias Greene, the "Toby" of *Typee,* who had written him on 9 January after seeing advance notices of the Cleveland lecture. The letter urged Melville to come to Sandusky in the course of his tour, assuring him that arrangements could be made for him to speak there even though the local Young Men's Association had broken up. The suggestion did not bear fruit nor did Melville see Toby, although Mrs. Greene heard the lecture in Cleveland.[22] At Detroit, mean-

21 "Melville and His Public: 1858," *American Notes and Queries,* II (August 1942), 70. "Greeley was labeled 'a bore' " by the local reviewers "and accused of giving 'positively a diabolical lecture.' " As noted in this same article, the Cleveland *Herald* of 9 January, announcing forthcoming lectures by Melville, Greeley, George D. Prentice, and Rev. T. Starr King, pointed out that each lecturer had achieved "an established reputation."

22 Greene's letter to Melville of 9 January and a later letter from his wife to Mrs. Melville, 14 November 1892, which recalls her hearing the lecture in Cleveland, are quoted in part in *Log,* II, 588–589; both letters are now in the Harvard College Library. A notation of Toby's Sandusky address appears on the fourth page of Melville's lecture engagement book.

while, the Young Men's Society had inserted paid advertisements in the *Daily Advertiser* and *Daily Free Press,* and both papers as well as the *Daily Tribune* announced the program (under the title of "Roman Statuary") in their news columns, referring to the lecturer as "a gentleman of the highest ability," "unusually attractive" in his "person and delivery." Melville, who stayed at the Biddle House while in Detroit, spoke in the Society's own hall, delivering the third lecture of the first course of the season. A single review, appearing on the front page of the *Free Press* of 14 January, recalled his "'Omoo,' 'Typee,' and 'Moby Dick,' books that made some sensation a few years ago from the graphic manner in which they described scenes and incidents among the far-off islands of the Pacific," but there is no criticism in the article of the lecture and its delivery nor comments on the reaction of the audience. The account is a valuable one, however; for its detailed summary of what Melville had said, occupying nearly two columns, is the fullest version of "Statues in Rome" published by any newspaper. Whether his reception in Detroit was cordial or otherwise, the prominent position and generous space given this notice would suggest that the occasion was considered one of some local importance.[23]

A further source of information about the Detroit engagement is the annual report of the Young Men's Society, published in April 1858 over the signature of its president, John B. Palmer. Despite "the severe pecuniary embarrassments under which our entire community has labored during the past lecture season," the report states, "we are happy to announce that our success has greatly exceeded our expectations," the Society having realized a net profit of $200.50 from its lectures. "This we ascribe partly to the superior order of the lec-

---

[23] The staffs of the General Information Department and the Burton Historical Collection of the Detroit Public Library assisted in locating references to Melville's Detroit engagement, which is mentioned briefly in *Log,* II, 589, and Carl Bode, *The American Lyceum* (New York, 1956), p. 171. Miss Irene Dudley of the Burton Historical Collection has also contributed materially to other phases of this study.

tures we have presented to the public, and partly to our adoption of the course or season-ticket system." The section of the report devoted to lectures, which notes that the committee in charge had written over a hundred letters in arranging the season's program, contains some revealing material concerning this phase of the Society's activities and the expectations of its audience. The limited size of the hall, which held only "about 400 persons," was thought to prevent the engagement of very well-known lecturers whose high fees could be met only if a larger atttendance were possible. "With a Hall that would hold 2000 or 2500, while we could secure the most popular lecturers of the country, we could so reduce the price of admission [25 cents per lecture] as to permit the attendance of the mechanic and his family, as well as the merchant and the professional man, and in this manner cultivate and minister to the taste for popular lectures, and make the Society, as it was intended to be, an institution for the *people*." As for public taste in Detroit at the time, the following words are significant:

Many of our citizens object to our lectures, on the ground that they are too much of a literary, and too little of a practical nature. There is something in this objection. During the last season, we presented two lectures on chemistry [by E. L. Youmans], which proved as acceptable as instructive. I am convinced that we erred in limiting the number as we did; and would respectfully suggest to our successors that a course of lectures on chemistry, anatomy, geology—or other subjects of a like nature,—illustrated by diagrams and experiments, so as to present these important subjects in a form at once popular and easily to be comprehended, would do more to cultivate a taste for lectures and a desire for knowledge, on the part of the really needy, than the purely literary courses we have been in the habit of offering. . . . It is not intended to recommend scientific to the exclusion of literary lectures; but simply an addition of the former to satisfy the peculiar wants of a large portion of the public.[24]

[24] *Twenty-Fifth Annual Report of the Board of Managers of the Detroit Young Men's Society* (Detroit, April 1858), pp. 8–12, 21. Palmer's objectives in advocating a larger auditorium and the engagement of

These remarks illustrate another facet of that "prevailing *practicality* of pioneer society" emphasized by the reviewer of the Cleveland *Morning Leader,* and may reflect some dissatisfaction with Melville's choice of subject, although there is no specific discussion of individual lectures or speakers in the report. The same attitude, it will be seen, was to be found also in the South when Melville lectured there following his appearance in Detroit. After crossing Indiana he proceeded down the Ohio River by steamer to Tennessee and an engagement for 22 January in Fowler's Hall at Clarksville. The invitation had come in a flattering letter of 12 October 1857 from the lecture committee of the Clarksville Literary Association. In replying on 20 October Melville had specified $50 as the "average sum" usually paid a lecturer, but in Clarksville the committee members were evidently determined to alter "the impression with our Northern Brethren that Literary men meet with poor appreciation in the South" and prepared to welcome him with the largest fee he had yet received, $75.[25] According to the Clarksville *Jeffersonian* of 27 January his lecture there was "one of the events of the season. The spacious Hall was crowded with a large and fashionable audience." Again a familiar criticism was expressed: his subject "was not one calculated to excite general interest or elicit much enthusiasm in any manner in which it could possibly be treated. But we believe we express the sentiments of all when we say that Mr. Melville's effort received general admiration, in so far as regards, the finished and scholarly character of the composition,

especially popular speakers are illuminated by a reference in the annual report for 1859, pp. 13–14, to the appearance of Bayard Taylor in Detroit on 1 February of that year: though the Society rented the larger Fireman's Hall to accommodate the expected crowd, "several hundred persons" were nevertheless turned away for lack of room.

[25] The letter from Clarksville and the draft of Melville's reply, both in the Harvard College Library, are quoted in part in *Log,* II, 583. Receipt of Melville's acceptance, along with answers from others invited to lecture in Clarksville, is mentioned in an article in the Clarksville *Chronicle* for 30 October 1857, located by Miss Lucy C. Howard, librarian of Austin Peay State College in Clarksville. Miss Howard also located and transcribed the review in the *Jeffersonian* of 27 January cited below.

and the mastery of the subject evinced by the lecturer." In contrast to the verdict of this brief review, however, is that of a longer article in the Clarksville *Chronicle* of 29 January. Somewhat reminiscent of the earlier notice in the Cleveland *Morning Leader,* its extravagant praise goes beyond anything that had yet been written of "Statues in Rome." With unintended irony the *Chronicle's* critic terms the lecture "so faultless in conception and execution, that its subtle yet marvellous beauty escaped only the most appreciative sensibility and the most cultivated discernment." Some listeners, the writer acknowledges,

objected to Mr. Melville's subdued delivery; but if we rightly reflect, we will observe a striking congeniality between this quiet manner and those mute forms that stand still and silent amid the venerable ruins of "ancient Rome."
Those who appreciate the sublimity of Nature, only when the storm is loosed, and are insensible to the grandeur of her noontide silence, felt not the beauty of Mr. Melville's lecture. Those who prefer, what they term truth, and practicality and subjects of every day interest, who relish the strong meat that makes bone and muscle, above that "Nectar of the Gods" that sublimates a finer essence, tasted not of the divine chalice that the lecturer held to their lips. Mr. Melville goes from us, with the appreciation of many pure tastes, and the kindly feelings of many hearts that penetrated through the natural reserve of his character to the noble nature beneath.[26]

Throughout the article the emotional temperament of the *Chronicle's* reviewer is conspicuous. He singles out for particular comment the speaker's tribute to the horse as depicted in the equestrian statues of Rome, and in summarizing Melville's philosophic musings in the Coliseum he asserts that "in all our reading" he cannot remember "a more beautiful passage." But "the closing remarks of the lecturer," upon which the critic

[26] A clipping of this article is preserved among the Melville papers in the Harvard College Library; it is quoted in part in *Log,* II, 590, where it is erroneously attributed to the Clarksville *"Daily Enquirer"* of 3 February (there was no Clarksville paper of that name). Mrs. Francis Gibbs of the Clarksville Public Library located the original article in the *Chronicle,* along with two brief advance notices in the issues of 15 and 22 January.

"hung entranced," had inspired his principal encomium: Melville's conclusion, as the article explains, was a vindication of "these spiritual productions of the ancient mind from their alleged inferiority to the utilitarian inventions of the present age. Never before was the superiority of art over science, so triumphantly and eloquently sustained. But we will not add more of our feeble praise to a production which, if published, would elicit commendation from the highest critical sources." This glowing tribute, however, is exceptional, both in its enthusiasm for the content of "Statues in Rome" and in its frank expression of the critic's personal tastes, usually subordinated, in most of the reviews examined, to at least the appearance of journalistic objectivity. The southern critic's concurrence in Melville's partisan defense of the ancients against the moderns, moreover, recalls the sentiments of the Cleveland reviewer who had deplored "the prevailing *practicality*" of modern society. But most auditors in the industrial North, on the other hand, were probably far less inclined to agree with the speaker's unorthodox views on the "utilitarian inventions of the present age" than were the Cleveland critic and the rhapsodic Clarksville reviewer. Even in Boston, it may be noted, Melville's challenging assertion of "the superiority of art over science" had "caused some little discussion in several groups of homeward-bound listeners, after the lecture was closed." [27]

From Clarksville Melville returned to Ohio by way of Paducah and Louisville for his lecture on 2 February in Cincinnati, speaking there in Smith and Nixon's Hall for the Young Men's Mercantile Library Association (fee $50).[28] The Cincinnati reviews of the following day were unusually thorough, offering detailed summaries of the lecture along with

[27] Reported by the Boston *Evening Traveller* of 3 December 1857.

[28] The entry "Fby 2ᵈ Cincinnati" on p. 5 of Melville's notebook of lecture engagements is followed by the name "Charles Wells." Miss Mary Downing of the Public Library of Cincinnati advises that Wells, identified in the Cincinnati directory for 1858 as secretary of the Cincinnati Type Foundry and a resident of Avondale, was not listed in the membership of the Mercantile Library Association. His name may have been given to Melville as that of a person to call upon while in the city.

discerning critical comments.[29] The program, according to the *Daily Commercial,* "proved a most agreeable entertainment to a select audience of at least a thousand persons. Had the weather been even reasonably propitious, the spacious hall, no doubt, would have been filled." The *Daily Gazette* agreed, "considering the condition of the streets and the bad weather," noting that of those attending, "a good proportion" were women. The *Enquirer* observed that the hall "was about two-thirds filled with a highly intelligent and cultivated auditory," adding that "report has spoken very favorably" of the lecture as "delivered in the cities of the East." The sponsoring organization itself, however, was disappointed by the attendance at this and other recent programs, as revealed in the annual reports for 1857 and 1858 submitted by its board of directors. During 1857 the audiences had been "generally small throughout the season, and the interest shown by our members and the public far less than usual—partly, perhaps, in consequence of the hardness of the times, but chiefly attributable to the number of lectures before other societies, and by individuals on their own account, by which the taste for such recreations has been surfeited." [30] The succeeding board had indeed considered do-

[29] Clippings of the reviews in the Cincinnati *Daily Commercial, Daily Gazette,* and *Enquirer,* together with advance notices appearing in the *Daily Commercial,* are among the Melville papers in the Harvard College Library; an item of "3 newspapers" bought at Cincinnati is included in Melville's memoranda of expenses during his first lecture season. The article in the *Daily Gazette* is reprinted in "Melville and His Public: 1858," *American Notes and Queries,* II (August 1942), 68–70; extracts from the *Commercial* and *Gazette* are given in George Kummer, "Herman Melville and the Ohio Press," pp. 34–35; excerpts from all three reviews and from the *Commercial's* announcement of 2 February are included in *Log,* II, 590–591. Miss Ethel L. Hutchins of the Public Library of Cincinnati identified the *Commercial's* announcement of 1 February, not previously reprinted, which is quoted below. The Cincinnati *Daily Times,* which also printed a brief advance notice on 2 February, may likewise have carried a review of the lecture, but Mrs. Alice P. Hook of the Historical and Philosophical Society of Ohio, which holds the only known file of that paper for this period, reports that the issue of 3 February is lacking and that there is no mention of Melville in the following issues.

[30] *Twenty-Third Annual Report* (Cincinnati, 1858), p. 18. Copies of these reports have been made available for examination by Miss Isabelle K. Ackerson, librarian of the Association.

ing away with the annual series of lectures, but concluded that the

custom . . . is of so long standing that whatever may be the opinions of the Board, the public do not seem prepared for their discontinuance. The system of Courses of Lectures, however, has proved by our experience and that of similar Associations in other cities, a failure. Of all the duties incumbent on the Board, the arrangement of the annual Courses of Lectures was always the most difficult and troublesome. The labor and time would not be thought of, had not the pecuniary results for some years been so generally unsatisfactory. The present Board, after due consideration, determined to abandon the system.

But the preceding board had already arranged a brief course of four lectures for the early months of 1858, Melville's being the third. "The first lecture," given by Charles Mackay on "Poetry and Song," had "attracted a large audience," the report continues, but the others, including Melville's, "were poorly attended, and the expenses over the receipts consumed nearly all that was realized on the first." [31]

These extracts from the Association's reports are of interest in their revelation of the obstacles confronting both lecturers and their sponsors during this period. The sagging revenues of the Association were a cause for concern, and an effort on the part of friendly newspaper editors to support its activities may account for the unusually full publicity given Melville's appearance in the city. The advance promotion in Cincinnati was certainly more extensive than that in other localities which he visited. On 1 February the *Daily Commercial* had announced his lecture in a four-paragraph notice, identifying the speaker as "one of the most popular writers in the United States" and furnishing a brief sketch of Melville's career. "His reputation as well as the interest of the subject . . . ," the article observed, "justify the public in expecting something of a

[31] *Twenty-Fourth Annual Report* (Cincinnati, 1859), pp. 11–12. The report lists total receipts for the four lectures of $589.25 and expenses of $580.00. In addition to the lectures by Mackay and Melville, Henry Fuller spoke on "The Credit System" and William Birney on "Reformers and Reform."

superior character." A second announcement in the next day's issue of the same paper remarked that "Mr. Melville's lectures are said to be admirably written, but none of our exchanges discourses upon the style of his delivery. If he would avoid the objection usually urged against our lecturers, he will speak *distinctly*, and with animation, that all may hear. The public is extremely desirous to see and hear Mr. Melville, and anticipates a rich literary repast this evening." From this admonition it may be inferred that complaints of inability to hear the visiting speaker were anything but exceptional in Melville's day, and this was probably as true in other cities as it was in Cincinnati. But Melville unfortunately arrived from the South with a worsening cold which was to hamper his delivery to a noticeable extent. The *Commercial's* reviewer took this handicap into account, subsequently describing his voice as being "as soft and almost as sweet, barring a slight huskiness proceeding from a cold, as the warbling of the winds in cocoa groves. His style of delivery is earnest, though not sufficiently animated for a Western audience, and he enunciates with only tolerable distinctness." The *Daily Gazette* noted that he "makes no attempts at eloquence, but appears upon the rostrum as though reading from one of his own descriptive works of what he saw. . . . The manner of Mr. Melville is too quiet, common-place and unobtrusive for a popular audience, but he talks as he writes—without the pretension of those who make lecturing a business." The *Enquirer* found his delivery "agreeable" in some respects "but not in others—it was monotonous and often indistinct, but not devoid of impressiveness, which sometimes approached the ministerially solemn."

The review in the *Commercial*, which considered the lecture "very superior" as "a literary production," includes a stenographic report of Melville's opening remarks, continuing with a digest of the body of the lecture copied without acknowledgment from the earlier account in the Boston *Daily Courier* —evidently one of the "exchanges" referred to in the advance announcement. To the *Daily Gazette*, which also furnished a long summary but one of its own composition, the introduction was "very finely expressed," and the lecture throughout "was rather interesting than otherwise, although the interest excited in the opening passages was not maintained to the close." The *Enquirer* prefaced its review by specifying Melville's "stories of the sea, such as 'Typee,' 'Omoo,' and 'Moby Dick,' " as the best of his works. "Of late years," however, the reviewer continued in an interesting survey of Melville's literary accomplishments,

Mr. M. has turned his attention to another species of composition more akin to the modern novel. "Pierre, or the Ambiguities," is an example of this; highly extravagant and unnatural, but original and interesting in its construction and characters. His last production, "The Confidence Man," is one of the dullest and most dismally monotonous books we remember to have read, and it has been our unavoidable misfortune to peruse, in the fulfillment of journalistic duty, a number of volumes through . . . which nothing but a sense of obligation would have sustained us. "Typee," one of, if not the first of his works, is the best, and "The Confidence Man" the last, decidedly the worst. So Mr. M.'s authorship is toward the nadir rather than the zenith, and he has been progressing in the form of an inverted climax.

"Fayaway" is the most attractive and best-known character Mr. M. has drawn, and there are few who do not have sentimental recollections of the fair, lithe, graceful Indian girl [*sic!*], with all the instinctive delicacy and refinement and cha[r]mfulness, which the highest circles of society often fail to exhibit.

This sketch of Melville's literary achievement, with its inaccurate recollection of his earlier works and its bias against his most recent writing, is probably fairly representative of the popular attitude during what the critic regarded as the wane of his success as an author. As for the lecture itself, which the *Enquirer* also summarized rather fully, it occupied "nearly two hours in delivery" but was "exceedingly interesting and eloquent, abounding in admirable specimens of such word-painting as his best works contain. His discourse was classic and beautiful, and by far the best that has yet been delivered this season before the Library."

Apart from the disappointment to the sponsoring organization of the small financial return, Melville's Cincinnati engagement, despite the now familiar objections to his manner and delivery, rivals his earlier appearances in Boston, Cleveland, and Clarksville as the most successful performance of his first season. On the following day, 3 February, still suffering from his cold, he left Cincinnati for Chillicothe, Ohio, where he spoke that evening in the Second Presbyterian Church. His lecture in Chillicothe was the fourth and last program of a new course sponsored by the local Gymnasium and Library Association (fee $40). "Wherever Mr. Melville has lectured," the weekly *Scioto Gazette* had generously affirmed in its announcement of 2 February, "he has received the general commendation of the press and the people. His fame as a writer is world-wide, and his fine descriptive powers, as exhibited in 'Omoo' and 'Typee' cannot fail to make his lecture a rich intellectual treat to his audience." A week later the same paper reported that "one of the largest audiences of the season" had assembled to hear him.

Mr. Melville's high reputation as an author led the audience to expect a rare intellectual treat, and they [were] not disappointed. He makes no attempt at eloquence, but the deep stillness that pervaded the large audience from the commencement to the close of the lecture, showed that his brilliant imagination and charming descriptive powers, could hold hearers as well as readers entranced.

Although laboring under a severe cold, his voice was still rich and mellow, and he had the most complete control of it. He speaks with earnestness and enunciates distinctly; even when he descended, as he sometimes did, almost to a whisper, his words were audible in the remotest parts of the room.

We can give no sketch of the lecture that would do it justice. Replete with rich imagery and charming descriptions, its beauty would be marred by presenting it in fragments, even as would the grand creations of genius it described.

The Chillicothe *Advertiser* of 5 February agreed that "the general expression with regard to the Lecture was of high appreciation. And in truth the Lecture was by no means void either of interest or instruction." But the reviewer had his private reservations nevertheless: "the Lecturer," he observed,

did not confine himself to those statues which immortalize the "Eternal City," but telegraphed his audience to Naples and Florence, and to Amsterdam with little regard to their convenience, and did not even take the trouble to render the travelling easy. . . . Altogether, to those familiar through writers of the day with Rome and its attractions, the lecture was a string of indifferent Pearls, genuine indeed, but sadly wanting in that polish which gives even to trite common places a passing interest and endows the germ of originality with the power of life and beauty. If the lecture was faulty, the delivery can hardly be said to have been less so. Perhaps we do injustice to Mr. M by expressing any opinion in regard to his delivery, since any one who has tried to speak in public, must know how a slight cold will entirely untune the voice, and so diminish his control over it as to render the speaker timid and reserved in his utterance, and it was quite apparent that Mr. M was afflicted with quite a severe cold, was aware that he could not command his voice and [was] therefore afraid to trust it.

Doubtless these objections did not occur to many of the audience. . . .[32]

The two Chillicothe notices, which are unusually full in comparison with those of other small cities visited by Melville, are interesting in their differing evaluations. It was of course not uncommon for local journalists of the day to choose opposite sides on controversial questions, and one is tempted to suspect that some nineteenth-century reviewers may have been at least as anxious to contradict their rivals as to do impartial justice to the visiting lecturer. In Chillicothe too, as previously in Clarksville, one of the critics notes a difference between his judgment and that of others in the audience, a situa-

[32] The notice in the *Advertiser,* which also includes a two-sentence digest of Melville's subject-matter, is reprinted in George Kummer, "Herman Melville and the Ohio Press," p. 35; an extract from the review in the *Scioto Gazette* is also quoted. Excerpts from both articles appear in *Log,* II, 591–592. Mrs. Alene Lowe White of the Western Reserve Historical Society located the advance notice in the *Gazette.*

tion which was to recur during Melville's subsequent tours. As examples of fair-minded reporting such comments deserve approbation, but they complicate the problem of determining whether Melville's reception in Chillicothe and elsewhere was as generally favorable or unfavorable as it was sometimes reported to be.

Having fulfilled his midwestern engagements for the season, Melville returned to New England by way of Pittsburgh, Philadelphia, and New York for his next appearance on 10 February in Charlestown, Massachusetts. For this lecture, under the sponsorship of the Mishawum Literary Association, he received his smallest fee of the season, $20. The program was briefly described in what appears to be a secretary's report, carried in the Charlestown *Advertiser* for 10 February, as "interesting and instructive." Melville's style, this account continues, "was neither dry nor verbose but elegant—mostly free from artificialities," and the lecture "was prepared with much taste, the best part being the beginning and end, between which the lighter matter was sandwiched." But to the less receptive "Reporter," writing in the *Bunker Hill Aurora* for 13 February, it was "well written but particularly dull. . . . Still Mr. Melville's fault was rather in the selection of his subject than in his treatment of it. No man could reasonably hope to interest a common audience upon such a subject. . . . Some nervous people, therefore, left the hall; some read books and newspapers; some sought refuge in sleep, and some, to their praise be it spoken, seemed determined to use it as an appropriate occasion for self-discipline in the blessed virtue of patience." [33] Not even the Chillicothe *Advertiser's* reviewer had been so harsh in his criticism of Melville's material as the anonymous "Reporter," and none of the earlier audiences had been so openly hostile as this account describes the listeners in Charlestown, to whom the lecture was merely a "painful *bore.*"

[33] The account in the Charlestown *Advertiser* is reprinted in J. H. Birss, "Toward the Whole Evidence on Melville as a Lecturer," *American Notes and Queries*, III (April 1943), 11–12; that in the *Bunker Hill Aurora* is given, with some omissions, in *Log*, II, 592.

On 18 February Melville appeared in Rochester, New York, speaking in Corinthian Hall and delivering the next to last lecture in the course sponsored by the Athenaeum and Mechanics' Association (fee $50). In an announcement the same day the Rochester *Union and Advertiser* observed that "Mr. M. comes to our city with a reputation which should entitle him to a full house and the vast number who feel an interest in his subject will not fail to be present," but this paper did not carry a report of the lecture. The local *Democrat and American* of 18 February noted the "high character borne by Mr. MEL-VILLE as an author," which was "formed years ago"; his " 'Omoo,' 'Typee,' etc., are found in every well-selected home library. He has abstained from producing books latterly, and entered the lecture field, where his success has been entirely commensurate with his exalted literary reputation previously attained." Although this paper anticipated "one of the most interesting lectures of the season," its review two days later treated the lecturer and his books more appreciatively than the topic he had chosen to discuss. Beginning with a reference to his "very entertaining narratives of adventures in some of the far-off islands of the sea, and various fictions smacking of salt-water and mystic philosophy," the newspaper critic reported that Melville himself

was very well received. . . . His discourse on the Statues of Rome, was well-written, and evinced not only a familiar knowledge of art in the Eternal City, but a critical appreciation of those sermons in stone. To a miscellaneous audience like that assembled to hear it, however, the lecture was not particularly in[t]eresting. The mass of people are not deeply versed in ancient history, and regard with less interest than the traveler . . . the remains of those immortal achievements. . . . The audience generally, were disappointed; and we think that the lecturer erred in his choice of a theme in this instance. Mr. MELVILLE is capable of doing better, and since he has entered the field as a "popular le[c]turer," will not abandon it without further efforts to win laurels therein.[34]

[34] The account in the *Democrat and American* and its announcement of 18 February are reprinted in "Melville and His Public: 1858," p. 68;

There is no summary of Melville's remarks in this brief review, nor does its friendly criticism touch at all on his voice or delivery. Both critic and audience were kinder to Melville in Rochester than their immediate predecessors had been in Charlestown, but once again his subject had failed to win popular approval. When he stopped in Albany on the following day his uncle found him "in excellent health and very fine spirits," [35] but as his first lecture season drew near its close he must surely have become aware, from his hearers themselves or from published reviews, that for most of his audiences he had indeed "erred in his choice of a theme."

On 23 February Melville made his last appearance of the winter at Liberty Hall in New Bedford, Massachusetts; the plans for an additional engagement in Malden, entered after New Bedford in his notebook but again canceled as on a previous occasion, had evidently not materialized. Once again the local press recalled his earlier connection with the sea: "If we are not mistaken," the New Bedford *Daily Mercury* remarked on the morning of the lecture, "Mr. Melville once tried his fortune as a hand upon a whaleship from our port." More than seventeen years before, he had embarked from New Bedford aboard the whaler *Acushnet*, a fact which must have come into his own mind as he now returned to the city to keep a less momentous appointment. Melville's program was the thirteenth Lyceum Lecture of the New Bedford course (fee $50), and his own sixteenth engagement of the season. To the *Mercury* the lecture was "interesting and instructive . . . more especially with many suggestive and thoughtful criticisms on art interspersed"; the *Evening Standard* found it "a well written and scholarly essay, which would doubtless be read with

the review is quoted in part in *Log*, II, 593, along with the advance notice of the lecture which appeared in the Rochester *Union and Advertiser* for 18 February. Miss Gladys E. Love and Miss Emma Swift of the Rochester Public Library have searched the files of the two Rochester papers and have also checked the annual report for 1858 of the sponsoring organization; it does not mention Melville.

[35] Peter Gansevoort to Maria Gansevoort Melville, 20 February 1858, as quoted in *Log*, II, 593.

much pleasure, but . . . not calculated to interest as a lecture"—an opinion reminiscent of those recently voiced in Charlestown and Rochester. That the reporter himself had lost interest during the evening may be indicated by his second-hand digest of Melville's remarks, which in its phrasing is heavily indebted to the Boston *Traveller's* earlier summary of 3 December 1857.[36] Melville himself probably did not see the comment in the *Standard,* but before leaving New Bedford he evidently bought a copy of the morning *Mercury,* since a clipping of its review has been found among his papers along with five Boston reviews of "Statues in Rome," two advance notices and three reviews from Cincinnati, and also the enthusiastic southern notice which had appeared in the Clarksville *Chronicle.*

Had Melville managed to collect all contemporary newspaper reviews of "Statues in Rome" he would have seen only a few more notices than the twenty-eight articles examined here. These reviews cover all of his sixteen engagements during his first season except those in Concord and New Haven, where the lecture was not reported, and in Montreal, where newspaper files are lacking; in Lawrence, Saratoga Springs, and Cincinnati there may have been additional articles in papers whose files are either lacking or incomplete. "Statues in Rome" was repeated on one occasion during Melville's second season, a double engagement at Lynn, Massachusetts, but only his companion address on "The South Seas" was reviewed by the local press. The extant reports, then, are concerned exclusively with his first lecture season.

Taken as a whole these reviews suggest that Melville had proved a popular drawing-card when, as a well-remembered author of "light literature" (to quote the *Ohio Farmer*), he

[36] A clipping of the article in the *Daily Mercury* is among the Melville papers in the Harvard College Library; it is quoted in part in *Log,* II, 593. Miss Marion H. Bonner of the New Bedford Free Public Library located and transcribed the article in the *Daily Evening Standard* and the advance notices appearing in both papers on the day of the lecture.

began his new venture as a lecturer. Though still a novice in the field he had consistently attracted good audiences except where bad weather or the appeal of competing local attractions had interfered, as in Lawrence and Cleveland. His appearances in Boston and Clarksville, it will be recalled, were described as among the events of the season; his audiences in Auburn, Ithaca, Clarksville, and Chillicothe were considered large and that in Cincinnati was better than the reporters had expected in view of weather conditions. Additional testimony to the attraction of his name in 1857–58 is afforded by the very number of his engagements and the fact that the fees for his paid appearances, which averaged better than $46, compare favorably with those of more experienced lecturers. But even a casual glance at the newspaper publicity clearly shows that Melville's name was still associated in the popular mind chiefly with *Typee* and *Omoo,* his first two books, which are those named most frequently in the articles sketching his literary career. The single review showing any awareness of his most recent works, those appearing since the publication of *Moby Dick* in 1851, mentions only *Pierre* and *The Confidence-Man.* Its author dismisses both with a sneer, recalling even the favorite *Typee* in a vague and highly inaccurate way as he traces the later decline, in his view, of "Mr. M.'s authorship."

Whether such an impression was general or whether "Statues in Rome" served to enhance Melville's reputation in the minds of those who still thought of him largely in terms of his South Sea adventures is somewhat difficult to determine. Most of the reviews discussing the new lecture distinguished between its merits as a literary composition and its suitability for the lyceum platform, and although Melville's fame as an author may have drawn listeners to the lecture hall there is no evidence to show that his hearers were similarly moved to increase their purchases of his books. That an author of the day should turn lecturer was less surprising than that the writer of *Typee* should choose to discuss "Statues in Rome." Recognizing that Melville was speaking as neither an artist nor a

professional art critic, to paraphrase his own statement in introducing his topic, the reviewers generally found his treatment a competent one and quarreled with none of his artistic
judgments. Although "Reporter" of the *Bunker-Hill Aurora*
complained that his "draughts upon the classical Dictionary
were frequent and heavy," other writers thought the discussion scholarly and "quite interesting to those of artistic tastes,"
as the Boston *Journal* described it, even if the general public
"would have preferred something more modern and personal."
Except for a single bit of conversation which Melville had
quoted, the more caustic "Reporter" would "hardly have
guessed that he had ever been in Italy at all," yet few of the
critics openly complained that the lecture had been something
other than a collection of anecdotes. Though three reviewers
found that Melville exceeded the customary time-limit of an
hour, only two writers called his lecture "faulty" or "particularly dull," and these were the critics in Chillicothe and
Charlestown whose reports, incidentally, were contradicted by
those of rival papers in their own localities. Three other articles
made no observations on the substance of the lecture, two
others expressed qualified approval, and the rest—twenty-one
in all—returned favorable verdicts amounting in some instances to very high praise.

Thus the lecture was termed "interesting and instructive,"
"exceedingly creditable," "very superior," "masterly," and even
"faultless" in various accounts, and its "beautiful word-painting" was frequently singled out both as something to be expected of Melville the writer and as an achievement fully
worthy of commendation. The language he had used was described in such terms as "racy and rich," "graceful," "fervid
and eloquent," or "highly finished," though one of the more
hostile reviewers thought his writing "sadly wanting" in polish,
and another critic, in complete disagreement, found it "perhaps too highly wrought." But even this admirable literary production, as "Statues in Rome" evidently seemed to many of
these journalists, was in their opinion "not calculated to inter-

est as a lecture" though it might have given complete satisfaction had it been published as an essay. Nine critics in all thought its subject "unattractive to the masses" and its treatment too remote or too bookish for a miscellaneous audience "not deeply versed in ancient history" or particularly interested in sculptural art. Yet in spite of these reservations the lecture was appraised as "the most chaste and classic of the season" in Auburn, "by far the best yet delivered" during the course at Cincinnati, and "superior to nine-tenths" of the programs heard in Cleveland, where as in Clarksville one of the critics openly deplored the fact that popular taste was incapable of responding on as high a level of culture as Melville's subject and treatment clearly demanded.

Although fourteen reports make no pronouncement on the reaction of Melville's audiences as distinguished from the evaluations of the newspaper critics themselves, the other fourteen are rather evenly divided on this point. Only four accounts speak of the outright disappointment of listeners—in Auburn, Charlestown, and Rochester. Six papers, in Lawrence, Boston, Auburn, and Clarksville, noted qualified popular approval, or at least "complimentary attention." And in Cleveland and Boston, as well as in Chillicothe, where one writer described the audience as "entranced," there were five separate reports of "apparent interest," "evident satisfaction," and "high appreciation." Some of the objections and qualifications had to do not with the subject but rather, as in Lawrence, Auburn, and Clarksville, with Melville's low voice. Some, notably in cities west of the Hudson, were concerned with his indistinct enunciation—by which may have been meant simply an unfamiliar eastern accent. Then too he had contracted a severe cold before reaching Cincinnati and Chillicothe, and the local reviewers were generous enough to take this handicap into account in making their evaluations. But throughout Ohio his delivery, that of an amateur "without the pretension of those who make lecturing a business," had been found "not sufficiently animated for a Western audience." Since an indistinct voice and a want of animation were objections "usually urged against our lecturers," as one of the Cincinnati papers remarked, these shortcomings were not peculiar to Melville among visitors to Ohio. Perhaps he had been more "at home in the lecture-room" at Boston, among his relatives and personal friends, where he not only "spoke in a clear and distinct voice" but delivered his lecture with "animation and effect" and even "considerable enthusiasm." As his granddaughter has recently pointed out, "it is quite likely that he was extremely sensitive to the response of an audience, and that the quality of his delivery varied with the quality of his hearers." [37]

Unfortunately for Melville, his visit to what was then the West had come at a rather unpropitious time. Not only had "the number of lectures" in cities like Cincinnati surfeited "the taste for such recreations" by 1858, but there were increasing objections throughout Ohio and also in Detroit to the cultural subjects chosen by most lecturers from the East. The Cleveland critic who deplored contemporary preoccupation with "the iron slavery of railroad speculation, money panics, and the tyranny of the almighty dollar" would have been forced to agree with his like-minded southern colleague in Clarksville: those who "preferred practicality and subjects of every day interest . . . tasted not of the divine chalice" which Melville "held to their lips." A lecturer on "Statues in Rome" might have fared considerably better had he come to Ohio before the vogue for utilitarian and scientific subjects set in there during the several years immediately preceding the Civil War.[38] Although the tastes of New England audiences were evidently somewhat different, it will be recalled that even in Boston Melville had provoked discussion by his exaltation of ancient art over modern practicality and science. The Boston listeners, a more select group than the popular audiences of the West, also differed considerably from those who heard Melville else-

[37] Eleanor Melville Metcalf, *Herman Melville: Cycle and Epicycle* (Cambridge, Mass., 1953), p. 173.
[38] Mead, *Yankee Eloquence in the Middle West,* pp. 21–22.

where in New England itself, notably at nearby Charlestown and in New Bedford. "Common people" who "care but precious little about Italy or the statues therein" were probably in the majority in these communities if not at New Haven or Boston, and such people, according to the *Bunker-Hill Aurora,* have "a decided preference for living things. Statues and Mummies don't interest them." It may be indicative of popular reaction to "Statues in Rome" that of all the cities which Melville visited during his first lecture season, those in New England included, Boston was the only one to which he returned for a speaking engagement the following winter.

Taking all these varying judgments into account, rather than the scattered or regional verdicts considered in previous scholarship, it seems unwarranted to conclude that Melville's first season was simply a "failure," just as it appears unwise to make broad generalizations about the effect of his reception as a lecturer upon his reputation as an author.[39] Like many another speaker before and since his day, he had met with widely different responses in different areas and cities, pleased some listeners by what repelled others, and received mixed and even contradictory reviews from the press. Most of the notices, though not penetrating in their analysis of "Statues in Rome," were judicious rather than sensational in treating Melville simply as a popular author turned lecturer instead of the figure he dreaded to be, the "man who lived among the cannibals." Except in Montreal the newspapers made no direct allusion to the controversy which had arisen a decade before over his remarks about missionaries, and only one reviewer, in Cleveland, had objected to the religious implications of the lecture itself. But few critics other than those in Boston, Cleveland, and Clarksville paid much attention to the philosophical aspects of Melville's preoccupation with antiquity, which are more likely

[39] In "Melville and His Public: 1858," an article appearing in 1942, the editors of *American Notes and Queries* asserted that Melville's "failure as a speaker" during this first lecture season "in no way harmed his reputation as an author" (p. 70). Even on the basis of evidence assembled up to that time the statement is ill-founded.

to interest the present-day student than the somewhat conventional descriptions of Roman statuary offered in the bulk of the lecture.

It seems reasonable to conclude that neither Melville's subject nor his power as a speaker had attracted the majority of those who came to hear him, and it is probably true that those who were drawn chiefly by recollections of *Typee* and *Omoo* would have been better pleased if, as during the following season, his topic had been "The South Seas." [40] With such a theme, treated so as to answer the demand for "something more modern and personal," and with his delivery improved through the experience gained during his first season, there was justification of the hope expressed by the friendly Rochester reporter who thought Melville's topic ill-chosen: "Mr. MELVILLE is capable of doing better, and since he has entered the field as a 'popular le[c]turer,' will not abandon it without further efforts to win laurels therein."

[40] David Mead similarly attributes "Melville's moderate success before Ohio's lyceums" to "his somewhat notorious reputation as an author rather than to his subject matter or his eloquence" (*Yankee Eloquence,* p. 76).

3

"A Rather Spacious Field"

The South Seas

AFTER Melville had given the final lecture of his first season at New Bedford on 23 February he paid a visit to his mother at Gansevoort, where in March of 1858 he suffered a "severe attack of what he called crick in the back," according to a memoir by his wife, and "never regained his former vigor & strength." The state of his health continued to be a matter of particular concern for the next several years. After his return to Pittsfield it was reported by two of his friends, Evert and George Duyckinck of New York, who visited him in July, that he was "busy on a new book"—probably the volume of poems for which he was to seek a publisher in 1860. In early September, when he and George Duyckinck enjoyed "a delightful three days ride," Duyckinck described him as "robust and fine looking . . . but somewhat impaired in health by an affection of the spine brought on by too many hours of brain work day after day, following a life of great bodily activity." Chief Justice Shaw, however, during a visit to Pittsfield later in the same month, thought his son-in-law to be "as well as I have seen him for years." By October Melville considered himself able to undertake a second season of lecturing, his need for money being the determining factor once again as it had been in 1857. In going over the records of his first season in his notebook of lecture engagements he computed his gross receipts at $645.00, less $221.30 for traveling expenses, leaving a net gain of $423.70 from his sixteen appearances, including the two for which he received no fee. The chance of earning as much again during the following winter was not one to be readily sacrificed by a man whose financial straits were known even to relatives outside his immediate household—provided, of course, that his health would permit the necessary traveling. On 8 November his father-in-law sent a check for $100 from Boston to help "in providing your family supplies for the approaching winter," remarking that "I presume you have an engagement to deliver a lecture here." By this date Melville had already publicized his readiness "to receive applications to lecture," as the Pittsfield newspapers subsequently noted, and had agreed, "by invitation of a large number of his fellow citizens," to "give his new lecture upon the South Seas, in this town, December 14th." [1]

During the previous lecture season, as articles in the press make clear, it was not an opportunity to hear a discussion of Roman statuary that had primarily attracted Melville's consistently good audiences. More intriguing was the privilege of looking at the "man who lived among the cannibals," as he had once described himself to Hawthorne in reflecting upon his popular reputation. To lecture on "The South Seas" was in keeping with what the public chiefly remembered about the author of *Typee* and *Omoo,* though Melville himself had become so weary of just this kind of fame that he had made a determined effort to exploit new fields of interest in his later books, in his magazine pieces, and more recently in his first lecture. None of these had caught the popular fancy, however, after the manner of *Typee,* as Melville had learned long before this, and a second lecture on a subject more to his own taste than to that of the public was obviously not advisable if he intended pursuing a new career on the platform. The point is worthy of some emphasis, along with the factors which influenced Melville's decision to speak on "The South Seas," in

[1] Leyda, *Log,* II, 593–596, provides more extensive quotations from the source material cited in this paragraph.

view of his evident uncertainty about his future course. Choosing this topic for his second season, in spite of his continued efforts to avoid it in his other writings, need not be regarded as proof that he had exhausted alternative material; [2] in fact he had used only a small portion of the journal of his recent Mediterranean trip in writing "Statues in Rome." The decision suggests rather that his pressing need for money made him more willing than he had previously been to take the expectations of the public into account. Then too, his relatives and friends may have been more persuasive after the mixed reception given "Statues in Rome" than they had seemed at the beginning of the season.

From the private correspondence of 1857 between Melville's cousin Henry Gansevoort and his uncle Peter, Henry's father, it is known that at least some of the family had reservations at the outset concerning the success of a lecture on Roman statuary. The younger Gansevoort had immediately sensed that to the public Melville's name was associated primarily with narratives of adventure; as the Rochester and New Bedford reviewers were to suggest later in the season, it was "the far-off islands of the seas" that first came to mind when his name was mentioned. Peter Gansevoort, although "persuaded" that Melville would make "an interesting & successful lecturer," had entirely agreed with his son's observation that "he would be more 'at home' in Narrative than in criticism," and in a letter of 17 December 1857 to his son he proposed that Melville prepare as a lecture "a Narrative of his recent tour on the borders of the Mediterranean & Constantinople &c" that could also "be hereafter woven into a Book." To compose such a work would not make the "requisition on his imagination" demanded by art criticism, Gansevoort felt, remembering the mental and

---

[2] Merrell R. Davis, "Melville's Midwestern Lecture Tour, 1859," *Philological Quarterly*, XX (January 1941), 46–57, justifiably concluded that essentially Melville "had no new material to draw on" concerning the South Seas (p. 56); his further suggestion that Melville may have "stopped writing because he could offer the public nothing new" (p. 57) does not take into account the unused material of the journal of 1856–57. For further discussion of this point see Chapter 6 below.

physical strain of the last few years brought on by Melville's exhausting labor as a creative writer.[3] This idea, which had doubtless occurred also to Melville as he looked over the extensive material recorded in his journal, must have been urged upon him both by Henry Gansevoort, as the father had requested, and also by his uncle in person during the several visits to Albany which Melville made in the course of the winter. But his experiences in Egypt, in Greece, and especially in Palestine had in fact stirred his imagination so profoundly that he was not disposed to treat them glibly from the platform in popular terms. Some of this material very likely went into the poetry he had begun to compose by the summer of 1858; some of it was to be reserved still longer, and when at last "woven into a Book" it was ultimately published in 1876, through a subsidy from Peter Gansevoort himself, as *Clarel, A Poem and Pilgrimage in the Holy Land.*

Thus the new lecture was not in the strictest sense a sequel to "Statues in Rome," though regardless of the shift in locale from ancient Rome to the Pacific of Melville's own day the two compositions have a number of elements in common. At first glance, however, the differences are more apparent than the similarities. From a comparison both of the reconstructed texts and of the newspaper criticisms it is seen that Melville, having learned from his initial venture something of what was expected of a popular speaker, had in fact brought himself to face his second season with the demands of public taste firmly in mind. The reviewers, along with their call for a more appropriate subject, had also emphasized the importance of a more pleasing delivery than he had been able to demonstrate during at least the opening weeks of his first tour. To begin with, of course, a man obliged to talk in a series of auditoriums with consistently poor acoustics must learn to make himself

---

[3] Relevant extracts from the correspondence, including phrases from the original draft of Peter Gansevoort's letter of 17 December, will be found in *Log,* II, 584–585, 586–587; Henry Gansevoort's comments of 23 December are discussed in the concluding paragraphs of Chapter 1 above.

heard by more than "those on the front seats." His voice must be loud and his enunciation must be distinct and clear. Again, especially when venturing west of the Hudson, he must overcome his "natural reserve" sufficiently to deliver his remarks with expression and animation—and preferably without being tied to a manuscript—in order to suit the taste of the West. To meet such requirements Melville would have to begin by preparing something "more modern and personal," as the critics had suggested, since the personal note must be struck first in content before it can be realized in delivery, and if at all possible by dealing with a theme into which some humor could be injected. To Melville "The South Seas" met these specifications more readily than any attempt to treat lightly and entertainingly the incidents of his Mediterranean travels, considering the chastened mood in which he had undertaken the trip. The new lecture is accordingly provided with just the kind of humorous personal anecdotes that had been found wanting in "Statues in Rome," thus avoiding the almost unrelieved seriousness of its predecessor. But in its social criticism Melville was as much in earnest as ever, both pieces containing equally severe judgments upon the shortcomings of contemporary Christian civilization. As the *Ohio Farmer's* reviewer had been perceptive enough to sense in hearing "Statues in Rome," Melville's "affection for heathenism" was indeed "both profound and sincere," and by tracing expressions of this same attitude through the two lectures one can easily grasp their continuity, given this basic clue, despite their seeming differences in matter and manner.

In composing "The South Seas," however, Melville was evidently quite conscious of the difficulties he faced in treating so vast a topic in an hour's time and in proceeding without benefit of a firsthand glimpse of the Pacific since his return from Hawaii in 1844. By 1851 he had made the major events of his life there the subjects of various books—his captivity among the Marquesan natives in *Typee,* his subsequent wanderings in *Omoo,* his whaling experiences in *Moby Dick,* and

his return as a naval seaman in *White-Jacket;* for each of these
accounts, moreover, he had been obliged to draw upon numerous literary sources to supplement what he himself had observed and remembered. In the opening paragraphs of the new
lecture he commented on the "somewhat expansive" theme he
had chosen and also on the possible expectations of his audience with regard to his previous writings in this "rather spacious field." "To do away with any erroneous anticipations as to
our topic," he remarked in beginning his discussion,

I hope you do not expect me to repeat what has long been in print
touching my own casual adventures in Polynesia. I propose to
treat of matters of more general interest, and, in a random way,
discuss the South Seas at large and under various aspects, introducing, as occasion may serve, any little incident, personal or
other, fitted to illustrate the point in hand.

These words establish the key of the composition which follows. The next eleven paragraphs are devoted to a brief survey of Pacific geography and exploration, beginning with the
history of the equivalent names "South Seas," used by Balboa,
and "Pacific Ocean," Magellan's later term. Melville's own
preference for "South Seas" is attributed to "a lingering regard
for certain old associations, linking the South Seas as a name
with many pleasant and venerable books of voyages, full of
well-remembered engravings," and also with the writings of
Charles Lamb, who had worked in "those haunted old offices
of the once famous South Sea Company" in London. Among
the writers and voyagers specifically mentioned are Captain
Dampier, John Harris, Admiral Burney, and Captain Cook;
Burney's *Chronological History of the Discoveries in the South
Sea or Pacific Ocean* (1803–1817) was Melville's principal
source for his discussion of Balboa and Magellan in this section of the lecture. Mixed with these literary references are
passing allusions to his own traveling both as a sailor and as a
passenger.

Emphasizing again the size of the Pacific and the problem
of choosing "a topic from so vast a storehouse," still but par-

tially known even in the mid-nineteenth century, Melville
turned next to an extended catalogue of what "we might tell,"
given sufficient time, of the fishes, the birds, and the "exceptional phenomena" of the Pacific, each of which could in itself
provide the substance of a lecture; in mentioning these topics
he touched incidentally upon two episodes of his service aboard
a whaleship. The paragraphs devoted to these subordinate
topics draw, in spite of the previous disclaimer, from what he
had already described in print, such as the fishes of *Mardi* and
the birds of "The Encantadas"; a subsequent picture of a Polynesian island as seen from the sea is set forth here in virtually
the same words used once before in *Typee*. Knowing Melville's
amazingly retentive memory for the phrasing of other authors,
one is at a loss whether to attribute these verbal reminiscences
of his own earlier works to unconscious recollection or to in-
tentional repetition. Throughout this portion of the lecture, it
will be seen, the "haze of obscurity" enshrouding the Pacific is
emphasized, along with the vastness of its area and the great
number of its islands, "thick as the stars in the Milky Way."

The next subdivision deals with the attractiveness of the
South Seas to white men and their reception by the natives,
who in Melville's opinion have good reason to "esteem us, with
rare exceptions, such as *some* of the missionaries, the most
barbarous, treacherous, irreligious, and devilish creatures on
the earth." This Swiftian judgment, he explains sarcastically,
is based upon the "brotherly affection" with which the whites
have always treated the islanders—thus "sustaining the honor
of a Christian flag and the spirit of the Christian gospel." Both
the humanitarianism of this passage and the incidental reference to the shortcomings of some aspects of the missionary
movement directly recall Melville's point of view in his earliest
books and the notoriety which resulted from his candid remarks about missionaries, which the Montreal resident who
objected to his lecture there the season before had obviously
not forgotten. In the present discussion, other Western immigrants to the Pacific included are the Buccaneers, long hid-

den by its "mantle of mystery," and the mutineers of the *Bounty*; among those who have considered following in their wake are several bodies of nineteenth-century reformers and cultists—Fourierites, Free Lovers, and Mormons, all the subject of great public curiosity at the time of the lecture—for whose schemes of social betterment Melville had already expressed his disdain in the concluding section of "Statues in Rome." Two more personal anecdotes are introduced at this point in "The South Seas," one concerning "a disciple of Fourier" who had "waited upon" Melville shortly after he published *Typee* in 1846, the other relating to "an acquaintance met in Italy" in 1857. Neither story is found elsewhere in his writings, including journals and correspondence, and it is possible that one or both may have been invented as "yarns" that would add color and personal interest to the lecture. They might have been put into "Statues in Rome" with equal propriety, but when writing it Melville had been making no particular effort to include anecdotes of this kind; their presence in "The South Seas" is an indication of the change in his attitude by the beginning of the second season.

Continuing his discussion of "visionaries," Melville then alludes to the Hawaiian legend of Kamapiikai, which he drew from Ellis' *Narrative of a Tour through Hawaii* (1827), and to a story which had long been one of his favorites, the voyages of Alvaro Mendaña, Viceroy of Peru and discoverer of the Marquesas and Solomon Islands; references to Mendaña are scattered through his works from *Typee* to *Clarel*. Then follows another personal anecdote unmentioned in his earlier writings, concerning a former Professor of Moral Philosophy whom he had once come upon in a secluded Pacific island, attended by three native wives. Other white dwellers among the islands include the notorious "beachcombers" of California fame and many old sailors "who could tell tales about these regions stranger far than any that have ever yet been written." Even his own *Typee* and *Omoo,* Melville adds here, "give scarcely a full idea of them except, perhaps, that part which tells of the long captivity in the valley of Typee." Some of these characters "exhibit sure vouchers of their stories in the shape of tattooing," he continues by way of introducing a discussion of tattooing and "the mysterious rites of the 'taboo,' " both of which he had previously taken up in chapters of *Typee* and *Omoo*. "By contrast, the modern progress in some of these islands is seen in the publication there of newspapers"—usually conducted, however, by white men who show little understanding of or sympathy with the native language and culture. "So the result of civilization . . . is found productive to the civilizers, destructive to the civilizees. It is said to be compensation—a very philosophical word; but it appears to be very much on the principle of the old game, 'You lose, I win': good philosophy for the winner."

The future prospects of Polynesia, according to the concluding paragraph, are at best uncertain, and are not likely to be improved either by current projects for annexing certain islands to the United States or by the continued inroads of whalemen and commercial enterprisers. "I shall close," Melville wrote,

with the earnest wish that adventurers from our soil and from the lands of Europe will abstain from those brutal and cruel vices which disgust even savages with our manners, while they turn an earthly paradise into a pandemonium. As a philanthropist in general, and a friend to the Polynesians in particular, I hope that these Edens of the South Seas, blessed with fertile soils and peopled with happy natives, many being yet uncontaminated by the contact of civilization, will long remain unspoiled in their simplicity, beauty, and purity. And as for annexation, I beg to offer up an earnest prayer . . . that the banns of that union should be forbidden until *we* have found for ourselves a civilization morally, mentally, and physically higher than one which has culminated in almshouses, prisons, and hospitals.

From even this brief résumé of "The South Seas" it is plain that Melville's preliminary remark about the "random way" in which he would proceed was aptly put. By introducing more personal anecdotes and by striving for a lighter, less formal tone he had intentionally sacrificed the comparatively tight organization of its predecessor. "Statues in Rome" had possessed a greater unity of subject matter to begin with, based as it was on recent observations of specific art objects, most of which could be appropriately described in the course of an imaginary journey through the Eternal City and its environs. "The South Seas" is much broader in approaching its more general material, from which Melville had been separated by a much longer span of time. The underlying assumptions of the two lectures are nevertheless strikingly similar. Along with their author's characteristic sympathy for paganism ancient or modern, already observed in both compositions, is found his correlative skepticism about Christianized civilization and its supposed "daily progress" toward "intellectual and moral perfection." In "Statues in Rome" he had developed the contrast between the art of the ancient world and the invention of the modern; "The South Seas" reveals his basic doubt concerning the worth of civilization itself. The allure of primitive life which drew him initially to these pagan Edens of the Pacific had been strengthened, in spite of personal hardship and danger, by direct observation of their "simplicity, beauty, and purity," which according to *Typee* had served for a time to confirm Melville's faith in the natural goodness of man. But seeing also the "contamination" of disease and crime brought with the white men wherever they had come, along with the spectacle of "pent-up wickedness" aboard the frigate on which he returned to the United States, made him increasingly critical, even before he began writing books, of "civilization" and its "almshouses, prisons, and hospitals."

Perhaps Europe and America had been presumptuous in sending missionaries to enlighten the South Seas, Melville suggested as early as *Typee;* the need might well be greater for a corps of native missionaries to be sent to the West! "Are there no Moravians in the moon," he asked later in *White-Jacket,* "that not a missionary has yet visited this poor pagan planet of ours, to civilize civilization and christianize Christendom?"

Similar expressions of brotherly regard for savages, so-called, are found in the brief review of Parkman's *California and Oregon Trail* that Melville wrote in 1849 and particularly in the character of Queequeg in *Moby Dick*. The two lectures are themselves extensions of his previous social criticism, culminating most recently in *The Confidence-Man;* their verdicts on nineteenth-century culture—though returned on the basis of two different standards, one classical and the other romantic —were in keeping with what he had been saying about the modern world ever since his return from the Pacific. In the years to come he was to hold the same fundamental ideas and attitudes, and notably in *Clarel* and in *Billy Budd* was to examine once again the contrasting values brought into question in the lectures.

There are other relations, too, between "The South Seas" and earlier products of the romantic side of Melville's imagination. Through Ishmael in *Moby Dick,* named for the Biblical figure who is the prototype of so many of the wanderers found in Melville's writings, he had uttered the "uncounted thanks" with which, in answer to "the long supplication of my youth," he had first beheld the "dear" Pacific; "to any meditative Magian rover," he had added, "this serene Pacific, once beheld, must ever after be the sea of his adoption." In the lecture the questing which had driven Ishmael, Ahab, and many another voyager of the earlier works has its echo in the attention given to stories of explorers such as Balboa and Magellan, Cook and Mendaña, and of seekers like the Spaniard Ponce de Leon and the Hawaiian Kamapiikai. Mention of the very size of the Pacific draws forth Melville's characteristic response to magnitude, as did the vastness of the Egyptian pyramids and the Roman ruins during his Mediterranean travels. Its islands are "an endless theme"; they are "numberless"; they lie enveloped in "mystery," "obscurity," and "a dark indistinctness." Melville had long been partial to settings of darkness and mystery and infinitude. His White-Jacket had declared his fondness for "an indefinite, infinite background," and the essay "Hawthorne and His Mosses" (1850) deals with "the infinite obscure" of the backgrounds of Hawthorne's tales, whose intense "power of blackness" influenced Melville's subsequent writing so profoundly.

Mention of the human derelicts who seek a solitary hiding-place in the obscurity of London or of the South Seas illustrates another aspect of the Ishmael motif; Melville's emphasis in the lecture upon the lesser-known islands as retreats cut off from the world is especially reminiscent of some of the short stories he had written between 1853 and 1856, together with several striking passages in the journal of his Mediterranean trip which followed. "Many of the sailors who are supposed to be lost," he declares in "The South Seas," are in fact living by choice on some secluded island. This recurrent theme of withdrawal and isolation, which bears a reciprocal relationship to the longing after Utopia touched upon in both lectures as well as to the prevailing "quest" pattern of his writing in general, reveals a yearning deep within his own nature. His sympathetic understanding of the compulsions which motivate the waifs and strays of the South Seas had been voiced most poetically in the chapter of *Moby Dick* containing the moving description of the *Pequod's* solitary blacksmith:

to the death-longing eyes of such men, who still have left in them some interior compunctions against suicide, does the all-contributed and all-receptive ocean alluringly spread forth his whole plain of unimaginable, taking terrors, and wonderful, new-life adventures; and from the hearts of infinite Pacifics, the thousand mermaids sing to them—"Come hither, broken-hearted; here is another life without the guilt of intermediate death. . . ."

Ishmael too had turned sailor as a "substitute for pistol and ball," longing like Melville himself to "sail forbidden seas, and land on barbarous coasts."

Now in 1858, however unwilling Melville the lecturer may have been to resume an old role before the public by writing and delivering "The South Seas," there is ample evidence to bear out the Cleveland reviewer's remark that he had "never forgotten his imprisonment" in Typee and "never recovered

from his captivity." This "attempt to speak" fifteen years later
of the immensity and obscurity of these waters made him feel,
in the words of the lecture, as though he were again "embarking on a voyage to their far distant isles." Though Melville had
once dated the beginning of his own development from his
twenty-fifth year, when he returned from the Pacific and commenced the writing of *Typee,* his earlier life as a wanderer had
in fact been his seed-time as an artist, providing not only the
themes of his first books but also the very basis for his subsequent view of the world. Sharply visualized recollections of
Polynesia and its people appear in nearly all his works from
Typee through *Billy Budd*—even those such as "Statues in
Rome" or *Clarel* whose settings are not the South Seas. By thus
continually " 'traveling' the Pacific again as both writer and
lecturer, Melville betrayed his indissoluble unity with the images of the journey." Such is the comment of James Baird,
whose recent study of Melville demonstrates the pervasive influence upon his imagination of his South Sea experiences.[4]
The same dominant imagery recurs both in the lecture and in
Melville's private writing of this or a later period, particularly
in those "Minor Sea Pieces" which address as "Ned Bunn" his
companion of *Typee,* Toby Greene. There, long after the visit
of the "Typee-truants" to the Pacific, he once more looked back
in memory to the

> Marquesas and glenned isles that be
> Authentic Edens in a Pagan sea,

again regretting the passing of "the world we roved":

> Hollows thereof lay rich in shade
> By voyagers old inviolate thrown
>   Ere Paul Pry cruised with Pelf and Trade.
> To us old lads some thoughts come home
> Who roamed a world young lads no more shall roam.

[4] *Ishmael* (Baltimore, 1956), p. 95. In relating Melville's Pacific
voyages to his subsequent writings Baird stresses a number of dominant
images, or *autotypes* (pp. 106–116): tropical landscape; Polynesian
physique, with its adornment of tattooing; the savage as artisan; the
savage's "superior humanity" in relation to the missionary.

In his verses as in the lectures, moreover, appears the familiar contrast between pagan simplicity and the dubious rewards of modern "progress":

> But tell, shall he, the tourist, find
>   Our isles the same in violet-glow
> Enamoring us what years and years—
>   Ah, Ned, what years and years ago!
> Well, Adam advances, smart in pace,
> But scarce by violets that advance you trace.

So too in *Clarel* the remembrance of things past is voiced in the words of Rolfe, who turns back like Melville himself to memories of earlier adventures

> In mid Pacific, where life's thrill
> Is primal—pagan; and fauns deck
> Green theatres for that tattooed Greek
> The Polynesian.

Melville's "affection for heathenism," to quote the *Ohio Farmer* again, was indeed both "profound and sincere," and in his later work as in "Statues in Rome" and "The South Seas" he continued to write of it "as if the world were little indebted" either to Christianity or to modern progress. The real continuity between the two lectures, as well as their link with the body of his writing, is to be found in his sympathy toward paganism and his regret at the disappearance from modern life of the imaginative richness, the "primal thrill," he associated with the ancients and the Polynesians alike. The chief interest of "The South Seas" to the modern student therefore lies in its reassertion of the same underlying attitudes and emotions that Melville had been expressing in work after work ever since his return from the Pacific. Except for a few personal anecdotes whose authenticity is somewhat questionable, the material of the lecture is not new, though its subject and Melville's method of handling it were to make the lecture more interesting to contemporary audiences than its predecessor had been, as will be seen from the critical reviews to be examined. Most of the commentators at the time were unconcerned with the fundamental ideas or themes of either lecture; their successors today have paid even less attention to "The South Seas" than to "Statues in Rome" in spite of what both reveal about their author's state of mind at a little-known and little-understood point of his career.

4

Melville's Second Lecture Season

1858–59

MELVILLE's second season as a lecturer opened on 6 December 1858 at the Getty House in Yonkers, New York, with the reading of his new lecture on "The South Seas" before the Yonkers Library Association. For a smaller fee than had been usual during the previous season, $30, he appeared as the fourth lecturer of the winter course in Yonkers, speaking to an audience described as "not only large, but very sympathetic." The words are those of the reporter for the Yonkers *Examiner,* which printed the only review of the lecture in its issue of 9 December.[1] The article emphasizes the favorable response to Melville's humor but voices the reviewer's personal objections to his style and delivery:

His success in this field [humor], if it be newly tried, is such as should encourage him. . . . It has been related of Clay, that at the close of one of his speeches, the effect produced by his eloquence was so intense, that the vast assemblage was unable to manifest any outward applause. Thus was it with Mr. Melville's audience[;] though in continuous merriment, their hilarity was too great to allow of other exertion. The facetious tone of Mr. Melville is beyond description. . . . We need say but little as to the literary ability displayed. He has evinced his excessively florid style in his "Typee". Each noun has its adjectives, each sentence

[1] Reprinted in J. H. Birss, "Herman Melville Lectures in Yonkers," *American Book Collector,* V (February 1934), 50–52; excerpts are given in Leyda, *Log,* II, 596–597. Holmes and Curtis were also on the roster of speakers at Yonkers that season.

its parenthesis, till we are aghast at the profuseness, and cannot but be reminded of the sailor who emphasized every other word by an expressive prefix.

Mr. Melville's delivery is anything but pleasant. To use a common simile, the close[s] of his sentences have a descending and rising cadence, which can be likened to nothing on earth but the graceful twist in a porcine afterpart. It may be Polynesian style, but it is hardly *good reading*. On the other hand, his voice is susceptible of a modulation, which cannot be acquired without much care.

The reviewer's objection to Melville's delivery is reminiscent of complaints made during the previous season, and his criticism of the "excessively florid style" suggests that the "literary" touches found in "Statues in Rome" were not absent from its successor. But what the Yonkers reviewer particularly disliked was the absence of new and original material in "The South Seas." His summary, with interpolated comments, of Melville's remarks makes clear that he considered much of the lecture a mere rehash of standard information already familiar to students of history and to readers of Buffon and of Wilkes' *Narrative of the United States Exploring Expedition*. And Melville, he complains, "could not forbear making a splenetic allusion to the missionaries, concerning whom his feelings are well-known, and are too bitter to be impersonal." Other than this he "mentioned a love-story, peculiarly adapted to ladies, which he would not tell, and spoke of the 'Devilfish,' which he did not see"; with respect to content, the reviewer concluded, "this lecture was *'parvum in multo.'* " A similar criticism of Melville's material occurs in a letter to the editor of the *Examiner* printed in the same issue as the review; dated "South Sea View, Yonkers, Dec. 8th," it is signed " 'Herr Honeytown.' " *"Who,"* the letter demands,

is H. Melville, and *where* and *what* is the South Sea? . . . Can the devil's fish tell us? Can we glean it from that legend so interesting to the "ladies of my audience, for it is a love legend of Kamekamehaha, Tahiti and Otaheite?" [*sic*] We must be in our second childhood, for up to Monday evening last we were ignorant of the fact that the Pacific Ocean extended from Tierra del Fuego to Kamschatka, and that the said pool was . . . *"infested* with islands, densely *peopled* with sharks, and *some natives."* Equally so were we in regard to the fact that its ever green arcadias were still free from the corruptions of civilization and annexation. . . . Really we have much to learn, and how shall we ever digest the ponderous philosophy, how shall we obtain the primeval purity, or how shall we scan the Cleopatran hieroglyphics of our New Zealander painted a la Melville? . . . Job must have his disciples in Yonkers, and Bildad the Shuhuhite, from the placid Pacific has come to the rescue. Let us yawn! . . .[2]

Thus Melville, in attempting to be entertaining, had for once in his more recent career been too obvious for some of his listeners rather than too abstruse or subtle. And in returning to the familiar subject matter of *Typee* and *Omoo* he had once more brought to mind his own controversial judgments on Polynesia of twelve years before. The *Examiner's* reviewer, in response, took pains throughout his digest of the lecture to expose what he considered Melville's unjustified bias against the treatment of South Sea natives at the hands of civilized whites. At the conclusion of the lecture, he points out, Melville had called upon

all good people to join in the prayer, that those Islands of the South Sea, which were yet in their natural condition, should ever so remain, that their innocence and repose should be neither destroyed nor disturbed, that they might be preserved from the misery of enlightenment. The good people did not say "amen." On the contrary, it appeared to us that, if expressed, the wish of the audience, the same as that of every true man, would be for the glorious period when Polynesia, having tasted the vices, will turn to the virtues of civilization, and thereby possess, not the bliss of ignorance, as *this* philanthropist desires, but the happiness of rectitude, and the reward of integrity.

So in Yonkers, as in Montreal and Cleveland during the previous season, Melville's familiar views on the missionary enter-

[2] The letter was printed under the heading of "A 'South Sea' View of the Monday Night Lecture." Mr. Thomas E. Dutelle of the Yonkers Public Library supplied its text for this study.

prise had colored both his remarks and the verdict of at least one of his audience. But though his opinions are overtly restated in the passages of "The South Seas" objected to by the Yonkers reviewer, and though the same remarks were fully reported in a number of cities which he was still to visit, there is no further indication in later reports that Melville's criticism again provoked the hostile reaction so obvious in this first review of the new lecture. Nor is there recognition, either in contemporary reviews or in present-day Melville scholarship, that Melville's renewed defense of primitivism against "the misery of enlightenment" complements his attack on modern science and practicality in "Statues in Rome," either the unspoiled primitivism of the South Seas or the virtues of the ancient world being preferable, in his view, to the impieties of modern "progress." It is surprising that this aspect of the lectures, an outgrowth of the scrutiny of modern society offered in *The Confidence-Man,* should so long be ignored.

After his lecture in Yonkers, Melville made a number of calls in New York, where he was scheduled to speak in February, with the object of securing additional invitations in that area. On his return to Pittsfield he found an inquiry from the Chicago Young Men's Association offering not only an engagement in Chicago but the possibility of other appointments in nearby cities,[3] and to this letter Melville replied favorably on 8 December. Meanwhile, in the words of the local *Berkshire County Eagle* of 19 November and 10 December, "by invitation of a large number of his fellow citizens of Pittsfield" he was to "give his new lecture upon the South Seas" in that city, and "we need say nothing to induce Pittsfield people to hear such a man upon such a subject." Melville's lecture on 14 December (fee $50) was the second in a new series which was

[3] The idea of attracting eastern lecturers to Chicago by securing additional engagements for them in the area had originated with S. D. Ward, a former secretary of the Chicago Young Men's Association: see Carl Bode, *The American Lyceum* (New York, 1956), pp. 173–174. Melville's Chicago correspondent was James Grant Wilson, a successor to Ward, who had written on 1 December 1858. A draft of Melville's reply, now in the Harvard College Library, is quoted in *Log,* II, 597.

being established there, and "Burbank's Hall was filled" for the occasion, according to the *Eagle's* report on 17 December, "although the night was the most stormy and uncomfortable of the winter." The lecture, "pleasant and instructive," was "written in the style of Mr. Melville's best books, quaint, simple, and polished . . . and sparkling with original thoughts." The Pittsfield *Sun,* which had printed an advance announcement on 9 December, did not carry reviews of local lectures, but the *Eagle's* brief account clearly indicates a large attendance and a favorable reception on the part of Melville's neighbors. No summary of his remarks appeared in the *Eagle* beyond a reference to his "outline of the geography, natural history, 'civilization,' and other general characteristics of the 'South Seas,' enlivened with incidents of personal adventure." [4]

Melville's two engagements in Yonkers and Pittsfield were his last appearances of 1858; during his previous season he had already lectured six times by the end of December. His first appointment in 1859 was for 31 January in Boston, where he again spoke in the Tremont Temple, this time delivering the ninth lecture of the course sponsored by the Mechanic Apprentices' Library Association (fee $50). The Boston notices of the following day consist largely of brief digests of the lecture, the longest being the summary in the *Journal.* The editorial comments, though few, are uniformly favorable, the only disagreement occurring in reports of the size of the audience. "The reputation of the lecturer called out an audience somewhat larger than usual," according to the *Atlas and Daily Bee,* "though not so numerous as should have been the case"; both the *Daily Advertiser* and the *Daily Courier* also mentioned "a large audience." The *Post* and *Journal,* on the contrary, described it as "not large," the *Journal* adding that it was "about equal to the usual attendance at this and the Mercantile course" and the *Evening Traveller* reporting that the hall "was not more than half full." The *Advertiser* observed that "Mr. Melville was compelled from want of time to pass over many

---

[4] The brief notices and reviews of the Pittsfield lecture are quoted in *Log,* II, 596–597.

things which no doubt would have been exceedingly interesting to the audience. The lecture was a fine production, and
received the close attention of all who heard it." The *Evening
Transcript,* in a brief paragraph, remarked that it "contained
much fine writing, and vividly described the manners and customs of the natives"; the *Traveller* noted that it "abounded
with numerous anecdotes and facts of great interest." The
Herald found the program "interesting" and the *Atlas and
Daily Bee* described it as "quite interesting," adding that Melville's remarks "frequently elicite[d] applause"—something unmentioned in any previous review of his lecturing. The *Journal*
agreed that he was "frequently applauded," concluding that the
lecture "gave the most ample satisfaction." No comments on
Melville's voice or delivery appear in any of these accounts,
which are unanimous in their reports of an entertaining evening and which go beyond anything in the earlier Boston reviews of "Statues in Rome" in their clear and specific indication of manifest popular approval.[5]

Following his Boston engagement Melville left for Gansevoort to visit his mother, accompanied by his seafaring brother
Thomas, just returned from a cruise. On 7 February he was in
New York for his lecture that evening before the New-York
Historical Society (fee $55), the fourth in a special series given
in January and February for the benefit of the Society and
arranged by a committee of which his friend George Duyckinck
was an active member.[6] In December Melville had written to
Duyckinck in an effort to advance the date to an earlier week

[5] All the Boston reviews appeared in newspapers of 1 February 1859.
That in the *Daily Journal* is reprinted, somewhat inaccurately, in Raymond
Weaver, *Herman Melville: Mariner and Mystic* (New York, 1921), pp.
373–375; those in the *Advertiser, Courier,* and *Traveller,* along with an
advance notice in the Boston *Herald* of 31 January, are quoted in part in
Log, II, 598–599. A clipping of the review in the *Atlas and Daily Bee,*
among the Melville papers in the Harvard College Library, was identified
by Mr. Louis Polishook of the Boston Public Library, who also located
additional reports in the *Herald* and *Post;* Miss Jean Simonds of the
Boston Athenaeum located the notice in the *Evening Transcript.*

[6] The series was in addition to the Society's regular lectures for its
membership, given on the first Tuesday of each month. For further details see Willard Thorp, *Herman Melville: Representative Selections* (New
York, 1938), p. 435.

in January, when he had only the single Boston engagement scheduled, feeling some uneasiness about his ability to arrive in Baltimore on 8 February "in time," as he put it, "to immortalize myself there also." But the date had remained fixed, and Melville's hope of an additional engagement in Jersey City, to be secured through Duyckinck's friend David Davidson, had come to nothing. "I should be glad to lecture there—or anywhere," he had told Duyckinck. "If they will pay expenses, and give a reasonable fee, I am ready to lecture in Labrador, or on the Isle of Desolation off Patagonia." In January Duyckinck, on his own initiative, had urged his friend Rosalie Baker to get Melville "an invitation to lecture at Sag Harbor," but again no engagement resulted.[7]

The lecture in New York was perhaps Melville's most successful engagement, according to all available evidence. He spoke in the Historical Society's new building at Second Avenue and Eleventh Street, where the lecture room, according to the New York *Evening Express* of the following day, "was nearly filled by an audience highly respectable, and comprising some of our most eminent *literati.*" The capacity of the hall was 600 persons; an advance notice in the *Daily Tribune* of 5 February had stated that the number of tickets to be sold was limited to 500. Melville's cousin Henry Gansevoort, who attended, complained in a letter to his sister that the rooms "were about half filled owing to the want of proper advertising but those who were present evinced their gratification by applause and attention." A brief notice in the *Tribune* similarly observed that Melville "was listened to with great attention by

7 For the correspondence cited see *Log,* II, 597–599; Thorp, *Herman Melville,* pp. 396–397. Melville had agreed to go to Chicago for a fee of $50; according to Duyckinck he would lecture at Sag Harbor "for fifty dollars and his travelling expenses." During the previous season he had in most instances paid his own expenses, keeping detailed if not altogether accurate records as he traveled and finally subtracting the total from his accumulated fees to determine his net profits for the season. (These records, laid within the notebook of lecture engagements, in the Harvard College Library, are printed in the Appendix.) To charge for expenses in addition to his fee was thus a new policy which Melville initiated during his second season.

a fair audience," and to the *Evening Post* his hearers "seemed much interested with the discourse." The *Post,* in a six-sentence outline of Melville's remarks, detected "some 'yarns' that bordered upon the 'Munchausen,' though they were undoubtedly true," and the *Express,* which gave a much more extensive summary, described the lecture as a whole as "ably treated, full of rich, valuable information, and delivered with ease and grace." [8] A fourth paper, the weekly *Century,*[9] considered it "a very interesting lecture, none the less so for its modest and unpretending composition and delivery." Prefacing its digest of what Melville had said, which is comparable to the long notice in the *Express,* the *Century* characterized his remarks as

a bird's flight of an old traveller over the vast region of waters of the Pacific, alighting here and there for a memorable observation of some natural or moral phenomenon, a bit of personal experience or a reminiscence of some striking trait in the annals of former voyagers. The public expects to hear something from the author of "Typee" and "Omoo" of the wonders he has seen, and would not object to see the curtain raised upon portions of his adventures. To satisfy this sentiment, in his capacity of lecturer, he talks for an hour very pleasantly about the "South Seas," touching now and then upon former topics among his old cannibal friends and Tahitian missionaries—opening the door half way to curiosity, and then, like Autolycus with his ballad, off with a whisk and a "Do me no harm, good man." Mr. Melville, of course, finds it impossible to tell us everything of a region literally half

[8] A clipping of the *Daily Tribune's* review is among the Melville papers in the Harvard College Library. Thorp, *Herman Melville,* pp. 435–436, reprints the review and an advance notice from the same paper; the Reference Department of the New York Public Library located the articles in the *Express* and *Post,* no reports having been carried by other New York dailies. (Files checked are those of the *Commercial Advertiser, Herald, Journal of Commerce, Morning Courier and New York Enquirer,* and *Times,* examined by the library staff, and the *Sun,* searched by the New-York Historical Society; the Brooklyn *Eagle* and *Star,* according to the Long Island Historical Society, did not report the lecture.)

[9] In its issue of 12 February 1859. An extensive search among other weekly and semi-weekly publications issued in New York has located no additional reviews. (The Free Public Library of New Brunswick, New Jersey, the Harvard College Library, the New York Public Library, and the Massachusetts, New-York, Western Reserve, and Wisconsin Historical Societies assisted in checking files of these papers.)

the globe, in the small portion of an evening allowed him. But he tells us a great deal.

To these uniformly favorable newspaper reviews may be added the private comments of Henry Gansevoort, for whom the evening had been "a treat long to be remembered." In his judgment Melville had resumed his "true vein" by abandoning criticism and turning to a more popular subject in "The South Seas." "He was emphatically himself" in the new lecture, reminding Gansevoort "of his vivid and colloquial sketches (always too short) told under the inspiration of Madeira after dinner—or drawn forth by some proper association elsewhere." His manner was informal, unpretentious, and even careless, Gansevoort continued, and the lecture was successful in its very simplicity. "He spoke ably for one hour," presenting his material "in such glowing and gentle colors that every mind seemed to quit its local habitation the while for a short journey through the countries he described." [10] This unstinted praise contrasts sharply with Gansevoort's earlier reaction to "Statues in Rome," and there is nothing in the New York newspaper reports to contradict his assertion of his cousin's gratifying success among the "eminent *literati*" of the city. The favorable reviews in Pittsfield, Boston, and New York, if Melville himself consulted them, surely offered encouragement after the disappointments of the previous season, although his satisfaction must have been offset by his failure to obtain as many engagements during the winter as had been tendered him when he first began lecturing the year before.

On the evening following his lecture in New York, Melville appeared in Baltimore for the tenth lecture of the local Mercantile Library series, speaking in the Universalist Church for the largest fee yielded by any of his engagements: $100. Neither the Baltimore *Clipper* nor the *Republican* reviewed the lecture,

---

[10] Gansevoort's comments appear in his letter of 8 February 1859 to his sister Catherine (Gansevoort-Lansing Collection, New York Public Library). The letter, the advance notice in the *Tribune,* and excerpts from two newspaper reviews are quoted in *Log,* II, 600–601.

but flattering notices appeared the next day, 9 February, in both the Baltimore *American and Commercial Advertiser* and the *Sun*. The *American,* remarking on the "fine audience" drawn to hear Melville, "who had delighted them from time to time through several years past with his graphic and graceful books," published an unusually long front-page summary of the lecture, giving a "phonographic" report of its opening passages in Melville's own words, slightly condensed. The *Sun* concluded its much briefer version with another favorable comment: "The lecture abounded in interesting personal narratives, and held the interest of the audience to the close." [11] Thus in Baltimore, as in at least three of his four previous readings of the new manuscript, Melville had again satisfied both the public and the press, and at last seemed on the way toward establishing the reputation of being a consistently well-received lecturer. From Baltimore he returned to Pittsfield, to find an inquiry awaiting him about the possibility of his reading two lectures in Lynn, Massachusetts, later in the season. To his Lynn correspondent he replied affirmatively on 12 February,[12] and on 18 February he left for a series of four engagements in Illinois and Wisconsin, first stopping en route in Albany with Peter Gansevoort and then probably continuing to Galena, Illinois, for a brief visit with an aunt living there.

Melville's initial midwestern lecture of the season was given in Chicago on 24 February (fee $50), when he spoke in Metropolitan Hall for the Young Men's Association before "a large and fashionable audience." Here the atmosphere was quite different from that of the eastern lecture halls, for after

[11] A search of the Baltimore *Clipper* has been made by the Serials Division of the Library of Congress; the report in the *Sun* was located by Mr. Fred Shelley of the Maryland Historical Society, who also checked the file of the *Republican.* Jay Leyda gives a short extract from the account in the *American* in *Log,* II, 601, and reprints that paper's extensive summary of the lecture in *The Portable Melville* (New York, 1952), pp. 575–583. George E. Gifford, Jr., "Melville in Baltimore," *Maryland Historical Magazine,* LI (September 1956), 245–246, reprints from the *Sun* both an announcement of the lecture on 8 February and the summary of its content included in the report of the following morning.

[12] *Log,* II, 602.

Melville had finished speaking, "Professor Charles Whit-
ney . . . announced his entertainment to take place this evening . . . and gave an admirable impersonation of the eccentric John Randolph, closing with a rendition of Boker's fine
ballad of Sir John Franklin." And here Melville, for the first
time since he had substituted "The South Seas" for "Statues in
Rome," received a totally unfavorable notice, one repeating the
familiar objection of the previous season to both his subject
matter and his delivery. The reviewer of the Chicago *Daily
Journal,* having noted the large attendance, chose to

exercise our charity, and forbear any criticism upon or summary
of the lecture; convinced that the one would prove no less dis-
tasteful to Mr. Melville than would the other to the many admirers of [his] really charming books. . . . Whether it was due
partially to the lecturer's vocal powers, and partially to an involuntary comparison between him and his immediate predecessors, the
matchless word-painting and clear-ringing cadences of the handsome Bayard [Taylor] still ringing in our ears,[13] or wholly to the
intrinsic defects of the lecture, we shall not undertake to say.

But this opinion, although a sample of the reaction Melville
was to provoke in at least three other midwestern papers (especially in cities where "the handsome Bayard" had also appeared), was not unanimous. The Chicago *Daily Press and
Tribune,* although agreeing that he had once more failed to
make himself heard, differed from the *Journal* on the merits
of his performance in other respects. In a front-page review by
a critic struck with the "novelty" of a lecture by "the author of
'Typee,' " this paper concluded that his discourse, "in the warm
coloring, the voluptuous odors and romantic drapery with
which he invested it, was fully up to the standard of public ex-

    [13] The unfavorable comparison of Melville with Taylor, which was to
be repeated in Rockford, Illinois, where both men lectured after their
appearances in Chicago, involved two lecturers personally acquainted. As
a young man of twenty-five Taylor had once been flattered by an invitation to dine in Melville's company; since that time, in 1850, his books of
travel and particularly his widely popular lectures had greatly increased
his fame while that of Melville was dwindling. In 1865 Taylor was to
invite Melville to join "The Travellers," a club made up of men who "had
seen much of the earth's surface." (See *Log,* I, 395; II, 672.)

pectation." The entertainment was "admirable," the reviewer continued, although those "who sat at some distance from the stage . . . whether owing to defects in the construction of the hall, which the speaker was not aware of, or to a lack of vocal powers on his own part . . . lost a large share" of it. A six-paragraph summary of Melville's remarks followed this familiar criticism.

No report was printed by the Chicago *Daily Democrat,* although that paper had carried an advance notice of Melville's local appearance, and no files of either the *Daily Herald* or the *Daily Times* have been located.[14] But from the two reviews examined it is clear that once again Melville was encountering a decidedly mixed reception beyond the Alleghanies, even with a lecture seemingly more appealing to popular audiences than his previous discourse on ancient statuary had been. Whether the tastes of the "West" were as alien to "The South Seas" as to the art of Rome, or whether the larger audiences gathered in unfamiliar halls dispelled the "sympathy" which had prevailed in the eastern cities, the reaction to the new lecture from this time on was by no means so favorable as it had been in Boston and New York. Melville seems to have been at his best when in familiar territory and among friends, where his quiet, unprofessional manner on the platform and his particular form of humor attracted rather than repelled his hearers. But in other areas, where a louder voice and more animation and eloquence were demanded, and especially in cities where his presentation was compared to the more polished style of "those who make lecturing a business," a different reception

14 Extracts from the two Chicago reviews, both of 25 February, have previously been given in Merrell R. Davis, "Melville's Midwestern Lecture Tour, 1859," *Philological Quarterly,* XX (January 1941), 46–57; a passage from the *Tribune's* review is also quoted in *Log,* II, 602. Mr. Paul H. Patterson of the Indiana State Library has searched the files of the Chicago *Weekly Times,* which did not cover the lecture. No review appeared in the Episcopal *Chicago Record,* whose editor was Melville's Chicago correspondent James Grant Wilson, though Wilson printed an announcement of lecturers to address the Young Men's Association in the January number (II, 152).

was again in store for him. Moreover, from the newspaper notices appearing in Milwaukee and in Rockford, Illinois, it seems apparent that though he continued to attract large audiences he could not match the appeal of more experienced speakers, and that many of those who did attend were led to expect a more sensational treatment of "The South Seas" from the author of *Typee* and *Omoo* than Melville's manuscript would offer them.

Melville left Chicago on 25 February for Milwaukee, where he spoke that evening in Albany Hall under the sponsorship of the local Young Men's Association (fee $50). An old family friend, William Cramer, editor of the Milwaukee *Daily Wisconsin,* was probably instrumental in bringing him to the city. The advance notice in Cramer's paper on the afternoon of the lecture identifies Melville as "the widely-known author of *Typee* and *Omoo*" and a member of a distinguished family; it urges that the lecturer "be greeted with a full house," which "always gives a stranger a good impression of the intellectual culture of the city," and by way of inducement reminds its readers that while in the South Seas Melville "had an opportunity to see something of the life of the Feejee Islanders, who are noted for their cannibalism." In Milwaukee as in Chicago, however, the attention of Melville's hearers seems to have been distracted by other entertainers, for the time of his lecture was advanced a half-hour in order to free the hall for a later performance that evening by "Father Kemp's Old Folks' Concert Troupe." In the next day's reviews it was agreed that for Melville's lecture the hall, which had a seating capacity of "about 800," [15] was "filled . . . with an unusually large audience," to quote the *Daily Sentinel,* and one which the *Daily Wisconsin* itself found "very large and appreciative." The *Daily News* did not cover the lecture, but the *Daily Free Democrat* demurred as to Melville's Milwaukee reception: of the "large audience," this paper observed, "many, perhaps the most . . . were disappointed in the lecturer and his discourse." The

<hr>

[15] Davis, "Melville's Midwestern Lecture Tour," p. 47.

Democrat's critic, like two of the Rockford reviewers a few days later, was disgruntled by what he considered a failure to arouse the "thrilling interest" promised by the advance notices. Instead, the lecture was

a literary effort below mediocrity, and too bookish to please, unless he intended it as a reading. In fact it seemed to us as though he had one of his romances before him, and had selected the most uninteresting passages to read for our edification. He spoke of his subject generally, as he said he would at the outset, and so general were his remarks that they failed to create much interest in the minds of his hearers. He commenced by saying that he should not detail any of his own personal adventures, which, to our notion, was a great mistake, for had he stated some of the scenes which he passed through himself, and thereby invested his lecture with some life, instead of telling us what the primary geographies told us in our school-days, he would have created a better impression in Milwaukee. But there were few illustrations of any kind in his discourse, and those given were bare, and colored more by his own attempts at word-painting, than by any inherent or thrilling interest appertaining to them. On the whole, we think there are few who knew much more about the South Seas, after he concluded, than before he began. "Typee" and "Omoo" have not been so widely read, but that some of their personal reminiscenses [*sic*] would have borne repitition [*sic*] on this occasion, and there are those who would have preferred them to such bombast as his asserted reply to the young Fourierite. The lecture was attentively listened to, but the appreciation of it, we think, was testified by the limited applause at the close. The Association, we think, received more profit from the lecture than the audience.[16]

The verdicts of the other Milwaukee papers, however, are in complete contrast to that of the *Democrat*. The *Daily Wisconsin*, as might be expected, was laudatory, its front-page

[16] Ralph M. Aderman, "When Herman Melville Lectured Here," *Historical Messenger* (Milwaukee County Historical Society), IX (June 1953), 5, citing the account books of the Young Men's Association, notes that total receipts for the evening, $50.45, were less than Melville's fee of $50 plus expenses; "even so," he adds, "Melville fared better than E. P. Whipple, the lecturer of the preceding week, who attracted a $39.50 audience." Leyda, *Log*, II, 603, holds that receipts at the door were in addition to fees already paid by subscribers to the lecture series.

comments recalling Henry Gansevoort's earlier description of Melville's success in New York:

It was a pleasant, richly colored story, as it were, (rather than a stilted lecture). . . . There was no labored effort to set before the audience profound logical syllogisms, nor soaring rhetorical flights; but it was such a feast as one would like to sit down to in a club room, and with the blue smoke of a meerschaum gracefully curling and floating away, to listen attentively, though dreamily to, for hours, even till the night wore away. While it was entertaining, too, it was also instructive, in laying open a field of adventure and wanderings to which one rarely has his attention called. We will say, therefore, that we are indebted to Mr. Melville for an evening spent in delicious literary languor during the delivery of his romantic stories of the South Seas.

The writer continues with an unusually full though somewhat inaccurate summary, regretting that the lecture cannot be published "word for word, since much of its merit consisted in the graceful and musical diction, every word of which is as necessary to its harmony and beauty, as is every note to a song of great merit." This review may be discounted as showing the friendly bias of the *Wisconsin's* editor, but the same cannot be said of the equally favorable though less extensive account in the *Sentinel*. This paper too had prepared "a full report of the lecture, but owing to political matters," its printed summary was somewhat abbreviated. Melville "sustains the idea we have formed of him" from his books, the *Sentinel* affirms in contrast to the *Democrat*, finding "a soft, voluptuous ease" his "predominant characteristic. Romance is breathed into the sterile topography of his subject, and the same drowsy enchantment that makes his writings so fascinating radiates from the speaker, and while we listen, it is to the murmur of the musical waves in coral grottoes, and to the sighing of tropical airs laden with the richness of dream land." [17]

[17] All three accounts of the Milwaukee lecture appeared in issues of 26 February 1859. Davis, "Melville's Midwestern Lecture Tour," pp. 48–51, reprints in full the account given in the *Daily Wisconsin,* and elsewhere in the same article quotes extracts from the *Free Democrat.* Leyda, *Log,* II, 602–603, adds excerpts from the *Sentinel's* article, a clip-

The inflated language of the *Sentinel,* like that of the *Daily Wisconsin,* might have been no more pleasing to Melville himself than the fulminations of the *Democrat,* but at least there is an unmistakably hospitable tone in both that is lacking in the reviews of his Rockford lecture of three days later. In Chicago, it will be recalled, Melville had unhappily chanced to follow the popular Bayard Taylor, whose Milwaukee engagement fortunately did not take place until six days after the presentation of "The South Seas." But in Rockford Melville appeared on Monday evening, 28 February, speaking in Warner's Hall (capacity 800), and on the next night Taylor was to discuss "Life in Northern Europe" in the larger Metropolitan Hall, booked to accommodate the many more listeners he was expected to draw. As Merrell Davis has pointed out, Melville's lecture, the fifth of the local course (fee $50), "seems to have been a late addition to the regular series sponsored by the Young Men's Association of Rockford. The newspaper accounts indicate that he may have been brought to Rockford as a substitute for E. P. Whipple, who had failed to arrive for his scheduled lecture on February 18." [18] The critic of the *Rock River Democrat,* which had carried an advance notice of the lecture, was "unable to attend," [19] but unusually full and revealing articles appeared in three other local papers. As in

---

ping of which is among the Melville papers in the Harvard College Library. Aderman, "When Herman Melville Lectured Here," cites advance notices (p. 3) as well as the three reviews. Mrs. Esther J. Nelson of the State Historical Society of Wisconsin reports that the German-language *Banner und Volksfreund* of Milwaukee did not review the lecture.

[18] "Melville's Midwestern Lecture Tour," p. 47. The Rockford and Quincy engagements may have been secured through James Grant Wilson of the Chicago Young Men's Association, to whom Melville had written his acceptance of the invitation there "hoping that, as you suggest, you will be able to make additional appointments for me in your quarter . . ." (see notes 3, 14, above). It may be added that an entry for the season of 1857–58 in Melville's notebook of lecture engagements mentions "Rockford About middle of Jan. 3ᵈ week," but this note was later lined out— probably when the date of the next entry, that of Clarksville, Tennessee, was definitely fixed.

[19] As noted in the issue of 1 March (Davis, "Melville's Midwestern Lecture Tour," p. 52, note).

Chicago and Milwaukee, the critics were divided in their opinions. The one favorable notice appeared in the *Daily News* of the following morning, which reported that "a large and appreciative audience . . . listened with great pleasure to the discussion of a subject invested with all the gorgeous coloring, and glowing romance of Mr. Melville's peculiar genius." But with this first report the *Republican* of 3 March and the *Register* of 5 March, both appearing after Taylor as well as Melville had lectured in Rockford, emphatically disagreed, the latter paper remarking that Melville "may have pleased the large audience who listened to him, but he certainly did not us. We think the *News* must have got an advance report of the gentleman's lecture." The thrust at the *News* was well-taken, for its six-paragraph summary had in fact been copied with only a minor change or two from that in the Chicago *Daily Press and Tribune* of 25 February. Even the opening sentence of the account in the *News* is indebted to the Chicago paper: "A lecture, by a novelist, who ignores women, and yet possesses the splendid imagination which colored 'Typee,' and 'Omoo,' might very well be considered a novelty of the rarest kind; and for this, or some other reason, has been anticipated with much interest by our citizens." From this evidence it appears probable that the critic of the *News*, like his colleague of the *Democrat*, failed to cover the lecture in person; his second-hand report, therefore, possesses little authority.

The two unfavorable reviews were written by critics whose expectations, like those of the reviewer for the Milwaukee *Free Democrat*, were disappointed by what Melville had to say. "It has rarely been our lot," lamented the *Republican*, "to witness a more painful infliction upon an audience. . . ."

We had expected to hear a personal narrative . . . ; some interesting details of the lives, manners and customs of the people; the relation of real personal adventure. . . . Instead of these there was a simple presentation of historical facts, few in number, very common placed, and to be found in books on the shelves of almost any library; the facts slightly exaggerated, all of which were of course, very acceptable to the audience, who must have

gone away highly satisfied that the South Sea bubble had at length
burst.

Mr. Melville . . . lacks depth, earnestness, consecutiveness,
and finish, without which qualities no man need hope of being
a permanently successful lecturer. Lecturing is evidently not his
forte, his style as well as the subject matter being intensely "Polynesian" and calculated to "Taboo" him from the lecture field in the
future.

A caustic summary follows, objecting among other things to
Melville's "telling what *might* be said if there were time to say
it in during the evening, which, happy for the audience, there
was not," and concluding with a completely devastating comment: "We failed to recognize one really good point throughout the entire lecture." Immediately following this thoroughly
hostile review, by far the most unfavorable Melville had received since he had begun lecturing, is a laudatory notice of
Bayard Taylor's obviously more popular appearance in the
larger auditorium, which "was crowded to its utmost capacity
by a very fine audience, anxious to listen to the greatest of living travelers. . . . The aisles of the Hall, and the stage on
either side of the speaker's stand, were occupied also, there
probably being twelve hundred people present."

The contrast between Melville's performance and Taylor's,
which the Chicago *Daily Journal* had previously drawn, was
similarly emphasized in the Rockford *Register,* reviewing both
lectures in a single article. This notice throws further light on
the circumstances of Melville's local reception, calling attention to the fact that the citizens of Rockford had been "well
favored with Lectures during the past few weeks." The critic
"had never listened to Mr. Melville, but from the display of his
various productions, with euphonious titles, which preceded
him on the posters," he too had looked forward to an account
of "interesting personal experience," presumably à la Bayard
Taylor. But like the *Republican's* reviewer, whose comments
are perhaps echoed in the *Register,*

we were disappointed in this, and instead we received a record in
manuscript of a few general, historical facts which could be

gained by visiting almost any well selected library. The first portion of his lecture was devoted to an exposition of the greatness and vastness of his theme. The middle portion was made up of a few *inklings* of what he saw, and what he *might* have said on what he saw, *if he had time!* Here we noticed an inconsistency. He was constantly telling that he must omit much that he would like to say, but never for once did an omission in his speech make an advance in his manuscript. The omissions were not put in. The latter portion of the lecture was made up of the announcement that the inhabitants of the different South Sea Islands were different in their manners and customs, and had many traditions, not one of which did he give us, and generous advice to Mormons, Free Lovers, and other Reformers, as to the impracticability of their attempting to locate thereon. Lecturing is evidently not Mr. Melville's sphere. And no man has a right to set himself up as a lecturer at $50 per night, who cannot for one minute take his eyes from his manuscript.

Taylor's lecture on the following evening, the report continues, "was widely different" from Melville's, being "the most interesting one of the Course, and it certainly was the most paying one." [20]

That Melville himself saw the hostile Rockford reviews is unlikely, as he was due in Quincy, Illinois, for his next lecture on 2 March before either was published. Although the articles express the opinions of the newspaper critics and not necessarily those of the general public, Melville, as Merrell Davis remarks, "would certainly have met with opposition had he wished to return later to the town of Rockford." [21] Perhaps not everyone in the audience attended his lecture with the same expectations, but it seems likely that the public as well as the press had been influenced by advance publicity keyed, as usual, to the fame of *Typee* and *Omoo.* "What 'reputation' H. M. has

[20] Davis quotes the critical passages appearing in the Rockford *Register* and *Republican,* alludes to the notice in the *Daily News,* and notes that the *Rock River Democrat's* reporter was " 'unable to attend.' " Excerpts from both the *Register* and the *Republican* appear also in *Log,* II, 603–604. The quotation from the *Daily News* has not previously been reprinted. Miss Louise C. Johnson of the Rockford Public Library assisted in making this material available for study.
[21] "Melville's Midwestern Lecture Tour," p. 53.

is horrible," Melville himself had written to Hawthorne in 1851. "Think of it! To go down to posterity is bad enough, any way; but to go down as a 'man who lived among the cannibals'!" [22] But so, in effect, he was billed, even by his Milwaukee friend Cramer, when he turned to lecturing—naturally enough, at this time, in view of his current subject. Yet of the "lives, manners and customs" of cannibals he had actually said little to an audience already surfeited with lectures and obviously far more readily attracted by the polished Taylor, "the greatest of living travelers," than by a man who had not visited the Pacific in fifteen years. Whether his reception in Quincy resembled that in Rockford is not known, for neither the *Daily Herald* nor the *Daily Whig and Republican* reviewed the lecture there although both had carried announcements. From these advance notices it is learned that Melville's appearance, scheduled for the City Hall, was sponsored by a "Lyceum" organization; his fee of $23.50 was the smallest he had received since he had spoken in Charlestown for $20 during the previous year. The only comment from Quincy that has been found occurs in the diary of Orville H. Browning, who "went to City Hall" with a friend "and heard Herman Melville Esqr lecture on the South Sea Islands—Erratic but interesting." [23]

From Quincy Melville returned to Pittsfield with but one more engagement yet to be filled, that in Lynn, Massachusetts, on 16 March. When he had replied in February to the inquiry of his Lynn correspondent, W. H. Barry, he had agreed to deliver both "The South Seas" and "Statues in Rome" for "thirty dollars for each lecture," [24] and a fee for "2 lec. 60.00" was later recorded in his notebook. The Lynn *News* of 1 March announced that Melville, "author of 'Typee', 'Omoo', etc., will

[22] Julian Hawthorne, *Nathaniel Hawthorne and His Wife* (2 vols., Boston, 1885), I, 405.
[23] Quoted by Davis, p. 54, note, from Browning's *Diary* as edited by Theodore C. Pease and James G. Randall in *Collections of the Illinois State Historical Library*, XX, 357.
[24] *Log*, II, 602. Barry, according to the Lynn city directory of 1860, was a shoe manufacturer.

lecture in Lynn soon" on " 'The South Seas', and 'Status [*sic*] of Rome'," but this paper carried no further mention of either performance. The *Weekly Reporter* of 12 March, identifying Melville as "the celebrated adventurer," embellished the title of the first lecture by giving it as "The South Seas and the Cannibal Islands," a billing reminiscent of the misleading posters displayed in Rockford. "Statues in Rome" was neither mentioned nor reviewed in the *Reporter,* but a week later a story by "Noggs" covered the "first lecture" as delivered in Sagamore Hall. The occasion was "tolerably well attended," but the lecture "didn't touch the innermost, as did those of Emerson and Lowell. It was more 'of the earth, earthy,' or rather of the water, aqueous. It was good, though, of its kind, and went off very well." [25] On this temperate note ended Melville's second season as a lecturer, which except for the hostility of some midwestern critics, had been far more successful than his first and nearly a hundred dollars more rewarding financially.

Although Melville presented "The South Seas" in only ten cities during 1858–59, as against the sixteen engagements of his previous lecture season, there are nearly as many surviving reports of the second lecture as there had been of "Statues in Rome": twenty-five as compared with twenty-eight. These cover all his appearances except that in Quincy, which was not reported; in Chicago there may have been at least one additional article—in the *Herald* or *Times,* of which files are lacking, but no other possibilities are known. The reviews as a whole indicate even more clearly than those of "Statues in Rome" how Melville's reception differed between the East and the "West." After his first engagement in Yonkers, where the reviewer seems to have been less pleasurably impressed than

[25] Miss Ludovine Hamilton of the Lynn Public Library located the notice in the Lynn *News;* the items from the *Weekly Reporter* are quoted in *Log,* II, 604. Mr. Clifford K. Shipton of the American Antiquarian Society, in checking a file of the weekly *Bay State* also published in Lynn, found no mention of Melville's engagement, and no further information about the lecture has been located in the collections of the Lynn Historical Society.

the audience, the eastern notices were uniformly favorable, but those in the West, meaning in this case Illinois and Wisconsin, were decidedly mixed.

As in 1857–58, Melville attracted good attendance throughout his tour, although not as many listeners came to hear him in Chicago and Rockford as had thronged to hear the reigning professional lecturer of the day, Bayard Taylor. The audience at Yonkers was "large"; in Pittsfield, despite bad weather, the hall was "filled"; in Boston, though the reports varied, the turnout was at least "about equal to the usual attendance" at local lectures. In New York, where his cousin blamed lack of adequate advertising, the audience was only fair, though it consisted of "eminent *literati*," and in Baltimore the attendance was "fine." The Chicago audience was "large and fashionable," that in Milwaukee was "unusually large," the Rockford attendance was again "large," and the final lecture at Lynn was, as the Yankee reviewer put it, "tolerably well attended." Although the number of engagements was smaller by six than in the previous season the net receipts were more than 20 per cent larger: $518.50 as against $423.70 for 1857–58. And Melville was evidently considered to be still a drawing-card in spite of the occasional objections that certain audiences and reviewers had voiced to "Statues in Rome." This inference is confirmed by the evidence of larger fees paid him during the second season, which average nearly $50 per lecture plus additional payments for traveling expenses—during 1857–58 he had assumed his own expenses. The low figures of $30 at Yonkers, $23.50 at Quincy, and $30 each for the two lectures at Lynn were offset by standard $50 fees at Pittsfield, Boston, Chicago, Milwaukee, and Rockford; $55 at New York; and his largest fee, $100, at Baltimore.

During the second season, speaking as he was on the theme with which his name was popularly associated, Melville received only one unfavorable criticism of his choice of topic. This was from the Rockford *Republican,* which in its own words "failed to recognize one really good point throughout the entire lecture." Both Melville's subject matter and also his style, according to this paper, were "intensely 'Polynesian' and calculated to 'Taboo' him from the lecture field in the future." Four of the twenty-five reviews, including the *Republican's,* strongly objected to the way in which "The South Seas" was treated. The first paper to sound this note was the Yonkers *Examiner,* which at the very outset of the season called Melville's discourse *"parvum in multo,"* charging a want of originality in its material. Thus his reasons for calling the Pacific "The South Sea" were in the *Examiner's* view merely his "following a precedant [*sic*] set by old authors," and his mention of "the early explorers in that region . . . we can confirm as correct, for we remember of reading of them in our school days"; again, his "vivid description of the sword-fish, pelican, and whale, . . . upon referring to Buffon, we find to be eminently truthful," and his "fine" account of tattooing is "corroborated in every particular by Lieut. Wilkes in his Narrative of the U.S. Exploring Expedition." Similar objections appear later in three of the Milwaukee and Rockford papers, whose reporters may well have seen the *Examiner's* critical notice among their exchanges. The Milwaukee *Free Democrat,* which found the lecture "too bookish to please"—a phrase seized upon by twentieth-century commentators—fancied that Melville, besides merely repeating "what the primary geographies told us in our school-days," "had one of his romances before him, and had selected the most uninteresting passages to read for our edification." More "personal adventures," more "illustrations," would have put "some life" into the lecture—even had this obliged him to draw still more repetitiously upon *Typee* and *Omoo* for material. Two of the Rockford critics likewise objected to Melville's "simple presentation of historical facts," which "could be gained by visiting almost any well selected library." Much of the lecture, said the *Register,* "was made up of a few *inklings* of what he saw, and what he *might* have said on what he saw, *if he had time!*" Although these criticisms are all similar to what had previously been written in Yonkers, no other paper repeated the *Examiner's* objections to Melville's views about missionaries and other agents of civilization and "enlightenment" in the Pacific. The three dissenters in Milwaukee and Rockford took issue instead with his slighting references to Fourierism, and the Rockford reviewers went on to draw a most unfavorable contrast between the lecture in general and that of Bayard Taylor. Their objection here was also familiar: to a lack of "personal narrative . . . of real personal adventure—always pleasing—which so emphatically marks the fact of the narrator's having actually been in the places described, and seen and known for himself." Just such a complaint against "Statues in Rome" had been made during the previous season—especially by the *Bunker-Hill Aurora* of Charlestown, which found little evidence in that lecture of Melville's having been in Italy.

The only other major objection to "The South Seas" came from the Chicago *Daily Journal,* whose reporter did "not undertake to say" whether his dissatisfaction "was due partially to the lecturer's limited vocal powers, and partially to an involuntary comparison between him and . . . the handsome Bayard . . . or wholly to the intrinsic defects of the lecture." No other reviewer considered the lecture "bookish" or found it "uninteresting" when measured against Melville's earlier writings. To a rival Chicago paper, the *Daily Press and Tribune,* it was "admirable entertainment" and "fully up to the standard of public expectation." The other Milwaukee papers, too, were more than favorable: the *Daily Sentinel* praised in it "the same drowsy enchantment that makes his books so fascinating" and the *Daily Wisconsin* liked it as "a pleasant, richly colored story . . . (rather than a stilted lecture)." The eastern papers, except for the report in Yonkers, had found the discourse "pleasant and instructive," as in Pittsfield, applauding the "numerous anecdotes and facts of great interest" (Boston) and its "rich, valuable information" (New York). Other eastern reviewers used such terms as "a fine production," "quite interesting" and "replete with interest," containing "much fine writing" and composed "in the style of Mr. Melville's best books, quaint, simple, and polished." The Baltimore *Sun's* reviewer took an opposite view from those of the three hostile critics in Milwaukee and Rockford who wanted more personal anecdotes, holding that the lecture "abounded in interesting personal narratives," and the New York *Evening Post* particularly mentioned Melville's colorful " 'yarns' that bordered upon the 'Munchausen,' though they were undoubtedly true." As for his supposed failure to gratify popular expectations, witness again the comments of another New York listener, the reviewer for the *Century:*

> The public expects to hear something from the author of "Typee" and "Omoo" of the wonders he has seen, and would not object to see the curtain raised upon portions of his adventures. To satisfy this sentiment, in his capacity of lecturer, he talks for an hour very pleasantly about the "South Seas," touching now and then upon former topics among his old cannibal friends and Tahitian missionaries—opening the door half way to curiosity, and then, like Autolycus with his ballad, off with a whisk and a "Do me no harm, good man."

One suspects that this writer would indeed have welcomed a still wider opening of the door, but only because of his satisfaction with what Melville did in fact say in the lecture. The defeated expectations of the western reviewers who disliked even what they heard seem to have been aroused by sensational advance notices of the speaker which reminded the public of his dramatic escape from cannibalism à la *Typee.* Even Melville's Milwaukee friend Cramer had been responsible for just that kind of publicity, which was calculated to attract a curious audience though it was of the very sort that Melville himself had long sought to avoid. But by consenting to talk on "The South Seas," as he very well knew, the "man who lived among the cannibals" was risking if not actually inviting its repetition.

As for complaints about voice and manner, so numerous during the previous season, the reviews in only one city, Chicago, mentioned Melville's failure to be heard by his audience, while those in Yonkers and Rockford objected respectively to his delivery and to his reading from manuscript. The caustic writer for the Yonkers *Examiner,* who frowned on Melville's "excessively florid style" even in *Typee,* thought the lecture no better in this regard. Although he commented favorably upon Melville's "facetious tone" and the expressive "modulation" of his voice, he disapproved of the peculiar "cadence" of his sentences, which "may be Polynesian style, but . . . hardly *good reading.*" In short, "Mr. Melville's delivery is anything but pleasant." There are no observations on this aspect of the lecture from Pittsfield, Boston, or Baltimore, where Melville was evidently well received; in New York its "modest and unpretending composition and delivery" were praised and he was said to have spoken "with ease and grace." Before such an audience as that in New York Melville was "emphatically himself," on the testimony of Henry Gansevoort, to whom the lecture there seemed like "his vivid and colloquial sketches (always too short) told under the inspiration of Madeira after dinner— or drawn forth by some proper association elsewhere." But again in the West, especially when in competition with the popular Taylor, he could evidently not bring himself to speak "in so unpretentious a manner, so originally and so carelessly" (in Gansevoort's phrasing), as he had done among the more sympathetic listeners in New York.

Both Chicago reviewers complained of his subdued delivery, one remarking that those at a distance from the stage "lost a large share" of his remarks, "whether owing to defects in the construction of the hall . . . or to a lack of vocal powers on his own part." Such complaints, unique in 1858–59, had been familiar during the previous season. Two of the western reviewers, on the other hand, were favorably impressed by Melville's "graceful and musical diction" and the "soft, voluptuous ease" of both his books and his lecture. These reports are from Milwaukee, where he had friends, and where both his audience and his own manner may well have been more conducive to a good performance than was the case in Chicago and later in Rockford. The *Daily Wisconsin* compared the lecture to "such a feast as one would like to sit down to in a club room"— a comment reminiscent of Henry Gansevoort's observations about the pleasing informality of Melville's engagement in New York. The *Sentinel* likened his voice to "the murmur of the musical waves" and "the sighing of tropical airs"—but after his next appearance in Rockford the sole comparisons made there were between his lecture and Taylor's, from which it was "widely different." That lecturing "is evidently not Mr. Melville's sphere" was the conclusion of two Rockford critics. "He lacks depth, earnestness, consecutiveness, and finish," said the *Republican,* "without which qualities no man need hope of being a permanently successful lecturer." "And no man has a right to set himself up as a lecturer at $50 per night," the *Register* added, "who cannot for one minute take his eyes from his manuscript. He may have pleased the large audience who listened to him, but he certainly did not us."

This acknowledgment of a possible difference between the reaction of the audience in general and that of the newspaper critic deserves some comment, particularly since even the hostile Yonkers reporter had acknowledged Melville's success "as a humorist" and the "continuous merriment" of his "very sympathetic" listeners there. And though the two Chicago critics had agreed that Melville failed to make himself heard they went on to return opposite verdicts as to the merits of what he had said. The Milwaukee critics also differed, two of them praising the performance and the third calling it "a literary effort below mediocrity" which "failed to create much interest" and left "many . . . perhaps the most . . . disappointed in the lecturer and his discourse." This was the *Free Democrat's* reporter, who granted that the lecture "was attentively listened to, but the appreciation of it, we think, was testified by the limited applause at the close." The friendly *Daily Wisconsin,* on the other hand, opened its review by mentioning the "appreciative audience, who seemed greatly to admire" Melville's "fascinating pictures" of the South Seas; the *Daily*

Sentinel, which praised the lecture, had nothing to say about the response of the audience. From other cities there is no indication of differing opinions among the critics or between the reviewers and other listeners. Two of the Boston reporters mentioned frequent applause, one observed "the close attention of all who heard" Melville there, and another declared that the lecture "gave the most ample satisfaction." In New York it was "listened to with great attention" by an audience who "seemed much interested" and who, said Henry Gansevoort, "evinced their gratification by applause and attention." At Baltimore Melville "held the interest of the audience to the close," and in Quincy Orville H. Browning thought him "erratic but interesting." At Lynn, where the reviewer felt that he "didn't touch the innermost" in the manner of Emerson and Lowell, the lecture was said to be "good, though, of its kind, and went off very well." Thus from all indications the lecture was generally well received by both press and public in Boston, New York, Baltimore, and Lynn. The reviewer in Pittsfield also liked the lecture, and Melville's neighbors there presumably agreed. At least one listener was interested in Quincy and others in Chicago, Milwaukee, and even Yonkers were entertained, although a private correspondent of the paper in Yonkers joined its reviewer in complaining about lack of substance in the lecture. Only in Rockford, therefore, was the press preponderantly hostile. To sum up the verdict in a different way: five of the twenty-five reviews were unfavorable; of those remaining, disregarding the borrowed story carried by the Rockford *Daily News,* three articles offered neither criticism of the lecture nor indication of its local reception while sixteen were completely favorable notices, some of them highly laudatory.

From the evidence here examined it seems clear not only that in his second season Melville had chosen a more popular subject in "The South Seas" but also that he had developed through experience into a more effective and probably a more confident public speaker, though his performance was still likely to vary according to the response of his audience. The

press notices reveal little that resembles the widespread dissatisfaction with "Statues in Rome" during the season before
on the ground of its inappropriate content; only in Chicago,
moreover, had there been any recurrence of the frequent complaints of the first season that Melville's voice had not reached
his listeners. Though his delivery and manner were still too
restrained for some western tastes, he had nevertheless improved upon what success he had scored with "Statues in
Rome" in the larger eastern cities, winning frequent applause
with "The South Seas" and praise for his ability as a humorist
and power as a storyteller. The humor and the narrative skill
had long been in evidence, not only in his books but notably
in conversation with his intimate friends, though the material
of "Statues in Rome" and the new experience of speaking in
public had not drawn them forth fully when he first began
lecturing. But even in "The South Seas" Melville could still
not bring himself to gratify completely the popular taste for
personal anecdotes that Bayard Taylor so well supplied, and
in this respect the lecture left some of its warmest admirers
with a measure of disappointment. From Melville's own point
of view, however, it had been a concession to popular taste for
him to talk on the subject at all, and there is reason to think
that by the end of the season he was thoroughly tired of it.

On 20 April 1859, barely a month after Melville returned
to Pittsfield following his last lecture at Lynn, he received two
visitors who had been born and brought up in the Hawaiian
Islands, where their fathers were missionaries. These were
Titus M. Coan and John T. Gulick, both in their mid-twenties,
on vacation from Williams College. The two young men, older
than their classmates, had been reading Melville's works and
were probably aware that he had been lecturing on "The South
Seas"—the one subject which they were most eager to hear
him discuss. Melville, however, "would not repeat the experiences" of which they had been "reading with rapture in his
books," as Coan reported the interview. "In vain I sought to
hear of Typee and those Paradise islands, but he preferred to

pour forth his philosophy and his theories of life . . . and I confess I was disappointed in this trend of the talk." Coan's thwarted expectations and the nature of Melville's quite characteristic response serve to epitomize the separation between curious audience and reluctant speaker that existed even during this second and more successful season of lecturing. What really occupied his mind at the time he was ostensibly seeking to please his public is summed up too in Gulick's impression that "the civilized world" and "our Christendom in general and in particular" had left Melville "disgusted" by their contrast with "the ancient dignity of Homeric times." It was just this turning away from contemporary civilization and "progress" that had led him in "Statues in Rome" to announce that he preferred the Laocoön to a locomotive, and to conclude "The South Seas" by expressing his opposition to all attempts at "civilizing" Polynesia. Yet only two or three reviewers and presumably an equally small segment of his listeners had caught the deeper undertone of either lecture, being eager as they were for stories of personal adventure rather than for Melville's private philosophy of life.

5

The Final Lecture Season, 1859–60

Traveling

VERY little is known of Melville's activities during the spring, summer, and autumn of 1859, though Henry Gansevoort found him "looking well and hearty" during a visit to New York in May and Evert Duyckinck described him in July as "doing nothing in particular." Following the close of his second lecture season and his visit from the two Hawaiian-Americans in April he evidently occupied himself to some extent with writing poetry, in preparation for which he was reading and studying the verse of such writers as Emerson and Herrick and the English and Scottish ballads collected by Professor Child that were added to his library in 1859. On 18 May he had unsuccessfully submitted two "Pieces" to an unidentified magazine, according to his accompanying letter; these were most likely two of his early poems, though they may possibly have been the manuscripts of "Statues in Rome" and "The South Seas," neither of which has survived among the family papers. At some time in the autumn, when Lemuel Shaw paid a visit to Pittsfield, Melville discussed his finances once more with his father-in-law, and with a view toward settling a long-standing obligation turned over to him the deeds to the Pittsfield property, which was subsequently conveyed to Shaw and in turn to Mrs. Melville. By early November he had written a third lecture, entitled "Traveling," and despite a recurrence of illness had arranged at least one engagement to

deliver it during the coming season. Since only a single comparatively brief newspaper summary, eight paragraphs in
length, exists, however, it is impossible to examine this lecture
as thoroughly as its two predecessors. What is clear from the
report is that in the new composition Melville had produced
neither a further treatment of Polynesia to follow "The South
Seas," where he had already reached his self-imposed limits in
recalling his adventures in the Pacific, nor a return to the material recorded in his Mediterranean journal on which "Statues
in Rome" had been based, but rather a discussion of travel in
general, unconcerned with any particular geographical area.
The illustrations, it is true, are primarily associated with his
most recent journey, as seen from a few references to Italy and
the Levant. But in the third lecture Melville apparently
avoided mentioning both the recollections of Palestine that
were to provide the background of *Clarel* and the impressions
of Egypt and Greece that are treated in several of his shorter
poems. The verses grouped under the title "Fruit of Travel
Long Ago" may well have been written by the autumn of 1859
as part of the manuscript volume of poems which he offered
for publication during the following spring.

The subject of travel should have been a congenial one to
Melville, at least under more favorable circumstances, for during the past twenty years he had managed to see much of the
world. At first, as a seaman, he had sailed for money and for
adventure, to Liverpool in 1839 and to the Pacific in 1841.
During his next voyage, to Europe in 1849, he had gone as a
passenger to London to arrange for the English publication of
White-Jacket, and then through the British Isles and to the
continent in search both of immediate pleasure and of materials
to be used in future writing. But the Mediterranean voyage of
1856–57 had been undertaken primarily for the sake of his
still-uncertain health, though the writing of "Statues in Rome"
and his lecturing for three seasons turned out to be unexpected
by-products of the winter abroad. In the words of the newspaper version of the lecture itself, "there are several requisites"

for the "good traveler" which he no longer possessed at the time "Traveling" was written. "One must be young, care-free, and gifted with geniality and imagination, for if without these last he may as well stay at home." In the following spring, when poor health once again obliged him to take to the ship, he was to add an even more fundamental requirement: "The prime requisite for enjoyment in sea voyages, for passengers, is 1st health—2^d good nature. Both," as he wrote to Evert Duyckinck shortly before leaving, are "first-rate things, but not universally to be found." In the lecture, the full title of which was advertised as "Traveling: Its Pleasures, Pains, and Profits," Melville was probably hampered as he had been in writing its two predecessors by the familiar conflict between his real feelings and the necessity of pleasing his public, for at the back of his Mediterranean journal is a penciled observation on the same theme which could scarcely have been repeated from the platform: "The pains lie among the pleasures like sand in rice, not only bad in themselves, but spoiling the good." [1]

As far as can be determined from the newspaper report, Melville treated his subject in the order indicated by his subtitle, discussing in turn the pleasures, the pains, and the profits of travel. Its pleasures consist, he explains, in experiencing the delight of beholding novel objects, which "bewilder and enchant" the spectator and yield not only pleasure but also instruction, provided that he is sufficiently receptive to novelty and fortunate enough to travel under favorable circumstances. He must be prepared, however, to encounter certain unavoidable discomforts and annoyances: the affliction of insects, the bother associated with passports, the "persecutions and extortions of guides," the continual drain on the purse; such are the pains of travel. Along with the rogues and rascals inevitably to be met with, there will also be honest and humane men, "but not in an overwhelming majority." As for the profits of travel, it operates to lessen prejudices and to liberalize one's ideas of

[1] See *Journal of a Visit to Europe and the Levant,* ed. Howard C. Horsford (Princeton, 1955), p. 268.

dress and modes of living, teaching "profound personal humility, while it enlarges the sphere of comprehensive benevolence
until it includes the whole human race." In such ways it
promotes the acquisition of just views, particularly if one sup-
plements his own firsthand experiences by "reading and comparing all writers of travels." Travel exposes the individual to
"change and novelty," which Melville specifies as "often essential to healthy life." In sum: "The sight of novel objects, the
acquirement of novel ideas, the breaking up of old prejudices,
the enlargement of heart and mind,—are the proper fruit of
rightly undertaken travel."

Melville's incidental remark that travel "to a large and generous nature is as a new birth" had been amply borne out in
his own experience during his earlier if not his more recent
years. The words are true enough with respect to his youth
and even to his visit to Europe in 1849, though they are contradicted in part by his most recent trip abroad, which had
evidently not been "rightly undertaken" in terms of the lecturer's advice to his public. Throughout the conventionalities
of the talk runs an undercurrent of half-concealed private sentiments which occasionally rise to the surface, as when Melville alludes to an improperly conditioned voyager of "a somewhat sour nature" who "might be set down even in Paradise
and have no enjoyment," or when he observes that "every individual sees differently according to his idiosyncrasies." Perhaps the most straightforward bit of philosophizing in the entire discussion, and one characteristic of Melville's thinking
ever since his visit to Typee, is his statement that the "legitimate tendency" of travel "is to teach profound personal humility" and at the same time enlarge the sphere of benevolence
till it embraces "people of all shades of color, and all degrees
of intellect, rank, and social worth" throughout the world. This
humanitarian outlook is reminiscent of Melville's fundamental
position when he returned from the South Seas to write *Typee,
Omoo, Mardi,* and his review of "Mr. Parkman's Tour"; it is
illustrated in different ways in *Redburn, White-Jacket,* and

Moby Dick; it suggests his current outlook, moreover, immediately before the outbreak of the Civil War, on a problem of
pressing national importance and popular concern. Here again
the lecture demonstrates the essential unity of his thought
through its recollections of his earlier writings and in this case
by touching obliquely upon a theme which was to occupy him
once more in the prose Supplement to *Battle-Pieces,* his Civil
War poems (1866), and still later in passages of *Clarel.* Unfortunately for Melville as lecturer, however, in the words of
Willard Thorp concerning the substance of "Traveling," all he
had to say about humanitarianism and release from narrow
prejudices "was hardly acceptable doctrine to an age whose
representative traveller is Mark Twain of the Quaker City excursion, bent on asserting the superiority of American manners and institutions" to anything seen abroad.[2]

One other element of the lecture deserves attention in the
light of Melville's personal situation in 1859 and in the perspective afforded by his earlier life and writings. In speaking
of the broadening effects of travel he introduces an illustration
taken from his surroundings at Pittsfield, whose features had
previously been employed both in *Pierre* and in several of his
contributions to magazines. Suppose a person should be born
in that valley of Greylock known as The Hopper, he declares,
and should for the first time ascend the mountain and behold
the landscape to be seen from its summit. "Every man's home"
is such a valley, "which however fair and sheltered, shuts him
in from the outer world." But "the pleasure of leaving home"
to discover the great world beyond "has also as a pendant the
pleasure of coming back to the old hearthstone, the home to
which, however traveled, the heart still fondly turns, ignoring
the burden of its anxieties and cares." Here Melville recurs to
the interlinked motifs of departure, discovery, and return
woven into the patterns of both his life and his art; "traveling,"
as Charles Feidelson has said, "is at once the rationale and the

[2] "Herman Melville's Silent Years," *University Review,* III (Summer
1937), 256.

chief theme of his work," [3] though as for Melville himself the pleasure of departure had always fought a losing battle, especially during his English visit of 1849, with the longing for return to his home and family. His earlier books, those based most directly upon his own voyages, are essentially reports of discovery, or at least the excitement attendant upon discovery, conveying the intensity of Melville's response to the bewilderment as well as the enchantment of "novel objects." But in the later works, their reminiscent postscripts, less concerned with the world of geography than with exploring the world of mind, the characteristic mood and tone are those of disenchantment. Had Melville first visited his Edens of the South Seas ten years later than he actually did, he too might have found himself "set down even in Paradise" incapable of enjoyment.

In Melville's writing between 1851 and 1856, including *Pierre* and *The Confidence-Man,* done at the time his previously good health had begun to fail, the benevolence toward mankind seen in the earlier works was giving way before his increasing doubts as to the prevalence of "honest and humane men." A number of the short stories of this period particularly anticipate the darker aspects of "Traveling," notably "The Piazza" (1856), whose central episode prefigures to some degree an illustration used in the lecture, that of the person dwelling in the valley of Greylock who by ascending the mountain becomes a traveler. The narrator of "The Piazza," drawn by curiosity to climb a mountain overlooking his valley home, finds living near its summit a dispirited girl, tired of a prospect that had once delighted her and envious of his own dwelling to be seen below. He himself returns to his old hearthstone like the traveler in the lecture, but with mixed feelings about his experience. As the story closes he is left pacing his piazza as though "weathering Cape Horn," contemplating some private crisis whose nature is scarcely hinted at. The brief illustration

[3] *Symbolism in American Literature* (Chicago, 1953), p. 173. Feidelson sees Melville himself in Lombardo, the author discussed at length in *Mardi,* whom Melville there compares to "a resolute traveler, plunging through baffling woods."

in the lecture lacks these somber reflections, however, for there Melville is emphasizing the positive rewards of travel. As though enlarging upon a remark in his Mediterranean journal that "seeing is beleiving [*sic*]," [4] he lists among the benefits accruing to the traveler "that of seeing for one's self all striking natural or artificial objects," acknowledging that even books of travel do not in themselves satisfy but only "stimulate the desire to see."

This assertion of the importance of direct experience is characteristic of Melville's empirical bent. In "The Tartarus of Maids" (1855) he had alluded to John Locke's figure of the mind of the newborn child as a blank tablet—"something destined to be scribbled on," as he had put it; here he declares that travel can serve "as a new birth." Like Henry James, fascinated with the plasticity of consciousness, he seems to have regarded the mind as a comparatively passive instrument; the preoccupation of both authors with the impressionistic American traveling abroad is related to their fundamentally empirical outlook. But for Melville the effect of sense-impressions is decidedly not the same for all travelers (which is to say for all men), since "every individual sees differently according to his idiosyncrasies." This acknowledgment in the lecture recalls the remarks in *Moby Dick* and *Pierre* that "it is all in what mood you are in," that "each man reads his own peculiar lesson according to his own peculiar mind and mood." Such is exactly the case with the two characters in "The Piazza," the inference being that the individual consciousness is highly subjective and yet something less than self-determining. That Melville felt obliged even in the lecture to admit the possible negative influence of time, circumstance, and constitution suggests that his belief in the invigorating power of change and novelty, "often essential to healthy life," had in recent years undergone considerable qualification. At the conclusion of the third lecture season, as though by some ironical twist of fate, the doctrine was once more to be put to the test. In May of 1860 Mel-

[4] *Journal of a Visit to Europe and the Levant,* p. 268.

ville was again on shipboard, but hardly "care-free" and "with no concern but to enjoy," as the lecture had prescribed. Seeking only restoration of health, as in 1856, he had undertaken a voyage on the clipper commanded by his brother Tom. But after sailing around Cape Horn as far as California with his brother, he left the ship to return home to his family by steamer via Panama, having failed, so his mother reported, to benefit "at all" from the voyage. From his reservations in the lecture about what is needed to make "a good traveler," and from his later remarks to Duyckinck about the requirements of health and good nature, one feels that his expectations of profit had not been high.

It may have been more than coincidental that Melville's voyage of 1860 followed his one season of lecturing that must be judged an out-and-out failure. His first of only three readings of "Traveling" took place before the Young Men's Association of Flushing, Long Island, on 7 November 1859 for a fee of $30, lower than what he had become accustomed to by this time. According to his sister Augusta, who "had not an opportunity of hearing" the lecture at Flushing but "read it in M S. & thought it highly interesting," Melville "stayed over night and part of a day at Mr. [William R.] Prince's where he was most hospitably entertained & presented with a bouquet of lovely flowers." [5] Although the lecture had been previously advertised in Flushing, no newspaper accounts of its reception there have been located.[6] Melville did not give "Traveling" again during November, and since both his sister and his Pittsfield neighbor Mrs. Morewood took note of his poor health at this time in their correspondence, there is some possibility that he may have been avoiding public appearances until he felt

[5] Augusta Melville to Catherine Gansevoort, 4 January 1860, quoted in Leyda, *Log,* II, 609.

[6] See J. H. Birss, " 'Travelling': A New Lecture by Herman Melville," *New England Quarterly,* VII (December 1934), 727f, note. The same article, pp. 725–728, reprints the sole newspaper report of the lecture, that appearing in the Cambridge, Massachusetts, *Chronicle* 25 February 1860.

stronger. But he himself left no record in his notebook to indicate what negotiations, if any, were then in progress. Whatever the situation had been, at the end of the month his brother-in-law John C. Hoadley wrote at least one letter to a business associate seeking an engagement for Melville, and in December Chief Justice Shaw was also writing, but December and January passed with no appearances booked. On 29 December A. M. Livingston of Salem, Massachusetts, replied to an inquiry from Shaw by saying that although the Young Men's Union there had completed its arrangements for the season the Salem Lyceum still had "one or two vacancies, and I have reason to believe that Mr. Melville will be invited to fill one of them—I think also he will be invited to lecture before the Peabody Institute, in S[outh] Danvers." Melville did not speak in Salem, but appeared in nearby South Danvers on 14 February 1860, according to his notebook, for a $25 fee. His lecture there was not reported, however, either in the local *Wizard* or in the three Salem newspapers, nor is it mentioned in the history of the Peabody Institute.[7] A week later, on 21 February, he delivered "Traveling" for the last time, speaking before the Dowse Institute in Cambridgeport, Massachusetts, where his fee of $55 was in keeping with what he had usually received during the previous seasons. The Cambridge *Chronicle* for 25 February furnished the summary of the lecture already mentioned, but offered no evaluation of its own or indication of the size or response of the local audience.

Such is the limited history of Melville's third season of lecturing, which yielded a total of only $110 in fees for his three engagements. The lack of further concrete evidence in the form of manuscript records, correspondence, or printed reports is disappointing to the student, as the season itself must have been to Melville, and to speak with finality about the exact circumstances involved is therefore out of the question. Obviously the situation confronting him as a lecturer had changed

[7] Miss Florence M. Osborne of the Essex Institute at Salem examined the history and made a search of the newspaper files.

materially since his first season on tour. In 1857–58, despite his lack of experience and the handicap of an inappropriate subject, he had secured sixteen engagements and cleared $423.70. In 1858–59 he had been able to command generally higher fees plus an additional sum for expenses, yet while his receipts rose to $518.50 the number of his engagements dropped to ten. Now in 1859–60 had come a precipitous fall-ing-away in both engagements and fees. During this season there was no appearance in Boston, which had welcomed him during each of the first two seasons; he did not return to New York or Baltimore, where "The South Seas" had been so well received, nor speak even before his own neighbors in Pittsfield, who had filled a local hall to hear him the winter before. One possible explanation has already been mentioned: that Mel-ville's poor health may have made it necessary at the very be-ginning of the season, when negotiations were naturally most active, to decline invitations. But it seems even more likely, considering the activities of Hoadley and Shaw in Melville's behalf, that except for the early engagement in Flushing there were no invitations to decline. In view of the genuine success of "The South Seas" during the previous year in Boston, New York, and Baltimore this may seem rather surprising, although it should not be forgotten that later in the season had come the unfavorable reviews from the West, particularly from Rockford—among the notices most recently seen by lecture committees examining newspaper exchanges when making plans for the following autumn and winter. And during the first two seasons, disregarding the double engagement at Lynn in 1859, which was booked in advance, there had been no re-turn invitations; even in Boston he had appeared each time before a different sponsoring organization.

This fact points in turn to another consideration. In 1857 and again in 1858 Melville's appearance on the lecture plat-form had been hailed as a "novelty," an "event," and even a "sensation," as one Boston paper had declared at the outset. But novelties wear off, among lecture-goers as among travelers,

and after twenty-six engagements over two seasons Melville in
1859 could no longer summon up the same kind of public expectations. By the late fifties, as the newspaper announcements and reviews consistently show, he was best remembered
for *Typee* and *Omoo,* though for more than a decade since
their appearance he had been trying in various ways to establish his fame on a broader base of achievement. His most recent
books, published in the shadow of the roundly condemned
Pierre and lacking the magic of *Typee,* had not made expenses;
since last returning from Europe he had published neither
book nor article. Thus there was nothing other than the lecturing itself to bring the name of Melville freshly before the
public—no new literary work to challenge statements like that
of the Cincinnati reviewer who described his authorship as
tending "toward the nadir rather than the zenith." Melville's
greatest single asset when he turned lecturer therefore remained his identity as "the author of *Typee,*" the "man who
lived among the cannibals"—phrases which he had tried vainly
to supplant in the popular mind, and which were now inevitably losing their immediacy with every passing year. In
1857 their appeal was still strong enough to secure him initial
lecture engagements, but the attraction of sheer novelty, unless
offset by other factors equally powerful, actually works against
the likelihood of repeat performances. It is therefore significant
that with the exceptions noted, Melville did not speak on "The
South Seas" where he had previously offered "Statues in
Rome," nor on "Traveling" where "The South Seas" had been
heard. Unquestionably his performance had improved during
the second season, when with the aid of a more popular topic
he had scored a real success in the larger eastern cities. But
even this was not enough; "The South Seas" was not another
Typee, and some newer and more positive appeal was evidently
necessary to assure him an extended career on the platform.

It will be noted, moreover, that Melville's final performances
took place along the eastern seaboard, two of them near Boston,
rather than in the South or West. Beyond the Alleghanies his

voice—perhaps his accent—had more than once proved a handicap, his manner had been too quiet for popular taste in several cities, and his subjects of the first two seasons were out of touch with the times. Ohio and Michigan wanted lecturers on "practical" and "scientific" subjects rather than "literary" speakers from the East; Illinois wanted "the greatest of living travelers," Bayard Taylor, the reigning lion of the platform, speaking on his most recent experiences abroad, rather than warmed-over *Typee* or a general discussion of "Traveling." Unwilling to write a popularized narrative of his Mediterranean trip, unable to match the voice and manner of professional speakers when before strange audiences, and unconvinced that even at higher rates of return the game of lecturing was worth the candle, Melville surely realized before the close of 1859 that his three-year experiment had at last run its course. A year later, in advance of his arrival in San Francisco aboard his brother's ship, the local press suggested that "our Mercantile Library Association, or some other society, might possibly secure his services for a series of lectures." [8] But if an invitation was actually tendered during his brief stay in San Francisco, Melville was not disposed to comply. Barely a week after reaching the city he was on his way home, with another chapter of his career approaching its close.

[8] The *Daily Evening Bulletin,* 12 October 1860, as quoted in *Log,* II, 627; the suggestion was later repeated in the *Daily Alta.* The declaration that Melville did lecture in California at this time appears in several newspaper articles published after his death in 1891; his friend J. E. A. Smith of Pittsfield, whose faulty memory has led biographers astray on more than one occasion, is probably responsible for the erroneous statements.

6

"Toward the Whole Evidence on Melville as a Lecturer"

THE voyage of 1860, which marks the end of the lecturing, also marks the terminal point of this search for "the whole evidence on Melville as a lecturer." From the investigation a great deal was to be learned, as Newton Arvin recognized fifteen years ago. Though after nearly a century much is now lost to view, with disappearance of the manuscripts of the lectures along with the great bulk of the correspondence between Melville and local lecture committees, much remains: the Mediterranean journal, the notebook of lecture engagements, almost every contemporary review of the lectures, a few letters, and a scattering of other documentary materials bearing upon the man and his work between his return from the Mediterranean and his second voyage to the Pacific. Out of this considerable body of evidence has emerged a far more complete story of Melville's public appearances and their reception than could be told before all these materials were brought together and sifted; at the same time the partial recovery of the content of the lectures, made possible by collating the newspaper summaries, has enlarged the knowledge of Melville's writing before and after his lecturing as well as of what he prepared for the platform. Both features of this study have served to fill in significant gaps in the record between 1856 and 1860 which previously confronted the student of Melville. To relate the picture that has been sketched here to the larger canvas of

Melville's life and times is a task awaiting some future in-
terpreter, though even within the limits of a comparatively re-
stricted investigation there have been clear indications of several cardinal issues. Among them is the relation to one another
of Melville's contemporary reputation and his venture at lecturing; a second matter is the value of the lectures and lecturing in his own eyes; a third is their significance to the student
of Melville's later career. A few words on each of these points
will appropriately conclude this discussion.

Had Melville consented to begin lecturing when *Typee* was
still new to the public mind, as he was in fact requested to do,
the story told here of the content and reception of his lectures
would surely have been very different. Between 1846 and
1850 he would have attracted to the lecture hall the same men
and women who were then reading and arguing about his suc-
cessive books, whether charmed by the adventures related or
aroused by the author's controversial opinions about missionaries in the Pacific, discipline in the United States Navy, or
politicians and issues at home. In the late forties Melville
could thus have carried with him into the lyceum movement
all three of the requirements for a successful program that
Emerson specified: "a great deal of light, of heat, and of people." [1] But the idea of taking time from his writing itself to explore a new medium was not one to move a successful young
author busy at his chosen work and fascinated with his craft.
In the fifties, however, Melville's prospects had drastically
changed as his health declined and his creative energy flagged.
When a need for money and weariness of writing finally drove
him to the platform in 1857, his name, as earlier research has
pointed out, still carried weight with the American public. But
he was no longer the center of active controversy, not because
he had ceased to publish controversial books but because the
public was not buying and reading *Pierre* or *The Confidence-
Man* as it had read *Typee* and *Omoo*. Though Melville was

[1] *The Heart of Emerson's Journals,* ed. Bliss Perry (Boston, 1909),
p. 296.

"well remembered," it was not for his serious novels but primarily as an author of "light reading"—or in his own depreciative phrase of some years before, of "Peedee, Hullaballoo, and Pog Dog." In the absence of some new or significant achievement to rival the success or even the notoriety of his earlier years, such fame as he still possessed was suffering the attrition of time: details of his books had grown dim, and even his quarrel with the missionaries was no longer an active issue. Audiences of 1857 and 1858 would still turn out for a glimpse of Melville, but in none of his progams did they find sufficient reward either to rejuvenate his reputation or to keep him permanently in demand as a speaker. Lecturing may have "in no way harmed his reputation as an author," as some students have asserted; [2] certainly it did little, especially in 1859–60, to sustain it.

By the time Melville brought himself to think of lecturing as worth a trial, the situation confronting any would-be lecturer was less auspicious than it would have seemed ten years before. The financial panic of 1857 "hampered the lecture movement somewhat" even in New England, as Carl Bode has recently written, [3] while in other sections of the country the pressure of hard times forced some lyceums and other sponsoring organizations to curtail or abandon their customary programs. And by this time the lyceum, originally dedicated primarily to adult education, had altered significantly in character and emphasis. The discussion of art and letters which had once dominated its platform was giving way, especially in states beyond the eastern seaboard, to more utilitarian programs, and in some cities like Cincinnati the market for lectures had been considerably overexploited in recent years. Despite the imminence of civil strife, however, there was little threshing-out in the lyceums of current political and social questions, and speakers considered radical, such as Wendell Phillips, found

<hr>

[2] "Melville and His Public: 1858," *American Notes and Queries,* II (August 1942), 70.

[3] *The American Lyceum* (New York, 1956), p. 132.

it difficult in some cities to secure any kind of a platform. The independent Henry Thoreau, viewing the situation in 1858, held it "no compliment to be invited to lecture before the rich Institutes and Lyceums. The settled lecturers are as tame as the settled ministers. The audiences do not want to hear any prophets; they do not wish to be stimulated and instructed, but entertained. . . . They want all of a man but his truth and independence and manhood." [4]

Light entertainment and perhaps some utilitarian instruction, but less culture and nothing controversial—these were the watchwords of the day when Melville followed Curtis and Holmes to the platform. The popular speaker, as he himself was warned by the press in 1857, must supply something "modern" and "personal"; for such fare, served properly and to taste, the public was willing to pay handsomely in spite of hard times. Melville himself accumulated a grand total of $1273.50 in fees during his three seasons on tour; against this had to be charged not only the expense of travel during 1856–57 but also the physical effort and emotional stress which lecturing demanded. In one year alone, 1856, Emerson, who was still actively writing, made about $1700 from lecturing; Bayard Taylor, who was much more in tune with the public and its demands than either Emerson or Melville, could confidently expect to "clear $5000 each season." [5]

Since money had been the principal object that turned Melville to lecturing, his record of comparatively low returns makes it surprising that he continued to lecture even for two seasons, let alone three. Perhaps his modest gains were worth the trouble for the first two winters, when he had little to do in Pittsfield. But by 1859 he had grown increasingly interested in poetry, and when he left for the Pacific in 1860 a collection

[4] *The Heart of Thoreau's Journals,* ed. Odell Shepard (Boston, 1927), pp. 311–312. Compare Vern Wagner's recent survey of "The Lecture Lyceum and the Problem of Controversy," *Journal of the History of Ideas,* XV (January 1954), 119–135. However valuable the lyceum was in other ways, according to Wagner, p. 135, it "was not the arena for serious and vital controversy" except during the single decade of the 1860's.

[5] Bode, *The American Lyceum,* pp. 218, 237.

of his verse was being copied for submission to a publisher during his absence. Poetry, not lecturing or fiction, had become his real concern even before he gave up lecturing; for the manuscripts of the lectures he showed no such solicitude as for the proposed volume of verse, though his expectations of its success were modest. He wanted none of the "clap-trap announcements and 'sensation' puffs" customary with publishers and lecture committees—"For God's sake," he admonished his brother Allan, "don't have *By the author of 'Typee' 'Piddledee' &c* on the title-page." Other contemporary writing, as he told Evert Duyckinck early in 1860, he considered "mealy mouthed" and intolerant of "plain speaking," a remark similar to what Thoreau had said about the character of the lyceum. But concerning the "Lyceums, Young Men's Associations, and other Literary and Scientific Societies" that Melville had satirized in *Pierre* he had nothing directly to say that is now known. Some years afterward, however, when at work on the third book of *Clarel,* he introduced two references to the lyceum, the speaker in each case being the acid-tongued Mortmain. In the course of a discussion of religion turning on the question of a future life, Mortmain remarks that he and his companions have

> "touched a theme
> From which the club and lyceum swerve. . . ."

Later he pours scorn upon the familiar motto of the lyceum movement:

> "Curse on this store
> Of knowledge! Nay, 'twas cursed of yore.
> *Knowledge is power:* tell that to knaves;
> 'Tis knavish knowledge: the true lore
> Is impotent for earth. . . ."

Melville is of course not to be identified wholly with Mortmain any more than with any other single character of *Clarel,* but certainly his own final opinion of lecturing was not markedly higher.

What then, it may well be asked, did he think of the three essays he had written for the lecture platform? All his books, he once told Hawthorne, were "botches" in his own eyes, spoiled by the necessity of trying to compromise between what he was most moved to write and what the public would buy; "dollars damn me," he had said, and the pursuit of the dollar was what sent him finally into lecturing. In referring on earlier occasions to *White-Jacket* and particularly to *Redburn,* which he despised as hack-work turned out solely for money, he twice likened himself to a wood-sawyer sawing such "wood" for sale by the cord—a figure that recurs in his stories and sketches written for the magazines a few years later, under the continuing financial pressure that lasted throughout the fifties. In his private scale of values the lectures probably ranked even below *Redburn, White-Jacket,* and the magazine work. Though after two seasons on tour he may possibly have offered "Statues in Rome" and "The South Seas" to an editor of some unnamed magazine, the truth of the matter is more likely that he destroyed the manuscripts of all three lectures in 1860 or after— a gesture indicative of the value he set on them. But though Melville looked down on all his work written wholly, or even partly, for money, he was too good a craftsman to turn out altogether shoddy products. Some of his highest achievements, for example, are to be found among the pieces written for magazines. No such claim is being advanced here for any of the lectures, although ignorance of their content has led some commentators to undervalue them as it has obliged all students to neglect them unduly. There are times when the work of an author's left hand affords valuable clues to the intentions guiding his right; such is the importance of these minor writings to the understanding of the mind that was still to produce both *Clarel* and *Billy Budd.*

When the significance of the lectures was last argued in print it was taken for granted that Melville did not regard them "as any part of his seriously imaginative writing." Such was the contention of the editors of *American Notes and*

Queries, B. Alsterlund and Walter Pilkington,[6] in commenting upon the study by Merrell Davis of "Melville's Midwestern Lecture Tour, 1859." What Davis took to be the "failure" of "The South Seas," not having access to reports of its favorable reception in Boston, New York, and Baltimore, he attributed in part to Melville's

inability to display upon the platform the narrative vividness which had so fascinated the Hawthornes some years before. But in a large part it may also be attributed to the fact that he had so completely exhausted his personal experiences that his attempts to please the public led him into commonplace generalities and verbal repetitions of himself. Consequently, these newspaper reports of his Midwestern lecture tour provide some evidence that he stopped writing because he could offer the public nothing new.[7]

But to accept this point of view, as Pilkington and Alsterlund pointed out, "one would have to assume that the lectures were Melville's idea of a kind of outlet for old stock in literary materials." Even with "The South Seas," a topic to which he returned only with considerable reluctance, such was hardly the case. First, Melville had deliberately avoided a "narrative" type of lecture, despite the promptings of his Gansevoort relatives and the conspicuous triumphs of Bayard Taylor with just that sort of offering. Second, Melville had not in fact lost altogether the "vividness" of his earlier stories—witness the comments of Henry Gansevoort and William Cramer, both of whom evaluated "The South Seas" favorably in the light of Melville's private storytelling over the years, or consider the favorable newspaper reports from Boston and New York. "Melville's criterion throughout this rostrum interlude," in the words of Alsterlund and Pilkington, "was moderation, restraint," and some listeners of course found such qualities little to their liking. Then too, as Mrs. Metcalf has rightly observed, the quality of his performance evidently depended directly upon the quality of his listeners. Third, though "The South Seas" was composed with

---

[6] "Melville and His Public: 1858," p. 67.
[7] *Philological Quarterly,* XX (January 1941), 57.

an eye on public taste, Melville had followed another standard in writing "Statues in Rome," when as Leon Howard has
pointed out he was making a serious attempt "to order his
thoughts on art." Lastly, after his three seasons on the platform
there still remained untouched, in his journal, page after page
of detailed notes on his Mediterranean trip—grist enough for
a series of Tayloresque travelogues had he felt moved to write
and deliver them.

While it is true that after 1859 Melville could not—or
would not—offer the public anything new about the South
Seas, he had obviously not "exhausted his personal experiences" so long as this other material lay unused, if not in lectures then possibly in additional magazine articles, either of
which could have been collected in the travel book envisioned
by Peter Gansevoort. But where his real interest was tending
involved no concern with narration in prose and no obligation
to please the public. Coupled with his turning to poetry, which
he was writing not for money but for his own satisfaction
alone, the significant anticipations of *Clarel* in the three lectures, especially the first, suggest that he was husbanding the
material for purely private purposes. In some shape or other
the conception of a major work related both to his recent travels and to his views on the course of modern civilization may
well have been taking form as early as 1857, when he wrote
"Statues in Rome," though the poem itself was probably not
begun until well after he had commenced to experiment with
his new medium through the writing of shorter verse. This
first lecture in particular, with its gathering together of earlier
themes and images and its suggestions of the writing still to
come, is a bridge between his prose written before the trip and
his later poetry. The other two lectures are less significant, being work of the moment to provide material for the platform
while he tried his hand at something new, though all three em-
body a projection of his immediate situation during this transi-
tional period of his career.

As the first literary fruits of the latter half of Melville's life the lectures are the product of a mind grown alien to mid-century America. Among the ancients whose civilization he so much admired Melville felt more at home, removed from the contemporary scene into the timeless world of mind. Distant too, in memory, was the Pacific of his youth, to which the voyage of 1860 proved no return; the reëmergence in his verse of the unforgotten story of the "Typee-truants" is a sign of how deeply the events of former days were engraved on his memory —too deeply, perhaps, for exploitation in public without pain. In the writing which lay ahead, the persistence of memories and the value of the past are major themes, not the fresh enchantment of a first glimpse of "novel objects" that had given *Typee* its popular appeal. A synonym for travel, according to the third lecture, is change, but to those interested in Melville's later thought it is his affection for things permanent and stable that strikes the dominant chord. Only after he had written *Mardi, Moby Dick,* and *Pierre* did this element take on significance in his work: in the magazine pieces written between 1853 and 1856. Essentially romantic at heart, he had come by 1857 to value, in the reported words of "Statues in Rome," that "tranquil, subdued air such as men have when under the influence of no passion"—strange words, seemingly, for the creator of Ahab and the chronicler of his "fiery hunt." But to the Melville of this period, unlike his earlier self, the best that life has to offer appeared to be receding inevitably into the past. This was true of his own vigor and youth; it was true also, he now felt, of Christianized civilization in general.

To the young collegians Gulick and Coan, Melville said as much in 1859. Their reports of the interview epitomize the real message of the lectures, whose meaning, lying beneath the surface, escaped most of those who paid to be entertained by the author of *Typee,* not instructed in the personal philosophy of Herman Melville. It was with just such an attitude, never abandoned in the years ahead, that he wrote slightingly to Curtis about man's "daily progress" toward perfection, rejected in two of the lectures the "social and political prodigies" of the contemporary reformers, and praised by contrast the more spacious days of South Sea exploration, the great cultural achievements of Greece and Rome, and the virtues of tolerance and humility. In 1866, after the purgation of the national life that he hoped had been worked by the Civil War, he was once more to exhort the public in his Supplement to *Battle-Pieces*. In concluding the volume, speaking with a voice like that of the young Melville though with Aristotelian overtones, he offered a prayer "that the terrible historic tragedy of our time may not have been enacted without instructing our whole beloved country through terror and pity; and may fulfillment verify in the end those expectations which kindle the bards of Progress and Humanity." But it is the older Melville, emergent in the fifties and studied here in his brief role as lecturer, that otherwise dominates the writing after 1860. When freed at last of the need to please an audience other than himself, Melville turned almost wholly away from the present for his subject matter. In his poetry exclusive of *Battle-Pieces* and in his late prose through *Billy Budd* the time and place are the past and the distant, the characterization and themes are quieter echoes of his earlier life and writing, the prevailing mood is no longer born of change but rather of reminiscence. For the proper study of this work the journal of 1856–57 and the lectures of 1857–1860 are the indispensable introductions.

· PART II ·

TEXTS OF LECTURES,
WITH COMMENTARY

STATUES IN ROME

[In the absence of a surviving manuscript of Melville's first lecture it is impossible to determine with certainty the exact title which he intended. Writing during his second lecture season to W. H. Barry of Lynn, Massachusetts, on 12 February 1859, he listed the titles of his "two lectures" as "The South Seas" and "Statues in Rome"—see Jay Leyda, *The Melville Log*, II, 602. But this single bit of evidence is not sufficient in itself to establish Melville's own usage, however, since in other letters which have not survived he apparently employed different phrasing. Some ten variants are to be found in newspaper references to the lecture, all of which derive ultimately from Melville's original wording, either in correspondence with local lecture committees on which advance publicity was based or else in his delivery of the lecture itself. There is disagreement as to the title not only among newspapers within the same city but even between the advance notices and the later review appearing in the same publication. Of the variant titles occurring more than once in newspapers the following are most frequent, in the order given: "[The] Statues in [*or* of] Rome," "[The] Statuary in [*or* of] Rome [*or* Italy]," and "Roman Statuary."

The composite text printed here is based upon the twenty-eight surviving contemporary newspaper reports of "Statues in Rome" discussed in Chapter 2 above. Two of these are of especial importance. (1) The introductory section of the lecture, comprising the first three paragraphs of the present reconstructed text, was reported almost verbatim, though with indication of some omissions, in the Cincinnati *Daily Commercial*, 3 February 1858. The *Commercial's* version has provided the basis for this portion of the text. (2) The remainder of the lecture, taken as a whole, was most fully reported in the Detroit *Daily Free Press*, 14 January 1858, which printed a detailed summary clearly revealing the over-all organization of Melville's material, though some parts of it, such as the introduction, were covered more thoroughly in other accounts. The *Free Press* report has accordingly provided the basis for the body of the present text, exclusive of the first three paragraphs. Extracts from other contemporary accounts have been introduced into the text here and there to replace or supplement the wording of the *Free Press* and the *Commercial*, however. This has been done wherever there is reason to believe that these other accounts offer a fuller or more accurate approximation of Melville's own language, as determined by collation of the several newspaper versions and by detailed comparison of their phrasing with that of similar passages in Melville's Mediterranean journal or in his published works. The consistent agreement, in essentials, among the newspaper reports indicates that Melville made little if any change in the pattern of the lecture during the course of the season.

In the absence of an authoritative version of any of the lectures, spelling and punctuation have been standardized throughout the composite texts. Citation of Melville's works in the accompanying annotation is by chapter number only, there being as yet no definitive collected edition. Citation of his Mediterranean journal is by date of entry or, if need be, to the published text edited by Howard C. Horsford: *Journal of a Visit to Europe and the Levant, October 11, 1856– May 6, 1857* (Princeton, 1955).]

IT might be supposed that the only proper judge of statues would be a sculptor, but it may be believed that others than the artist can appreciate and see the beauty of the marble art of Rome. If what is best in nature and knowledge cannot be claimed for the privileged profession of any order of men, it would be a wonder if, in that region called Art, there were, as to what is best there, any essential exclusiveness. True, the dilettante may enjoy his technical terms; but ignorance of these prevents not due feeling for Art, in any mind naturally alive to beauty or grandeur.[1] Just as the productions of nature may be both appreciated by those who know nothing of Botany, or who have no inclination for it, so the creations of Art may be, by those ignorant of its critical science, or indifferent to it. Art strikes a chord in the lowest as well as in the highest; the rude and uncultivated feel its influence as well as the polite and polished. It is a spirit that pervades all classes. Nay, as it is doubtful whether to the scientific Linnaeus flowers yielded so much satisfaction as to the unscientific Burns, or struck so deep a chord in his bosom; so may it be a question whether the terms of Art may not inspire in artistic but still susceptible

---

[1] So in "Hawthorne and His Mosses" (1850) Melville had written of "the mystical, ever-eluding Spirit of All Beauty, which ubiquitously possesses men of genius." His concept recalls the discussion of love of the beautiful in Plato's *Symposium* drawn upon in the early chapters of *Pierre*. Here the linking of beauty with grandeur also suggests the influence of eighteenth-century aestheticians.

minds, thoughts, or emotions, not lower than those raised in the most accomplished of critics.

Yet, we find that many thus naturally susceptible to such impressions refrain from their utterance, out of fear lest in their ignorance of technicalities their unaffected terms might betray them, and that after all, feel as they may, they know little or nothing, and hence keep silence, not wishing to become presumptuous. There are many examples on record to show this, and not only this, but that the uneducated are very often more susceptible to this influence than the learned. May it not possibly be, that as Burns perhaps understood flowers as well as Linnaeus, and the Scotch peasant's poetical description of the daisy, "wee, modest, crimson-tipped flower," [2] is rightly set above the technical definition of the Swedish professor, so in Art, just as in nature, it may not be the accredited wise man alone who, in all respects, is qualified to comprehend or describe.

With this explanation, I, who am neither critic nor connoisseur, thought fit to introduce some familiar remarks upon the sculptures in Rome, a subject which otherwise might be thought to lie peculiarly within the province of persons of a kind of cultivation to which I make no pretension. I shall speak of the impressions produced upon my mind as one who looks upon a work of art as he would upon a violet or a cloud, and admires or condemns as he finds an answering sentiment awakened in his soul. My object is to paint the appearance of

[2] These words open Burns' "To a Mountain Daisy." Melville's two-volume edition of Burns (Edinburgh, 1856) is now in the Harvard College Library. This reference to the daisy foreshadows the abundant flower imagery of his later poetry and prose. An especially striking parallel can be found in *Clarel*, I, xxxi, where Rolfe's meditation on science and religion resembles even to its imagery this earlier juxtaposition of science with poetry:

> "Yea, long as children feel affright
> In darkness, men shall fear a God;
> And long as daisies yield delight
> Shall see His footsteps in the sod.
> Is 't ignorance? This ignorant state
> Science doth but elucidate—
> Deepen, enlarge."

Roman statuary objectively and afterward to speculate upon the emotions and pleasure that appearance is apt to excite in the human breast.

As you pass through the gate of St. John, on the approach to Rome from Naples, the first object of attraction is the group of colossal figures in stone surmounting, like storks, the lofty pediment of the church of St. John Lateran.[3] Standing in every grand or animated attitude, they seem not only to attest that this is the Eternal City, but likewise, at its portal, to offer greetings in the name of that great company of statues which, amid the fluctuations of the human census, abides the true and undying population of Rome. It is, indeed, among these mute citizens that the stranger forms his most pleasing and cherished associations, to be remembered when other things in the Imperial City are forgotten.

On entering Rome itself, the visitor is greeted by thousands of statues, who, as representatives of the mighty past, hold out their hands to the present, and make the connecting link of centuries. Wherever you go in Rome, in streets, dwellings, churches, its gardens, its walks, its public squares, or its private grounds, on every hand statues abound, but by far the greatest assemblage of them is to be found in the Vatican.[4] In that grand hall you will not only make new acquaintances, but will likewise revive many long before introduced by the historian.

[3] Melville first visited this basilica 1 March 1857, returning two days later. His journal records his initial impressions: "Loneliness of the spot by Giovanni Gate (Naples) . . . . 12 Apostles gigantic—drapery—Did not visit Stairs &c." That his count of the statues was in error is to be seen from Murray's *Handbook for Travellers in Central Italy . . . Including . . . Rome* (London, 1843), p. 348, which describes the "massive entablature and balustrade, on which are placed colossal statues of our Saviour and ten saints." (This volume is cited hereafter as *Handbook*. Editions later than that of 1843 are unchanged insofar as the content of passages relevant to "Statues in Rome" is concerned.)

[4] According to the journal, 2 March 1857 had been Melville's first "Vatican Day (Monday)"; he remained "from 12 to 3 in Museum" and in the Vatican "till closed. Fagged out completely, & sat long time . . . recovering from the stunning effect of a first visit. . . ." He returned the following day and again on 9 and 16 March.

These are all well known by repute; they have been often described in the traveler's record and on the historic page; but the
knowledge thus gained, however perfect the description may
be, is poor and meager when compared with that gained by
personal acquaintance. Here are ancient personages, the
worthies of the glorious old days of the Empire and Republic.
Histories and memoirs tell us of their achievements, whether
on the field or in the forum, in public action or in the private
walks of life; but here we find how they looked, and we learn
them as we do living men. Here we find many deficiencies of
the historian supplied by the sculptor, who has effected, in
part, for the celebrities of old what the memoir writer of the
present day does for modern ones; for to the sculptor belongs a
task which was considered beneath the dignity of the historian.

In the expressive marble, Demosthenes,[5] who is better
known by statuary than by history, thus becomes a present
existence. Standing face to face with the marble, one must say
to himself, "This is he," so true has been the sculptor to his
task. The strong arm, the muscular form, the large sinews, all
bespeak the thunderer of Athens who hurled his powerful de-
nunciations àt Philip of Macedon; yet he resembles a modern
advocate, face thin and haggard and his body lean. The arm
that had gesticulated and swayed with its movement the souls
of the Athenians has become small and shrunken. He looks as
if a glorious course of idleness would be beneficial. Just so in
the statue of Titus Vespasian, of whom we read a dim outline
in Tacitus,[6] stands mildly before us Titus himself. He has a

[5] Although the impression given by the newspaper accounts is that
the busts Melville describes are for the most part in the Vatican, he was
probably referring to the bust of Demosthenes in the Hall of the Philosophers at the Capitoline Museum, where busts of Socrates, Seneca, and
Plato were also to be seen. His discussion of Demosthenes is indebted not
only to his general knowledge of classical history and biography but also
to his familiarity with Demosthenes' *Orations,* included in the set of
Harper's Classical Library which he had bought in 1849.

[6] This bust Melville had seen in the Hall of the Emperors at the Capitoline Museum; a note near the back of his journal mentions "Busts of
Titus & Tiberius (side by side)" (Horsford ed., p. 267). The "dim outline
in Tacitus" to which he alludes here suggests a principal source for his

short, thick figure and a round face, expressive of cheerfulness, good-humor, and joviality; and yet all know how different was his character from this outward seeming.

In the bust of Socrates we see a countenance more like that of a bacchanal or the debauchee of a carnival than of a sober and decorous philosopher. At a first glance it reminds one much of the broad and rubicund phiz of an Irish comedian. It possesses in many respects the characteristics peculiar to the modern Hibernian. But a closer observer would see the simple-hearted, yet cool, sarcastic, ironical cast indicative of his true character.[7]

The head of Julius Caesar fancy would paint as robust, grand, and noble; something that is elevated and commanding. But the statue gives a countenance of a businesslike cast that the present practical age would regard as a good representation of the President of the New York and Erie Railroad, or any other magnificent corporation. And such was the character of the man—practical, sound, grappling with the obstacles of the world like a giant.

In the bust of Seneca, whose philosophy would be Christianity itself save its authenticity, whose utterances so amazed one of the early fathers that he thought he must have corresponded with St. Paul, we see a face more like that of a disappointed pawnbroker, pinched and grieved. His semblance is just, for it was well known that he was avaricious and grasping, and

---

sketches of Roman notables. The *Ohio Farmer's* reviewer, taking note of Melville's acknowledgment, "could have sat for hours," he declared, "witnessing this skillful and appreciative master of ceremonies taking the robes from the pictured pages of Tacitus and putting them upon the lifeless marbles . . . breathing into them the breath of life, till Rome became living Rome again. . . ."

[7] Writing to Hawthorne in November 1851, Melville had likened himself to "the ugly Socrates"; in his later sketch "The Paradise of Bachelors" he had described a London waiter as having "a head like Socrates." His admiration for the character of Socrates outlasted his changing regard for other philosophers who attracted him at various times. The characterization here may be compared with that of old Ushant in *White-Jacket*, described in ch. 84 as "a sort of sea-Socrates," or with the passage in ch. 10 of *Moby Dick* in which the "calm self-collectedness of simplicity" in savages like Queequeg is called "a Socratic wisdom."

dealt largely in mortgages and loans, and drove hard bargains
even at that day. It is ironlike and inflexible, and would be no
disgrace to a Wall Street broker.[8]

Seeing the statue of Seneca's apostate pupil Nero at Naples,[9]
done in bronze, we can scarce realize that we are looking upon
the face of the latter without finding something repulsive, half-
demoniac in the expression. And yet the delicate features are
only those of a genteelly dissipated youth, a fast and pleasant
young man such as those we see in our own day, whom daily
experience finds driving spanking teams and abounding on
race-courses, with instincts and habits of his class, who would
scarce be guilty of excessive cruelties.

The first view of Plato surprises one, being that of a Greek
Grammont or Chesterfield. Engaged in the deep researches of
philosophy as he was, we should certainly expect no fastidious-
ness in his appearance, neither a carefully adjusted toga or
pomatumed hair. Yet such is the fact, for the long flowing locks
of that aristocratic transcendentalist were as carefully parted
as a modern belle's and his beard would have graced a Vene-
tian exquisite. He might have composed his works as if medi-
tating on the destinies of the world under the hand of a hair-

---

[8] So in ch. 124 of *Mardi* Melville's philosopher Babbalanja quotes
extensively from an unidentified "antique pagan"—actually Seneca—and
the historian Mohi finds in his words "the very spirit" of early Christianity.
Some of the early church fathers, as the *Encylopædia Britannica* points
out (14th ed., XXIV, 637), indeed "reckoned Seneca among the Christians; this assumption in its turn led to the forgery of a correspondence
between St Paul and Seneca which was known to Jerome (cf. Augustin,
Ep. 153 . . .)" and to which Melville alludes here. In 1854 he had
given his brother Tom the copy of *Seneca's Morals* used in *Mardi;* in a
volume of Seneca's works which he owned—a 1614 London edition, now
in the collection of Mr. Carl Haverlin—there is this marginal comment
in his hand (p. 204): "in Seneca . . . we meet with maxims of actual
life, & lessons of practical wisdom which not only equal but exceed any
thing in the Scriptures.—But . . . Seneca's life belied his philosophy. . . ." In *The Confidence-Man,* ch. 37, is an allusion to Seneca as
"a usurer."

[9] In this section Melville probably had in mind three bronze busts
which he had seen in the same Neapolitan museum on 21 February 1857.
Compare his journal entry for that day: "Plato (hair & beard & imperial)
Nero (villianous [sic]) Seneca (caricature.)."

dresser or a modern *valet-de-chambre,* as Louis XIV mused over documents while he smelled his Cologne bottle.[10]

Thus these statues confess and, as it were, prattle to us of much that does not appear in history and the written works of those they represent. This subject was illustrated by instances taken from modern times with which we are all acquainted because in this way we best obtain a true knowledge of the statues. They seem familiar and natural to us because the aspect of the human countenance is the same in all ages. If five thousand ancient Romans were mingled with a crowd of moderns in the Corso it would be difficult to distinguish the one from the other unless it were by a difference in dress. The same features—the same aspects—belong to us as belonged to them; the component parts of human character are the same now as then.[11] And yet there was about all the Romans a heroic tone peculiar to ancient life.[12] Their virtues were great and noble,

[10] The impression of Plato's personal appearance which Melville develops here may have been affected by a glimpse of several busts in the Capitoline Museum which bear Plato's name but are, in the words of Murray's *Handbook,* p. 434, "only bearded images of Bacchus." In *Moby Dick,* ch. 101, Melville had linked the epithets "transcendental" and "Platonic"; his reference here to "that aristocratic transcendentalist" anticipates Ungar's castigation in *Clarel,* IV, xx, of nineteenth-century liberal thought that ignores the existence of evil and imitates "Plato's aristocratic tone." Satirical portraits of the type had previously been drawn by Melville in *Pierre* and *The Confidence-Man* as Plotinus Plinlimmon and Mark Winsome. Yet his own regard for Plato himself, though not without major qualifications, was far higher than his opinion of Plato's latter-day disciples, for above all else he regarded Plato as a great original thinker. For further evidence on this point see note 52 below.

[11] "The grand points of human nature," Melville had written in ch. 14 of *The Confidence-Man,* "are the same to-day as they were a thousand years ago. The only variability in them is in expression, not in feature." When he visited Pompeii 18 February 1857 he found it "like any other town," as he observed in his journal. "Same old humanity," he added. "All the same weather [*sic*] one be dead or alive." And so to Ungar in *Clarel,* IV, xxi, man

> "abides the same
> Always, through all variety
> Of woven garments to the frame."

[12] Further development of this characteristic theme may be found in Melville's later poem "The Age of the Antonines," which another passage in "Statues in Rome" similarly anticipates (note 42 below). Melville's views of paganism and Christianity, influenced both by his personal ob-

and these virtues made them great and noble. They possessed a natural majesty that was not put on and taken off at pleasure, as was that of certain eastern monarchs when they put on or took off their garments of Tyrian dye. It is to be hoped that this is not wholly lost from the world, although the sense of earthly vanity inculcated by Christianity may have swallowed it up in humility.

Christianity has disenchanted many of the vague old rumors in reference to the ancients, so that we can now easily compare them with the moderns. The appearance of the statues, however, is often deceptive, and a true knowledge of their character is lost unless they are closely scrutinized. The arch dissembler Tiberius was handsome, refined, and even pensive in expression. "That Tiberius?" exclaimed a lady in our hearing. "He does not look so bad." Madam, thought I, if he had *looked* bad, he could not have been Tiberius. His statue has such a sad and musing air, so like Jerome in his cell, musing on the vanities of the world, that to some, not knowing for whom the statue was meant, it might convey the impression of a man broken by great afflictions, of so pathetic a cast is it. Yet a close analysis brings out all his sinister features, and a close study of the statue will develop the monster portrayed by the historian. For Tiberius was melancholy without pity, and sensitive without affection. He was, perhaps, the most wicked of men.[13]

---

servations in various parts of the world and by his interest in antiquity, are discussed in Part I above, particularly in Chapters 1 and 3.

[13] As in an earlier passage on "the diabolical Tiberius," in ch. 55 of *Redburn,* Melville was presumably relying here on the account of "unmatchable Tacitus." In *Redburn* he had written of Tiberius as "that misanthrope upon the throne of the world . . . who even in his self-exile, imbittered by bodily pangs, and unspeakable mental terrors only known to the damned on earth, yet did not give over his blasphemies but endeavored to drag down with him to his own perdition, all who came within the evil spell of his power." The passage occurs in a discussion of the sailor Jackson, whose characterization anticipates Ahab in *Moby Dick* and Claggart in *Billy Budd.*

When Melville saw the bust of Tiberius in the Hall of the Emperors at the Capitoline Museum 26 February 1857 he recorded in his journal the comment of his fellow-tourist: " 'That Tiberius? he dont look ["wicked

The statue which most of all in the Vatican excites the admiration of all visitors is the Apollo, the crowning glory, which stands alone in the Belvedere chapel. Every visitor to Rome, immediately on his arrival, rushes to the chapel to behold the statue, and on his quitting the Eternal City, whether after a few weeks or many years, always makes a farewell visit to this same loadstone. Its very presence is overawing. Few speak, or even whisper, when they enter the cabinet where it stands.[14] It is not a mere work of art that one gazes on, for there is a kind of divinity in it that lifts the imagination of the beholder above "things rank and gross in nature," [15] and makes ordinary criticism impossible. If one were to try to convey some ade-

---

at all" lined out] so bad at all'—It was he. A look of sickly evil,—intellect without manliness & sadness without goodness. Great brain overrefinements. Solitude." One hostile critic, reviewing Melville's appearance in Charlestown, Massachusetts, and finding the lecture "particularly dull," was grateful for the anecdote: "Excepting for [Melville's] conversation with the lady about the head of Tiberius, one would hardly have guessed that he had ever been in Italy at all."

[14] Notwithstanding Melville's admiring discussion of the Apollo there is no corresponding passage of impressions in his journal, where it is altogether unmentioned. Nor had he rushed to behold it "immediately on his arrival" in Rome, having walked first to the Capitol in disregard both of the Apollo's supposed appeal and of the "principle" mentioned in his journal entry for 30 March 1857: "that at Rome you go first to St. Peters." It is true, however, that he had found his first visit to the Vatican "stunning" (2 March 1857), and to this effect his glimpse of the Apollo had doubtless contributed. The contemporary enthusiasm for the Apollo reflected in the present passage was indebted to the writings of Winckelmann and of Byron, whose well-known description of the statue's "ideal beauty" in *Childe Harold's Pilgrimage,* IV, clxi–clxiii, is quoted in full for the admiring traveler in Murray's *Handbook,* p. 414. Melville's own youthful enthusiasm for Byron entered into his regard for the statue as early as 1839, when in the first of his "Fragments from a Writing Desk"—heavily indebted to *Childe Harold*—the narrator terms himself "beautiful as Apollo." In *Typee,* ch. 18, Melville later described the "beautifully formed" Marnoo as a suitable model "for the statue of the Polynesian Apollo," and in a magazine sketch of 1856, "The 'Gees," he used the expression "an Apollo Belvedere for beauty." It seems likely that his introduction to the statue itself merely confirmed his long-standing conception of its merit. Melville's account in the lecture of the reaction of spectators reminded the Cleveland *Herald's* critic "of the passage in the poet Campbell's letters, where he says that the first sight of the Apollo struck him dumb, and that he shed tears of joy copiously at the contemplation of such sublime beauty."

[15] *Hamlet,* I, ii, 136.

quate notion, other than artistic, of a statue which so signally lifts the imagination of men, he might hint that it gives a kind of visible response to that class of human aspirations of beauty and perfection that, according to Faith, cannot be truly gratified except in another world.

Milton's description of Zephon makes the angel an exact counterpart of the Apollo.[16] He must have been inspired to a great degree by his recollections of this statue, once the idol of religion and now the idol of art; and the circumstances of his having passed a year in Italy might not be deemed unfortunate for England's great epic. In fact, the whole of that immortal poem, "Paradise Lost," is but a great Vatican done into verse. Milton must have gleaned from these representations of the great men or the gods of ancient Rome high ideas of the grand in form and bearing. Many of those ideas from heathen personages he afterwards appropriated to his celestials, just as the Pope's artist converted the old heathen Pantheon into a Christian church.[17] Lucifer and his angels cast down from Heaven are thus taken from a group in a private palace at Padua,

[16] In *Paradise Lost,* IV, 844–848, the cherub Zephon administers to Satan a "grave rebuke" which to the cherub himself,

> "Severe in youthful beauty, added grace
> Invincible: abasht the Devil stood,
> And felt how awful goodness is, and saw
> Virtue in her shape how lovely. . . ."

Melville's ensuing comments about the effect of Milton's sojourn in Italy upon *Paradise Lost* are quoted here from the account of the Detroit *Daily Free Press,* which gives a more credible version of the passage than such other reports as the Boston *Journal's* brief sentence: "The elevating effect of such statues was exhibited in the influence they exerted upon the mind of Milton during his visit to Italy." Referring to the *Journal's* words, Henry F. Pommer, *Milton and Melville* (Pittsburgh, 1950), pp. 159–161 (note 22), though presenting several possible sources for the idea, considers it "difficult to find precisely what authority, if any," Melville had for this statement and thinks him "almost surely wrong" if he believed that Milton "was much influenced by statuary." Yet the affinities suggested to Melville have also impressed a recent critic: Wylie Sypher, *Four Stages of Renaissance Style* (Garden City, 1955), pp. 222–223, holds that Milton "derives his figures in *Paradise Lost* from the traditions of antique sculpture."

[17] The Pantheon, built by Agrippa, was consecrated as a Christian church by Boniface IV in 608 (Murray's *Handbook,* p. 286). A reflection upon its antiquity occurs in *Clarel,* I, xii.

among the most wonderful works of statuary. This was sculptured out of a single solid block by one of the later Italian artists. Three-score of the fallen lie wound together writhing and
tortured, while, proud and sullen in the midst, is the nobler
form of Satan, unbroken and defiant, his whole body breathing revenge and his attitude one never to submit or yield. The
variety and power of the group cannot be surpassed.[18]

Speaking of the Apollo reminds one of the Venus de
Medici,[19] although the one is at Rome and the other is at Florence. She is lovely, beautiful, but far less great than the
Apollo, for her chief beauty is that of attitude. In the Venus
the ideal and actual are blended, yet only representing nature
in her perfection, a fair woman startled by some intrusion
when leaving the bath. She is exceedingly refined, delicious in
everything—no prude but a child of nature modest and unpretending. I have some authority for this statement, as one

[18] *La caduta degli angeli ribelli,* by Agostino Fasolato, in the Palazzo
Pappafava at Padua. Melville saw the statue there on 1 April 1857, describing it in his journal as "the 'Satan and his host.' Fine attitude of
Satan. Intricate as heap of vermicelli." Photographs of the statue are re-
produced in Pommer, *Milton and Melville,* facing p. 31, and Leo Planiscig,
"Fasolato's Satan and Melville," *Art News,* L (1952), 21. Pommer, p. 138
(note 15), points out that in mentioning the "unbroken, defiant form of
Satan" Melville "probably confused one of the angels with Satan, who
is really at the bottom, in the form of an infernal monster." And as Pommer also observes, p. 32 and note 16, p. 138, it was probably Melville
himself rather than a reporter who introduced into the present passage—
as given in the Cincinnati *Daily Gazette*—"the phrase from Satan's first
speech in *Paradise Lost,*" i.e., I, 107–108:

> "And study of *revenge,* immortal hate,
> And courage *never to submit or yield.* . . ."

[19] This statue, like the Apollo, was mentioned in the first of Melville's
"Fragments from a Writing Desk." He saw it 26 March 1857 in the Uffizi
Gallery at Florence and returned two days later for a "last look." According to his journal, he was "Not pleased with the Venus de Medici" though
"very much astonished at the wrestlers & charmed with Titian's Venus."
His observation in the lecture that the Venus is "of the earth," contrasting
to the "divinity" of the Apollo, may be compared with a comment in
Murray's *Handbook for Travellers in Northern Italy,* where the Venus is
described as "an example of sculpture when the art had, in a great degree,
departed from its highest aim, that of addressing the sentiment by means
of tranquil expression and simple grandeur of form, and had entered on
the comparatively easy task of fascinating the senses by the display of the
soft and beautiful models offered by a less *idealised* nature" (1852 ed.,
p. 519).

day from my mat in the Typee valley I saw a native maiden, in the precise attitude of the Venus, retreating with the grace of nature to a friendly covert.[20] But still the Venus is of the earth, and the Apollo is divine. Should a match be made between them, the union would be like that of the sons of God with the daughters of men.[21]

In a niche of the Vatican stands the Laocoön, the very semblance of a great and powerful man writhing with the inevitable destiny which he cannot throw off.[22] Throes and pangs and struggles are given with a meaning that is not withheld. The hideous monsters embrace him in their mighty folds, and torture him with agonizing embraces. The Laocoön is grand and impressive, gaining half its significance from its symbolism—the fable that it represents; otherwise it would be no more than Paul Potter's "Bear Hunt" at Amsterdam.[23] Thus the

[20] This incident, which is unmentioned in *Typee,* appears only in accounts of the lecture given by the Boston *Journal* and by Henry Gansevoort. But the *Ohio Farmer's* reviewer, who thought that Melville "had never forgotten his imprisonment among the Pacific cannibals, and half regretted his extradition from that physical paradise," seems to allude to it. "We would venture a bet," he goes on to say, "that Mr. Melville, with all his admiration for the Medicean Venus, thinks Fayaway worth a score of cold uninhabited marbles." Among later critics, James Baird would agree with the Cleveland reporter. In *Ishmael* (Baltimore, 1956), pp. 95–96, he cites Gansevoort's version of this passage as illustrating the persistence in Melville's writing of images of his Polynesian experience: "even the Venus must be made one with Fayaway of Typee Valley, or one of her island sisters."

[21] See Genesis 6:2–4.

[22] The appeal of the Laocoön to Melville's imagination is suggested by the earlier reference in *Pierre,* Bk. XI, iii, to "a marble group of the temple-polluting Laocoon and his two innocent children, caught in inextricable snarls of snakes, writhed in eternal torments." A later instance occurs in *Clarel,* I, xxxvii:

> "From the mystic sea
> Laocoon's serpent, sleek and fine,
> In loop on loop seemed here to twine
> His clammy coils about the three."

As in the case of the Apollo, Melville's attitude toward the statue was probably influenced by the description of Byron, also quoted in Murray's *Handbook,* p. 414.

[23] While in Amsterdam on 24 April 1857 Melville "went to Picture Gallery. Wonderful picture of Paul Potter—the Bear." One critic of the lecture, the reporter for the Chillicothe *Advertiser,* objected to Melville's refusal to confine himself strictly to "those statues which immortalize the 'Eternal City'" instead of telegraphing his audience "to Naples and Flor-

ideal statuary of Rome expresses the doubt and the dark grop-
ing of speculation in that age when the old mythology was
passing away and men's minds had not yet reposed in the new
faith.[24] If the Apollo gives the perfect, and the Venus equally

ence, and to Amsterdam, with little regard for their convenience" and
without even taking the trouble "to render the travelling easy." No other
reviewers, however, complained of Melville's side-glances at works seen
elsewhere than in Rome.

[24] This observation, though reported only by the Clarksville *Daily
Chronicle,* is unquestionably genuine; in fact it directly anticipates the
comparison of ancient and modern religious doubt in *Clarel,* I, xxi. There
Rolfe, the speaker, begins his discussion with a reference to another
favorite of Melville's among the Roman writers, Cicero: Cicero's "fine
tomes" would "(change the gods)"

> "serve to read
> For modern essays. And indeed
> His age was much like ours; doubt ran,
> Faith flagged; negations which sufficed
> Lawyer, priest, statesman, gentleman,
> Not yet being popularly prized,
> The augurs hence retained some state—
> Which served for the illiterate.
> Still, the decline so swiftly ran
> From stage to stage, that *To Believe,*
> Except for slave or artisan,
> Seemed heresy. Even doubts which met
> Horror at first, grew obsolete,
> And in a decade. To bereave
> Of founded trust in Sire Supreme
> Was a vocation. Sophists throve—
> Each weaving his thin thread of dream
> Into the shroud for Numa's Jove.
> Cæsar his atheism avowed
> Before the Senate. But why crowd
> Examples here: the gods were gone.
> Tully scarce dreamed they could be won
> Back into credence; less that earth
> Ever could know yet mightier birth
> Of deity. He died. Christ came.
> And, in due hour, that impious Rome,
> Emerging from vast wreck and shame,
> Held the forefront of Christendom."

In a similar vein are other passages in Melville's poetry, such as this image
in *Clarel,* IV, viii, of the decline of modern faith:

> "that vast eclipse, if slow,
> Whose passage yet we undergo,
> Emerging on an age untried.
> If not all oracles be dead,
> The upstart ones the old deride. . . ."

shows the beautiful, the Laocoön represents the tragic side of humanity and is the symbol of human misfortune.

Elsewhere in the Vatican is the Hall of Animals.[25] In all the ancient statues representing animals there is a marked resemblance to those described in the book of Revelations. This class of Roman statuary and the pictures of the Apocalypse are nearly identical. But the ferocity in the appearance of some of these statues, such as the wolf and the slaughtered lamb, is compensated by the nature of others, like that of the goats at play around the sleeping shepherd. The quiet, gentle, and peaceful scenes of pastoral life are represented in some of the later of Roman statuary just as we find them described by that best of all pastoral poets, Wordsworth. The thought of many of these beautiful figures having been pleasing to the Romans at least persuades us that their violence as a conquering people did not engross them, and that the flame of kindness kindled in most men by nature was at no time in Roman breasts entirely stamped out. If we image the life that is in the statues and look at their more humane aspects, we shall not find that the old Roman, stern and hard-hearted as we generally imagine him, was entirely destitute of tenderness and compassion, for though the ancients were ignorant of the principles of Christianity there were in them the germs of its spirit.[26]

Thus, when I stood in the Coliseum, its mountain-chains of

[25] Melville first visited the Hall of Animals 2 March 1857, noting a "Wolf & sheep," and returned there a week later. His journal entry for 9 March, upon which the present passage is directly based, reads as follows: "Hall of Animals—Wolf & lamb, paw uplifted, tongue—fleece. Dog on stag, ey[e]ing him. Lion on horse.—But Playing Goats—the goat & kid—show a Wordsworthian appreciation of the gentle in Nature."

[26] Although the Boston *Post* was the only newspaper reporting Melville's lecture to bring out the Christian references in this and the following paragraph, there is little reason to question their authenticity. The specific identification, here and in the succeeding description of the Dying Gladiator, of tenderness and compassion with Christian attitudes seems not out of keeping with Melville's earlier treatment of the "antique pagan" in *Mardi* (note 8 above). After his first view of the Dying Gladiator, 26 February 1857, he remarked in his journal: "Shows that humanity existed among the barbarians of the Roman time, as it now among Christian barbarousness[?]."

ruins waving with foliage girding me round, the solitude was
great and vast like that of savage nature, just such as one experiences when shut up in some great green hollow of the Ap-
penine range, hemmed in by towering cliffs on every side. But
the imagination must rebuild it as it was of old; it must be re-
peopled with the terrific games of the gladiators, with the
frantic leaps and dismal howls of the wild, bounding beasts,
with the shrieks and cries of the excited spectators.[27] Unless

[27] This "rich scene of word painting," as the Auburn *Daily Advertiser* termed Melville's description of the Coliseum, was evidently the high
point of the lecture for many listeners; "in all our reading" the reviewer
for the Clarksville *Daily Chronicle* could not remember "a more beautiful
passage." That such writing was considered "eminently *lecturesque*," to
use the phrase of another reviewer, is indicative of the kind of material
which pleased the taste of Melville's day. This is the one section of the
lecture most often singled out not only for praise but also for extended
summary, paraphrase, and quotation in the various newspaper accounts.

To match the unusually full reconstruction which these detailed reports have made possible, there is a clear indication, from Melville's
journal entries and notes, of how the passage took form in his mind. Near
the end of the journal (Horsford ed., p. 268) he had written the following memorandum, which may indeed have been the germ of the entire
lecture: "*Coliseum*. great green hollow—restore it repeople it with all
statues in Vatican   Dying & Fighting Gladiators." The note was probably occasioned by his first visit to the Coliseum: on 26 February 1857,
when he also saw the Dying Gladiator in the Capitoline Museum, he described the Coliseum as like a "great hollow among hills. Hopper of Greylock. Slope of concentric ruins overgrown. Mountainous." On 5 March he
again visited the Coliseum, and when he returned on 12 March the idea
of "Repeopling it, &c," was included in his journal entry, with evident
reference to the earlier notations. His description in its final form compares the Coliseum not with the Hopper of Greylock, in the New England
Berkshires, but with a valley of the Appenines: "Grand scenery," he had
written of the Italian mountains on 29 March 1857. "Long reaches of
streams through solitary vallies [*sic*]. No woods. No heartiness of scenery
as in New England." Another adaptation seems indicated by his impression
of the ruins as "waving with foliage"; "summit wavy with verdure" was
what he had written of the Temple of Venus near Naples on 23 February.
As none of these passages in the journal are marked in any special way it
is impossible to say how much Melville depended upon its wording to recall or enrich his visual recollection of the scene he describes in the lecture. James Baird, *Ishmael,* p. 96, argues that the passage is also reminiscent of Melville's handling of Polynesian landscape in *Typee, Omoo,* and
Moby Dick. Pointing out similarities in imagery and phrasing, he suggests
that Melville either saw the Coliseum "with both Roman and Polynesian
vision, or, in retrospect, the image drifted into a Polynesian framework,
making a double image representing antiquity."

this is done, how can we appreciate the Gladiator? It was such a feeling of the artist that created it, and there must be such a feeling on the part of the visitor to view it and view it aright. And so, restoring the shattered arches and terraces, I re-peopled them with all the statues from the Vatican, and in the turfy glen of the arena below I placed the Fighting Gladiator from the Louvre, confronting him with the dying one from the Capitol. And as in fancy I heard the ruffian huzzas for the first rebounded from the pitiless hiss for the last, I felt that more than one in that host I had evoked shared not its passions, and looked not coldly on the dying gladiator whose eyes gazed far away to

> "where his rude hut by the Danube lay,
> *There* were his young barbarians all at play."

Some hearts were there that felt the horror as keenly as any of us would have felt it. None but a gentle heart could have con-ceived the idea of the Dying Gladiator, and he was Christian in all but the name.[28]

It is with varied feelings that one travels through the sepul-chral vaults of the Vatican.[29] The statues there are of various

[28] As with the Apollo and the Laocoön, Melville may first have heard of the Dying Gladiator in reading Byron; he refers to the statue as early as *Mardi,* ch. 135, and *White-Jacket,* ch. 87. While in Paris during his previous trip to Europe he had undoubtedly seen what in *Pierre,* Bk. XVI, ii, is called "that vaunted *chef d'œuvre,* the Fighting Gladiator of the Louvre," when he visited its "admirable collection of antique statuary" on 30 November 1849.

The brief quotation on the Dying Gladiator from Byron's *Childe Harold's Pilgrimage,* IV, cxli, appears in only one newspaper account, that of the Clarksville *Chronicle,* but there seems little doubt that Melville had the passage from Byron in mind. He may indeed have quoted it as extensively in his manuscript as it is given in Murray's *Handbook,* p. 435: compare the Auburn *Advertiser's* reference to his "beautiful poetical quo-tations."

[29] There is some question as to the precise reference intended in this passage. Although the two newspapers alluding to this portion of the lec-ture, the Boston *Journal* and the Detroit *Daily Free Press,* agree in their mention of "vaults of the Vatican," it seems likely that Melville had ac-tually been speaking of one or more quite different places. Among the pos-sibilities, all of which contain ancient sepulchral inscriptions and monu-ments, are the Galleria Lapidaria, a long gallery of the Vatican Museum; the crypt of St. Peter's, known as the *grotte Vaticane,* which he probably

characters: Hope faces Despair; Joy comes to the relief of Sorrow; Rachel weeps for her children and will not be comforted; Job rises above his afflictions and rejoices. The marbles alternate; some are of a joyous nature, followed by those that are of a sad and somber character. The sculptured monuments of the early Christians in these vaults show the joyous triumph of the new religion—quite unlike the somber mementoes of modern times. But just as a guide hurries us through these scenes with his torch-light, bringing out one statue in bold relief while a hundred or more are hidden in the gloom, so must I do to keep within the limits of an hour.

In passing from the inside of the Vatican to the square in front, we find ourselves surrounded by the mighty colonnade with its statues, from whence we see the balloon-like dome of St. Peter's and the great pile of confused architecture which is the outside of the Vatican. If one stands a hundred feet in front of St. Peter's and looks up, a vast and towering pile meets his view.[30] High, high above are the beetling crags and precipices of masonry, and yet higher still above all this is the dome. The mind is carried away with the very vastness.[31] But through-

visited during his "tour of interior" on 8 March 1857; and the Catacombs, whose "labyrinth" he had explored three days later. The appearance in the present passage of a guide with a torch-light suggests that Melville had at least referred briefly to one or both of the subterranean sites. Murray's *Handbook,* pp. 404–405, after pointing out that pagan and Christian works face one another across the Galleria Lapidaria, observes that the Christian inscriptions show "the influence of a purer creed . . . in the constant reference to a state beyond the grave, which contrasts in a striking manner with the hopeless grief expressed in the Roman monuments." But Melville, in his similar mention of "the joyous triumph of the new religion," prefers to emphasize the contrast between the early Christian monuments and "the somber mementoes of modern times."

[30] Upon arriving in Rome 25 February 1857 Melville had noted that the cathedral "looks small from Tower of Capitol.—Walked to St. Peters," his journal continues. "Front view disappointing. But grand approach. Interior comes up to expectations. But dome not so wonderful as St: Sophia's." On 3 March he arrived at the church too late for an ascent to the dome, but on the following day he returned to find "feilds [sic] and paddocks on top—figures of saints." On 6 and 8 March ("tour of interior") he was again at the church. Later, on 7 April, he was to find Milan Cathedral "More satisfactory" than St. Peter's.

[31] Melville's reaction is characteristic of his prevailing response to the magnitude of Roman buildings and the colossal size of some of the statues,

out the Vatican it is different. The mind, instead of being be-
wildered within itself, is drawn out by the symmetry and
beauty of the forms it beholds.[32]

But nearly the whole of Rome is itself a Vatican on a large
scale—everywhere are fallen columns and sculptured fragments. These are of different and varied character. Remarkable, however, among all are the sculptured horses of Monte
Cavallo, riderless and rearing, seeming like those of Elijah to
soar to heaven.[33] The most of these, it is true, were works of
Greek artists, and yet the grand spirit of Roman life inspired
them, for the marble horses seem to represent the fiery auda-
ciousness of Roman power. The equestrian group of Castor
and Pollux illustrates the expression of untamed docility, ra-

---

notably those of the horses which he describes in the succeeding paragraph. Similar remarks are to be found throughout his journal, especially
in his account of the overpowering effect upon him of the Egyptian pyramids. "In other buildings, however vast," he had written (Horsford ed.,
p. 123), "the eye is gradually inured to the sense of magnitude, by passing
from part to part." But with the pyramids "there is no stay or stage." They
stir "the sense of immensity," so that in comparison "all other architecture
seems but pastry. . . . As with the ocean, you learn as much of its vastness by the first five minutes glance as you would in a month, so with the
pyramid. Its simplicity confounds you." Compare also Melville's unfavorable discussion of the Crystal Palace near the conclusion of his lecture
(note 54 below), a further expression of his taste in architecture.

[32] Compare this expression of Melville's admiration with two comments among the penciled notes at the back of his journal (Horsford ed.,
pp. 267, 268): "The Vatican (a volume)" and "Vatican like long walks
in great Park—arbored with arabesques."

[33] As he beheld these "colossal horses from ruins of baths" on 28 February 1857 Melville thought his experience "like finding the bones of the
mastadon [sic]—gigantic figures emblematic of gigantic Rome." Richard
Chase, Herman Melville: A Critical Study (New York, 1949), p. 227,
pointing out that Melville consistently "thought of the earliest age as
the age of giants," compares this passage in the journal with ch. 104 of
Moby Dick on "The Fossil Whale," that "ante-mosaic, unsourced existence." Melville's journal entries on Monte Cavallo and the Baths of Caracalla are filled with comments on the magnitude of their ruins. On 1
March, when he saw a "colossal equestrian group" (Castor and Pollux),
he thought of such ruins found in the Baths as the "most imposing group
of antiques in Rome. . . . Gigantic Rome.—St. Peters in its magnitude &
colossal statuary seems an imitation of these fragments."

For the reference to Elijah, to whom "appeared a chariot of fire, and
horses of fire; . . . and Elijah went up by a whirlwind into heaven,"
see II Kings, 2:11.

ther than conquered obedience, which ancient artists have given the horse.[34] From this can be deduced the enlarged humanity of that older day, when man gave himself none of the upstart airs of superiority over the brute creation which he now assumes. The horse was idealized by the ancient artists as majestic next to man, and they longed to sculpture them as they did heroes and gods. To the Greeks nature had no brute. Everything was a being with a soul, and the horse idealized the second order of animals just as man did the first.[35] This ideal and magnificent conception of the horse, which had raised that animal into a sort of divinity, is unrivaled in its sublime loftiness of attitude and force of execution. We see other instances of this same profound appreciation of the form of the horse in the sculpture of the frieze of the Parthenon.[36]

Of other statues of large size much might be said. The Moses by Michelangelo appears like a stern, bullying genius of druidical superstition; that of Perseus at Florence would form a theme by itself.[37] This statue, by Benvenuto Cellini, is

[34] Valery's *Travels in Italy* (Paris, 1852), p. 566, notes that among the embellishments of the piazza of Monte Cavallo are "its superb colosses of *Castor* and *Pollux*," conjectured to be Greek productions, though "despite the Latin inscription, neither by Phidias nor Praxiteles." The passage is unmarked in Melville's copy (Osborne Collection, New York Public Library).

[35] The "most striking and beautiful thought" of this passage, as the Clarksville *Daily Chronicle's* reporter termed it, recalls Melville's earlier praise of the Liverpool truck-horses in *Redburn*, ch. 40: "what is a horse but a species of four-footed dumb man . . . ?" There is "a touch of divinity even in brutes," he had gone on to affirm, "and a special halo about a horse, that should forever exempt him from indignities." Later, in *Clarel*, IV, ix, there is an exchange of views growing out of Melville's own travel experiences. When Derwent observes that "poor Dobbin (Jew indeed / Of brutes) seems slighted in the East," Ungar counters with a reminder of Anglo-Saxon cruelty to horses (see "Traveling," note 5).

[36] Melville had seen this frieze in February of 1857 and was later to describe it in the third section of "The Parthenon":

> "What happy musings genial went
> With airiest touch the chisel lent
>   To frisk and curvet light
>   Of horses gay. . . ."

After visiting the studies of several contemporary artists working in Rome he remarked in his journal, 10 March: "Art perfect among Greeks."

[37] The famous figure of Moses, at the tomb of Pope Julius II in the

another astonishing conception, conceived in the fiery brain
of the intense artist and brought to perfection as a bronze cast
in the midst of flames which had indeed overshot their aim.
Another noble statue, conceived in a very different spirit, is
the Farnese Hercules, which in its simplicity and good nature
reminds us of cheerful and humane things.[38] This statue is not
of that quick, smart, energetic strength that we should suppose would appertain to the powerful Samson or the mighty
Hercules; but rather of a character like that of the large ox,
confident of his own strength but loth to use it. No trifles
would call it forth; it is reserved only for great occasions. To
rightfully appreciate this, or, in fact, any other statue, one
must consider where they came from and under what circumstances they were formed. In other respects they reveal
their own history.

Thus to understand the statues of the Vatican it is necessary
to visit often the scenes where they once stood—the Coliseum,
which throws its shade like a mighty thunder cloud, the gardens, the Forum, the aqueducts, the ruined temples—and remember all that has there taken place. I regret that the time
will not allow me to speak more fully of these surroundings.
But Roman statuary is by no means confined to the Vatican,
or even to Rome itself. The villas around the city are filled

---

Church of San Pietro in Vincoli, is unmentioned in Melville's journal.
Cellini's statue of Perseus holding the severed head of Medusa had interested Melville long before his glimpse of it in Florence on 24 March
1857. Describing Ahab in ch. 28 of *Moby Dick,* he had written that his
form "seemed made of solid bronze, and shaped in an unalterable mould,
like Cellini's cast Perseus." His present images of artistic conception "in
the fiery brain of the intense artist" and of "flames which had indeed
overshot their aim" not only recall Cellini's story of his work on the statue
while affected by a high fever but also suggest comparison with Melville's
own fire-symbolism in *Mardi,* "Hawthorne and His Mosses," and *Moby
Dick.*

[38] This colossal replica, ten feet high, was found in the Baths of
Caracalla and was once housed in the Farnese Palace, as Melville noted in
his journal 27 February 1857. He had previously seen it while in Naples
on 21 February, remarking on its size and describing it in his journal as
having a "gravely benevolent face." Compare the reference in *Billy Budd,*
ch. 2, to "that humane look of reposeful good nature which the Greek
sculptor in some instances gave to his strong man, Hercules."

with it, and, in those quiet retreats, we catch some of the last and best glimpses of the art.[39] Here, where nature has been raised by culture and refinement into an almost human character, are found many of those trophies which have challenged the admiration of the world; here, where once exhaled sweets like the airs of Verona, now comes the deadly malaria, repelling from these ancient myrtles and orange groves. This reminds us that in a garden originated the dread sentence, Death [40]—that it was amidst such perfumed grottoes, bowers, and walks that the guests of a Lucretia Borgia were welcomed to a feast, but received a pall.

Many of these villas were built long years ago by men of the heathen school, for the express purpose of preserving these ancient works of art. The villas which were to shield and protect them have now crumbled, while most of the statues which were to be thus preserved still live on. Notable is the Villa Albani, built as it was by one who had made art and antiquity the study of his life, as a place to preserve the splendid works he had collected.[41] Here are the remains of antiquity from

[39] In addition to the Villa Albani, which Melville singled out for special attention, he had visited a number of the villas near Rome. The grounds of the Villa Borghese, which he saw on 28 February 1857 and again on 13 March, he described in his journal as of "Great beauty. . . . Fine rich odours of bushes & trees. The laurel &c. The closed villa, statues seen thro' railing. Silence & enchantment. . . ." On 17 March he went to the Villa Aldrobrandini at Frascati, with its "Avenues of trees. Laurel cypress, pine, olive. Rich masses of foliage." During the next three days as he visited additional villas he made similar brief comments in the journal. On a page near the end of the volume (Horsford ed., p. 267) is the following note: "The cypress in the Villa D'Este / Whispering like Michael Angelo's 'Fates.' "

[40] Melville was to return to this theme in *Clarel,* I, xxx:

> "Within a garden walking see
> The angered God . . . where the vine
> And olive in the darkling hours
> Inweave green sepulchres of bowers."

Memory, he adds in the same passage, "Links Eden and Gethsemane. . . ."

[41] Melville had paid two visits to the Villa Albani, an eighteenth-century structure built by Alessandro Cardinal Albani outside the Porte Salaria. Murray's *Handbook,* p. 467, quotes a description of Cardinal Albani as "a profound antiquary" who, "having spent his life in collecting ancient sculpture, formed such porticos and such saloons to receive it as an old

Pompeii, and we might bring back the guests to the rooms where they sat at the feast on the eve of the fatal eruption of Vesuvius. It was not unusual for them at their feasts to talk upon the subject of death [42] and other like mournful themes forbidden to modern ears at such scenes. Such topics were not considered irrelevant to the occasion, and instead of destroying the interest of the feast by their ill-timed intrusion, they rather added to it a temporary zest. One of the finest of the statues to be found in this villa is the Minerva,[43] a creature as purely and serenely sublime as it is possible for human hands to form. Here also is to be found a bust of Aesop,[44] the dwarfed and de-

---

Roman would have done. . . ." The villa itself is termed "the third sculpture gallery in Rome, being surpassed only by the Vatican and the Capitol" (p. 468). Melville particularly noticed a statue of Antinous and a "small bronze Apollo" on his visit of 28 February 1857; on 14 March he mentioned a caryatid and admired the "long lines of foliage—architecture of villa, richness of landscape. Fine site." Richard Chase, *Herman Melville*, pp. 224–227, considers at some length the relations between these comments in Melville's journal and his later "After the Pleasure Party," in which these lines occur:

> "Entering Albani's porch she stood
> Fixed by an antique pagan stone
> Colossal carved."

[42] An exact parallel to this passage occurs in Melville's "The Age of the Antonines," the second stanza of which is quoted here from an early version sent by Melville to John C. Hoadley 31 March 1877:

> "Ere the sting was dreamed to be taken from death—
> Ere the saving of scamps was taught,
> They reasoned of fate at the flowing feast
> Nor stifled the fluent thought:
> We sham, we shuffle, while faith declines:
> They were *frank* in the age of the Antonines!"

According to Melville's accompanying letter, he had recently come across the poem "in a lot of papers. I remember that the lines were suggested by a passage in Gibbon (Decline & Fall)"—a book which had been in his mind during his visit to Rome, as indicated by his journal entry for 8 March 1857. Similarities between the poem and the lecture (see also note 12 above) and their common indebtedness to Gibbon may suggest an even earlier date for the genesis of the poem than that of 1862 advanced by Jay Leyda (*Log*, II, 760).

[43] Probably the "fine and imposing statue" at the Villa Albani mentioned in Murray's *Handbook*, p. 469, and thus the original of the "form august of heathen art" (an "armed Virgin") in "After the Pleasure Party," quoted in note 41 above.

[44] Also at the Villa Albani; Murray's *Handbook*, p. 470, finds the Aesop "perhaps the only example of an ancient statue of deformity." In

formed, whose countenance is irradiated by a lambent gleam of irony like that we see in Goldsmith's.

In conclusion, since we cannot mention all the different works, let us bring them together and speak of them as a whole. It will be noticed that statues, as a general thing, do not present the startling features and attitudes of men, but are rather of a tranquil, subdued air such as men have when under the influence of no passion. Not the least, perhaps, among those causes which make the Roman museums so impressive is this same air of tranquility. In chambers befitting stand the images of gods, while in the statues of men, even the vilest, what was corruptible in their originals here puts on incorruption.[45] They appeal to that portion of our beings which is highest and noblest. To some they are a complete house of philosophy; to others they appeal only to the tenderer feelings and affections. All who behold the Apollo confess its glory; yet we know not to whom to attribute the glory of creating it. The chiseling them shows the genius of the creator—the preserving them shows the bounty of the good and the policy of the wise.

These marbles, the works of the dreamers and idealists of old, live on, leading and pointing to good. They are the works of visionaries and dreamers, but they are realizations of soul, the representations of the ideal. They are grand, beautiful, and true, and they speak with a voice that echoes through the ages. Governments have changed; empires have fallen; nations have passed away; but these mute marbles remain—the oracles of time, the perfection of art. They were formed by those who had yearnings for something better, and strove to attain it by embodiments in cold stone. We can ourselves judge with what success they have worked. How well in the Apollo is expressed

---

Clarel, I, xii, Melville was to describe the deformed Celio's "fair head" as "set on crook and lump, / Absalom's locks but Æsop's hump. . . ."

[45] See I Corinthians 15:53. Throughout his journal of 1856–57 Melville had rung changes on the Pauline theme of corruption and incorruption.

the idea of the perfect man. Who could better it? Can art, not life, make the ideal? [46]

Here, in statuary, was the Utopia of the ancients expressed.[47] The Vatican itself is the index of the ancient world, just as the Washington Patent Office is of the modern.[48] But how is it possible to compare the one with the other, when things that are so totally unlike cannot be brought together? What comparison could be instituted between a locomotive and the Apollo? Is it as grand an object as the Laocoön? To undervalue art is perhaps somewhat the custom now.[49] The world has taken a practical turn, and we boast much of our progress, of our energy, of our scientific achievements—though science is

[46] "Can art, not life, make the ideal?": in ch. 33 of *The Confidence-Man* Melville had recently written that "as with religion" the art of fiction "should present another world, and yet one to which we feel the tie," and that art should exhibit to men "even . . . more reality, than real life itself can show." A passage in the later *Clarel,* I, xxvii, touches on the difficulty of his proposition:

> "But ah, the dream to test by deed,
> To seek to handle the ideal
> And make a sentiment serve need:
> To try to realize the unreal!"

Compare also a passage of "After the Pleasure Party":

> "For never passion peace shall bring,
> Nor Art inanimate for long
> Inspire."

[47] Melville's dislike of utopian political schemes as contrasted with the Utopia of ideal art is reflected in his manuscript poem entitled "A Reasonable Constitution" (Harvard College Library):

> "What though Reason forged your scheme?
> 'Twas Reason dreamed the Utopia's dream:
> 'Tis dream to think that Reason can
> Govern the reasoning creature, man."

Even in Plato's *Republic,* as in More's *Utopia,* he found an "almost entire reasonableness" offset by its "almost entire impracticality," as a note to the verse makes clear.

[48] In *The Confidence-Man,* ch. 22, the man with the brass plate reproaches the Missourian for his "way of talking as if heaven were a kind of Washington patent office museum."

[49] Living in a "utilitarian time and country," in the phrasing of the supplement to *Battle-Pieces and Aspects of the War* (1866), Melville had long felt the modern temper to be inimical to art. Compare his later allusion to "something retarding in the environment or soil" in his headnote to the poem "The American Aloe on Exhibition."

beneath art,[50] just as the instinct is beneath the reason.[51] Do all our modern triumphs equal those of the heroes and divinities that stand there silent, the incarnation of grandeur and of beauty?

We moderns pride ourselves upon our superiority, but the claim can be questioned. We did invent the printing press, but from the ancients have we not all the best thought which it circulates, whether it be law, physics, or philosophy? [52] As the

[50] In Boston, according to the *Traveller's* reporter, Melville's "proposition" about art and science "caused some little discussion in several groups of homeward-bound listeners, after the lecture was closed." "Never before," remarked the Clarksville *Daily Chronicle,* "was the superiority of art over science, so triumphantly and eloquently sustained." The Clarksville reviewer had "hung entranced" upon Melville's vindication of "these spiritual productions of the ancient mind from their alleged inferiority to the utilitarian inventions of the present age." For further discussion of Melville's thesis, see Chapter 1 above.

[51] In *The Confidence-Man,* ch. 3, Melville had similarly called instinct "a teacher set below reason." But in *Mardi* he had written of reason itself as a "noble instinct" (ch. 135) and also as "revelation" and "inspiration" (ch. 175), while in *Pierre,* Bk. XI, iv, there is a scornful reference to "the mere philosopher" and his "mere undiluted reason." What at first seems inconsistent terminology can be explained by distinguishing between Melville's conception of reason in the ordinary sense of the word—as something "reasonable," or even "rational," in man—and what he regarded as "right reason." "Right reason," as F. O. Matthiessen remarks in *American Renaissance* (New York, 1941), p. 457, note 6, is, "in the Coleridgean and Emersonian terminology . . . the highest range of *intuitive* intelligence, the gateway to divine madness" (italics added). This is what Melville had meant by "the sane madness of vital truth" in "Hawthorne and His Mosses." "So man's insanity is heaven's sense," he subsequently wrote in *Moby Dick,* ch. 93; "and wandering from all *mortal reason,* man comes at last to that celestial thought, which, to reason, is absurd and frantic . . ." (italics added). It was this same "mortal reason" that Melville evidently had in mind when he wrote "A Reasonable Constitution" (note 47 above).

[52] In private conversation 20 April 1859 with John Thomas Gulick, a student at Williams College, Melville reaffirmed this opinion: see Mentor L. Williams, "Two Hawaiian-Americans Visit Herman Melville," *New England Quarterly,* XXIII (March 1950), 97–99, and Chapter 4 above. "What little there was of meaning in the religions of the present day," Gulick quoted Melville as saying, "had come down from Plato. All our philosophy and all our art and poetry was either derived or imitated from the ancient Greeks." Similar pronouncements occur in Melville's poetry, as in Rolfe's declaration in *Clarel,* II, xxi,

> "That even in Physics much late lore
> But drudges after Plato's theme"

Roman arch enters into and supports our best architecture, does not the Roman spirit still animate and support whatever is soundest in societies and states? Or shall the scheme of Fourier supplant the code of Justinian? [53] Only when the novels of Dickens shall silence the satires of Juvenal. The ancients of the ideal description, instead of trying to turn their impracticable chimeras, as does the modern dreamer, into social and political prodigies, deposited them in great works of art, which still live while states and constitutions have perished, bequeathing to posterity not shameful defects but triumphant successes. All the merchants in modern London have not enough in their coffers to re-produce the Apollo. If the Coliseum expresses the durability of Roman ideas, what does their Crystal Palace express? [54] These buildings are exponents of

---

and in his own admonition in "Lone Founts" to

> "Stand where the Ancients stood before,
> And, dipping in lone founts thy hand,
> Drink of the never-varying lore:
> Wise once, and wise thence evermore."

[53] In *The Confidence-Man*, ch. 7, the "philanthropist" contrasts himself with "Fourier, the projector of an impossible scheme"; in "The South Seas" Melville was again to express his low opinion of Fourierism. François Marie Charles Fourier (1772–1837) had proposed the reorganization of society into small cooperative communities, "phalansteries," holding property in common.

[54] While in London in the spring of 1857, Melville had one day fallen into a reverie on the theme of this passage. The observations made in his journal at that time, as Raymond Weaver pointed out in editing *Journal up the Straits* (p. 172, note), form the basis of the present discussion: "Chrystal Palace—digest of universe. Alhambra—House of Pansi [Pansa, in Pompeii]—Temple of ——— &c&c&c.—Comparison with the pyramid [see note 31 above].—Overdone. If smaller would look larger. The Great Eastern. Pyramid.—Vast toy. No substance. Such an appropriation of space as is made by a rail fence. Durable materials, but perishable structure. Cant exist 100 years hence." So in *The Confidence-Man*, ch. 7, the inventor of the "Protean easy-chair," after seeing it placed on exhibition at the World's Fair, and observing that in the Crystal Palace was "the pride of the world glorying in a glass house," is impressed by "a sense of the fragility of worldly grandeur." Or as Melville himself had already pointed out in writing ch. 75 of *Mardi* ("Of Time and Temples"), "that which long endures full-fledged, must have long lain in the germ . . . and though a strong new monument be builded to-day, it only is lasting because its blocks are old as the sun. It is not the Pyramids that are ancient, but the eternal granite of which they are made. . . . For to make an eternity, we must build with eternities; whence, the vanity of the cry for any

the respective characters of ancients and moderns. But will the glass of the one bide the hail storms of eighteen centuries as well as the travertine of the other?

The deeds of the ancients were noble, and so are their arts; and as the one is kept alive in the memory of man by the glowing words of their own historians and poets, so should the memory of the other be kept green in the minds of men by the careful preservation of their noble statuary. The ancients live while these statues endure, and seem to breathe inspiration through the world, giving purpose, shape, and impetus to what was created high, or grand, or beautiful. Like the pillars of Rome itself, they are enduring illustrations of the perfection of ancient art.

> "While stands the Coliseum, Rome shall stand;
> When falls the Coliseum, Rome shall fall;
> And when Rome falls, the world." [55]

thing alike durable and new. . . ." Perhaps Melville considered his views vindicated when on 5 October 1858 another Crystal Palace, that built in New York for the World's Fair of 1853, was destroyed by fire.

[55] Murray's *Handbook,* pp. 294–295, points out that "the famous prophecy of the Anglo-Saxon pilgrims" embodied in these lines from Byron's *Childe Harold's Pilgrimage,* IV, cxlv, was recorded by the Venerable Bede. In Melville's *Clarel,* II, xxv, a Dominican adapts the phrasing to his own argument in defense of Roman Catholicism:

> "If Rome could fall
> 'Twould not be Rome alone, but all
> Religion."

THE SOUTH SEAS

[Since Melville begins his lecture with an explanation of its title, there is no question as to his intended usage. "The South Seas" appears consistently in newspaper reports of the lecture as well as in his correspondence concerning it.

The composite text printed here is based upon the twenty-five surviving contemporary newspaper reports of the lecture discussed in Chapter 4 above—primarily upon the long summary given by the Baltimore *American and Commercial Advertiser,* 9 February 1859, which has been conveniently reprinted, with minor emendations, in *The Portable Melville,* ed. Jay Leyda (New York, 1952), pp. 575–583. The *American's* account offers an almost verbatim report of the first eight paragraphs of the lecture, evidently from a shorthand transcription, followed by a combination of transcription and summary of the remaining passages. A comparison of the *American's* wording with that of Melville's sources, including in some instances his own earlier writings, attests to its accuracy, as will be seen from several of the accompanying notes. Extracts from other contemporary accounts have been introduced into the text here and there to replace or supplement the wording of the *American* wherever there is reason to believe that these versions offer a fuller or more accurate approximation of Melville's own language. As with "Statues in Rome," the consistent agreement, in essentials, among the newspaper reports indicates that he made little if any change in the pattern of the lecture during the season of 1858–59.

On standardization of spelling and punctuation in the composite texts and citation of Melville's works in the accompanying notes, see the headnote to "Statues in Rome" above.]

THE subject of our lecture this evening, "The South Seas," may be thought perhaps a theme if not ambitious, at least somewhat expansive, covering, according to the authorities, I am afraid to say how much of the earth's surface—in short, more than one-half. We have, therefore, a rather spacious field before us, and I hardly think we shall be able, in a thorough way, to go over the whole of it to-night.

And here (to do away with any erroneous anticipations as to our topic) I hope you do not expect me to repeat what has long been in print touching my own casual adventures in Polynesia.[1] I propose to treat of matters of more general interest, and, in a random way, discuss the South Seas at large and under various aspects, introducing, as occasion may serve, any little incident, personal or other, fitted to illustrate the point in hand.

"South Seas" is simply an equivalent term for "Pacific Ocean." Then why not say "Pacific Ocean" at once?—Because one may have a lingering regard for certain old associations, linking the South Seas as a name with many pleasant and venerable books of voyages, full of well-remembered engravings.[2]

To be sure those time-worn tomes are pretty nearly obsolete, but none the less are they, with the old name they enshrine, dear to the memory of their reader; in much the same way too that the old South Sea House in London was dear to the heart of Charles Lamb.[3]—Who that has read it can forget that quaint sketch, the introductory essay of Elia, where he speaks of the Balclutha-like desolation of those haunted old offices of the once famous South Sea Company—the old oaken wainscots hung with the dusty maps of Mexico and soundings of the Bay of Panama—the vast cellarages under the whole pile where Mexican dollars and doubloons once lay heaped in huge bins for Mammon to solace his solitary heart withal?[4]

[1] Melville's *Typee* (1846) and *Omoo* (1847).

[2] These "venerable books of voyages" were often cited in Melville's earlier works, beginning with references to "the olden voyagers" in the opening chapter of *Typee.* The "well-remembered engravings" are particularly reminiscent of his discussion "Of the Monstrous Pictures of Whales" in *Moby Dick,* ch. 55, based in part on just such old volumes.

[3] Melville's first significant reading of Lamb had taken place on shipboard in 1849 while he was en route to London, where Lamb's publisher was to present him with several books by and about the essayist. See Sealts, "Melville's Reading: A Check-List of Books Owned and Borrowed" (offprinted from *Harvard Library Bulletin,* 1948–1950), Nos. 315–318.

[4] In "The South-Sea House" Lamb had written of the old building's air of *"desolation* something like *Balclutha's"* (italics added). In Macpherson's Ossianic poem "Carthon," the father of Ossian burns Balclutha, a

But besides summoning up the memory of brave old books, Elia's fine sketch, and the great South Sea Bubble,[5] originating in the institution there celebrated—the words "South Seas" are otherwise suggestive, yielding to the fancy an indefinable odor of sandalwood and cinnamon, more relishing of the old, antique exploring and buccaneering adventures of the fresh, imaginative days of voyaging in these waters. In the adventures of Captain Dampier (that eminent and excellent buccaneer)[6] you read only of "South Seas." In Harris' old voyages,[7] and many others, the title is the same, and even as late as 1803 we find that Admiral Burney[8] prefers the old title to the new, "Pacific," which appellation has in the present century only become the popular one—notwithstanding which we occasionally find the good old name first bestowed still employed by writers of repute.

But since these famous waters lie on both sides of the Equator and wash the far northern shores of Kamchatka as well as the far southern ones of Tierra del Fuego, how did they

---

town on the Clyde: "I passed by the walls of Balclutha, and they were desolate." Lamb's passage, which Melville evidently had before him in preparing the lecture, goes on to describe the House, with its *oaken wainscots hung with . . . dusty maps of Mexico, dim as dreams,—and soundings of the Bay of Panama! . . .* with *vast* ranges of *cellarage under all, where dollars* and pieces-of-eight *once lay,* an 'unsunned heap,' *for Mammon to have solaced his solitary heart withal,*—long since dissipated, or scattered into air at the blast of the breaking of that famous BUBBLE!"

[5] A general term applied to a wave of speculative schemes commencing in 1719, when Parliament passed a law enabling persons owed money by Great Britain to convert their claims into shares in the South Sea Company—originally founded in 1711 for legitimate trading.

[6] William Dampier (1652–1715), buccaneer, privateer, and explorer, author of three volumes concerning his voyages. He is mentioned in *Mardi,* ch. 1, and *Moby Dick,* ch. 45 ("ancient Dampier"); in Sketch Sixth of "The Encantadas" Melville had listed him among those buccaneers "whose worst reproach was their desperate fortunes."

[7] John Harris, editor, *Navigantium atque Itinerantium Bibliotheca* (1748), cited (erroneously) in *Moby Dick,* ch. 55.

[8] James Burney, whose *Chronological History of the Discoveries in the South Sea or Pacific Ocean* (5 vols., London, 1803–1817) Melville had used as a source in his earlier writings, most recently "The Encantadas" in 1854, and probably had in his personal library at Pittsfield: see notes below.

ever come to be christened with such a misnomer as *"South Seas"*? The way it happened was this: The Isthmus of Darien runs not very far from east and west; if you stand upon its further shore the ocean will appear to the *south* of you, and were you ignorant of the general direction of the coastline you would infer that it rolled away wholly toward that quarter. Now Balboa, the first white man who laid eyes upon these waters, stood in just this position; drew just this inference and bestowed its name accordingly.[9]

The circumstances of Balboa's discovery are not uninteresting.[10] In the earliest days of the Spanish dominion on this con-

[9] Compare Burney, *History*, I, 9: "The particular position of the coast of that part of the American continent from whence the sea on the other side was first discovered, appears to have stamped on it the denomination of the SOUTH SEA. The isthmus of *Darien* lies nearly East and West; consequently, there the two seas appear situated, the one to the North, and the other to the South. If the new sea had been first discovered from any part to the South of the bay of *Panama*, it would probably have received some other appellation. A consequence resulting from the name thus imposed has been, that the Atlantic ocean, by way of contra-distinction, has occasionally been called the North Sea. . . . The two seas nevertheless, relatively to each other, are North and South only in the neighbourhood of the isthmus of *Darien:* in their general extent they are East and West."

[10] Balboa (*c.* 1475–1517?) discovered the Pacific in 1513; compare *Mardi*, ch. 169: "Balboa's band roving through the golden Aztec glades." Melville's present account of Balboa's discovery is indebted to Burney, *History*, I, 7–8 (italics added except as indicated): "the first actual information obtained by Europeans of this sea, was given to the Spanish conquerors by the native Americans. Basco Nunnex de Balboa, a Spanish commander at *Darien* [italics in original], to verify the intelligence he had received, marched with a body of Spaniards, and with Indian guides, across the isthmus. *He was opposed in the passage by the natives. They demanded who the bearded strangers were, what they sought after, and whither they were going?* The Spaniards answered, *'they were Christians, that their errand was to preach a new religion, and to seek gold; and that they were going to the southern sea.'* This answer not giving satisfaction, Balboa forcibly made his way. On arriving at *the foot of a mountain,* from the top of which he was informed that the sea he so anxiously wished to discover was visible; *he ordered his men to halt, and ascended alone.* As soon as he had attained the summit, *he fell on his knees, and* with uplifted hands *returned thanks to Heaven,* for having bestowed on him the honour of being the first European that beheld the sea beyond America. Afterwards, *in the presence of his followers, and of many Indians, he walked up to his middle in the water, with his sword and target; and called on them to bear testimony that he took possession of the South Sea, and all which appertained to it, for the king of Castile and Leon* [*South . . . it* in italics in original]."

tinent, he commanded a petty post on the northern shore of
the Isthmus, and hearing it rumored that there was a vast sea
on the other side of the land—its beach not distant, but of difficult approach, owing to a range of steep mountain wall and
other obstruction, he resolved to explore in that direction. His
hardships may be imagined by recalling the narrative a few
years since of the adventures of Lieut. Strain and party who in
like manner with the Spaniard, undertook to cross from sea to
sea, through the primeval wilderness.[11] A party of buccaneers
also likewise crossed the Isthmus under suffering, the utmost
that nature is capable of sustaining.[12] Balboa and the buccaneers, though not more courageous, were certainly more
hardy or more fortunate than the American officer, since, after
all they underwent, their efforts were at last successful.

The thronging Indians opposed Balboa's passage, demand-
ing who he was, what he wanted, and whither he was going.
The reply is a model of Spartan directness. "I am a Christian,
my errand is to spread true religion and to seek gold, and I
am going in search of the sea."

Coming at last to the foot of a mountain, he was told that
from its summit he could see the object of his search. He
ordered a halt, and, like Moses, the devout Spaniard "went up
into the mountain alone."[13] When he beheld the sea he fell

[11] In 1853, Lt. Isaac G. Strain (1821–1857) of the American navy
had volunteered to lead an exploring expedition across the Isthmus of
Darien from Caledonia Bay on the Caribbean side to the Gulf of San
Miguel on the Pacific; his objective was to determine whether that route
would be suitable for a ship-canal, and his conclusion was that it would
not. The party, as Melville was aware, suffered greatly during their crossing, and Strain himself died in Panama a few years later, weakened by
the hardships he had undergone.

[12] The "party of buccaneers" was described earlier in Sketch Sixth of
"The Encantadas" as "that famous wing of the West Indian Buccaneers,
which, upon their repulse from the Cuban waters, crossing the Isthmus of
Darien, ravaged the Pacific side of the Spanish colonies. . . ." Russell
Thomas, "Melville's Use of Some Sources in *The Encantadas,*" *American
Literature,* III (January 1932), 432–456, has demonstrated that Mel-
ville's knowledge of the buccaneers came largely from the works of Ad-
miral Burney (*History,* IV) and of Captain James Colnett, *A Voyage to the
South Atlantic and Round Cape Horn* (1798), both having been used also
in his previous writing.

[13] The quotation, as reported, is inexact. Compare Exodus 24:2,
"Moses alone shall come near the Lord"; Exodus 34:3–4, "no man shall

upon his knees and thanked God for the sight. The next day with sword and target, wading up to his waist in its waters, he called upon his troop and the assembled Indians to bear witness that he took possession of that whole ocean with all the lands and kingdoms pertaining to it for his sovereign master the King of Castile and Leon. A large-minded gentleman, of great latitude of sentiment, was Vasco Nuñez de Balboa, commander of that petty post of Darien.

If we should take sail, and set out for Cape Horn, probably the longest voyage that can be made on this planet, we would encounter much foul weather, and be subjected to the cold water treatment in its fullest rigor.[14] But having doubled the Cape and set sail for the North in the Pacific, we would be borne along by fair breezes that would send us skipping for joy, and in a short time would reach smooth seas and sunny skies, the air growing milder and more mild the further one goes north. The change during the run from Cape Horn to the Galapagos Islands [15] is more telling than in going from New York to Cuba, where in one week you are whisked from icicles to oranges.[16]

The European who first sailed upon those waters had this experience intensified. True, Magellan passed not round the yet undiscovered Horn, but through the straits which bear his name. But this only made the matter worse. For, in these straits, narrow, tortuous, and rockbound, dense fogs prevail and antarctic squalls, and the navigation is peculiarly danger-

---

come up with thee . . . and Moses . . . went up into mount Sinai, as the Lord had commanded him"; Deuteronomy 34:1, "And Moses went up . . . unto the mountain of Nebo, to the top of Pisgah."

14 Melville presumably drew here upon his own westward passage aboard the *Acushnet* in April 1841, and especially upon the tremendous storm encountered off the Cape in July 1844, when he returned aboard the *United States* (see *White-Jacket*, chs. 24–26).

15 The locale of "The Encantadas," described by Melville in Sketch First as an area of capricious winds and tides. This passage of the present text draws upon several newspaper accounts, of which one, the Milwaukee *Sentinel's* report, mentions specifically "the run from Cape Horn to the Islands"—presumably the Galapagos.

16 So the voyage of the *Fidèle* in *The Confidence-Man*, ch. 2, "extends from apple to orange, from clime to clime."

ous. Magellan worked through, however, and when he beheld ahead a fine open ocean, by good fortune smooth and serene, in his excess of emotion he burst into tears, stout sailor as he was, and this was the man who gave to this sea its second name—Pacific.[17]

Once, gliding through the tropics on the bosom of the Atlantic, the warm air and lulling calm made me say to myself, "Come, let us shut up the temple of Janus and dream"; and I thought that this ocean, rather than the South Seas, should have been named "Pacific." [18] But the names were owing to first impressions, and the Pacific when introduced to the public happened to put its best foot foremost, being then in a happy humor. The great sea hence will forever be called Pacific, even by the sailor destined to perish in one of its terrible typhoons.

Although the Pacific covers half the surface of the planet, yet with all its dotted isles and people it remained almost unknown to even a recent period. Captain Cook's account of his

[17] Melville's account of the voyage of Ferdinand Magellan (1480?–1521) into the Pacific is based upon Burney's *History*, I, 43, which states that Magellan "was so greatly rejoiced at finding a clear sea before him, that he is said to have shed tears." A later passage, I, 51, adds: "A long continuance of mild and temperate weather which they had experienced, occasioned the name of Pacific to be given to the sea in which they had been sailing." But this name Magellan and his companions "could design only for the sea within the mild latitudes: for from the strait they at first 'navigated with great storms. . . .' So tempestuous a sample of the climate could not entitle the higher latitudes to be comprehended under the appellation Pacific."

[18] Melville's brief reference to an Atlantic voyage in this passage was reported only in two Milwaukee newspapers, the *Daily Sentinel* and *Daily Wisconsin*. The *Sentinel's* phrase "through the tropics" suggests either his voyage through the South Atlantic on the *Acushnet* in 1841 or his return aboard the *United States* in 1844, his other Atlantic voyages up to this time having been through northern waters. But if the *Wisconsin* was correct in describing his view of the Atlantic as one seen from "the deck rail of a steamship," Melville was thinking not of the tropics but of one of his three North Atlantic crossings by steamer (1849–50, 1856, 1857). Merrell R. Davis, "Melville's Midwestern Lecture Tour, 1859," *Philological Quarterly*, XX (January 1941), 56, note, finds the description "suggestive of a passage in *Redburn*," ch. 13: "He Has a Fine Day at Sea . . ."; *Redburn*, however, was based on Melville's sailing voyage across the North Atlantic in 1849. In the absence of further evidence the passage remains obscure.

visit to Tahiti could produce, as late as 1780, upon the English people almost the full thrill of novelty.[19] Indeed, but little was known of the whole region till Cook's time. It was California that first brought the Pacific home to the great body of Anglo-Saxons. The discovery of gold in 1848, that memorable year, first opened the Pacific as a thoroughfare for American ships.[20]

The world of waters here is so broad, covering, it is estimated, over a hundred millions of square miles, and its living races so various, that one is puzzled where to choose [21] a topic from so vast a storehouse, upon which to expend the limited time of a single lecture. A haze of obscurity hangs over the Pacific even at the present day, and its geography is still but illy known. The ships which plough it for the most part go in established routes, and those vessels which leave these old roads continually run upon some island or cluster of islands unknown to the charts or to geographers. Even underwriters and shipping agents, if applied to about sailing to some of the islands in these seas, would not have a very distinct idea upon the subject. So with the student, also, and there is no full knowledge to be had of them anywhere. This, added to the immensity, makes one feel, in an attempt to speak of them, like

[19] James Cook (1738–1779), the celebrated circumnavigator, had first visited Tahiti in 1769. Accounts of his voyages were published in 1773, 1777, and 1784.

[20] Either Melville or the various newspaper reporters omitted mentioning here his previous claim, set forth in *Moby Dick,* ch. 24, that "the whale-ship has been the pioneer in ferreting out the remotest and least known parts of the earth. She has explored seas and archipelagoes which had no chart, where no Cook or Vancouver had ever sailed. . . . All that is made such a flourish of in the old South Sea Voyages, those things were but the lifetime commonplaces of our heroic Nantucketers. . . . *Until the whale fishery rounded Cape Horn,* no commerce but colonial, scarcely any intercourse but colonial, was carried on between Europe and the long line of the opulent Spanish provinces on the Pacific coast" (italics added).

[21] In the phrasing of "The world of waters . . . where to choose" Melville was probably echoing *Paradise Lost,* XII, 646–647 (italics added):

> "*The world* was all before them, *where to choose*
> Their place of rest, and Providence their guide. . . ."

Henry F. Pommer, *Milton and Melville* (Pittsburgh, 1950), p. 35, lists six other allusions in Melville's writings to the same Miltonic lines.

embarking on a voyage to their far distant isles. But what is known, and well known, affords an abundant theme for a lecture.

We might tell of tribes of sharks that populate some parts of the Pacific as thickly as the celestials do the Chinese Empire,[22] or we might introduce that gallant chevalier, the sword-fish—a different fish from that of the same name found in our northern latitudes, being more daring, the Hector of the seas —and tell of his martial exploits; the tilts he runs at the great ships; the duels he fights with the whale—sometimes leaving his weapon in their ribs, or by withdrawing it, leaving an open wound in the mass of flesh or wood to the great peril of the craft and crew, as in the case of the English ship *Foxhound*.[23]

[22] Melville had devoted ch. 13 of *Mardi* to the subject of sharks and may have drawn upon that account here: Merrell Davis, "Melville's Midwestern Lecture Tour," p. 55, compares the concluding sentence of the chapter, "The Pacific is populous as China," with the phrasing of the lecture as reported in the Chicago *Press and Tribune:* ". . . the 'south seas shark' as populous in those waters as the Chinese in China."

[23] A reworking of ch. 32 of *Mardi*, "Xiphius Platypterus," provided the substance of this passage on swordfish, as the following extract (italics added) will show: "of all the bullies, and braggarts, and bravoes, and free-booters, and *Hectors,* and fish-at-arms, and knight-errants, and moss-troopers, and assassins, and foot-pads, and gallant soldiers, and immortal heroes that swim the seas, the Indian Sword fish is by far the most remarkable. . . . Now, the fish here treated of is a very *different creature from the Sword fish frequenting the Northern Atlantic;* being much larger every way, and a more dashing varlet to boot. . . . I waive for my hero all . . . his cognomens, and substitute a much better one of my own: namely, *the Chevalier. . . .* Fire from the flint is our Chevalier enraged. He takes umbrage at the cut of some ship's keel crossing his road; and straightway *runs a tilt at it;* with one mad lunge thrusting his Andrea Ferrara clean through and through; not seldom breaking it short off at the haft, like a bravo *leaving his poignard in the vitals of his foe. In the case of the English ship Foxhound,* the blade penetrated through the most solid part of her hull, the bow; going completely through the copper plates and timbers, and showing for several inches in the hold." Merrell Davis, who first noted the parallel in his "Melville's Midwestern Lecture Tour," p. 55, shows in his *Melville's "Mardi": A Chartless Voyage* (New Haven, 1952), pp. 120–121, that the chapter in *Mardi* is based in turn on Bennett's *Narrative of a Whaling Voyage.* That the swordfish made a lasting impression on Melville's imagination is further confirmed by two passages of his poetry, which like the lecture but unlike *Mardi* mention "the duels he fights with the whale." In *Clarel* (1876), III, xxi, he was to write of

We might tell of the devil-fish, over which a mystery hangs like that over the sea-serpent of North Atlantic waters.[24] It is asserted by some mariners that he has horns and huge fins; and, sailors say, he dives to the profoundest abyss and comes up roaring with mouths as many and as wide open as the Mississippi. This I have not seen, but on one occasion, when off the coast of Patagonia early one evening, listening to a solemn ghost story from one of the crew of my vessel, we heard an awful roaring sound, something like a compromise between the snorting of a leviathan and the belching of a Vesuvius, and saw a bright train of light shoot along the water; the grizzled old boatswain, who was standing by, started and exclaimed, "There, that's a devil-fish!" [25] On another occasion I saw, a few feet beneath the surface, a large, lazy, sleepy-looking object, and was told that that too was a devil-fish. I am surprised that Professor Agassiz, the great naturalist,[26] does not pack his carpet-bag and betake himself to Nantucket, and from thence in a whaler to the South Seas, where he could find such a vast field for research!

"the slim Malay,
That perilous imp whose slendor proa
Great hulls have rued—as in ill hour
The whale the swordfish lank assay."

And in "Bridegroom Dick" (dated "1876") is this passage:

"the *Cumberland* stilettoed by the *Merrimac's* tusk;
While, broken in the wound underneath the gun-deck,
Like a sword-fish's blade in leviathan waylaid,
The tusk was left infixed in the fast-foundering wreck."

24 In 1847, when Melville was contributing to the humorous New York weekly *Yankee Doodle,* a sea-serpent allegedly seen off the New England coast had been a frequent subject for comment. Evert Duyckinck, writing to his brother George on 14–15 July, said that Melville would "probably in some shape or other take care of the sea serpent" in a future number of the paper (Duyckinck Collection, New York Public Library), but there were only occasional later references to it in *Yankee Doodle.*

25 Compare *Mardi,* ch. 13: "But look! fathoms down in the sea; where ever saw you a phantom like that? An enormous crescent with antlers like a reindeer, and a Delta of mouths. Slowly it sinks, and is seen no more. Doctor Faust saw the devil; but you have seen the 'Devil Fish.'"

26 Jean Louis Rodolphe Agassiz (1807–1873), Swiss-born American naturalist, professor of zoology and geology at Harvard and himself a noted lecturer.

We might speak particularly of the birds of those seas—the pelican, with his pouch stuffed with game like a sportsman's bag; the melancholy penguin standing on one spot all day with a fit of the blues; the man-of-war hawk, that fierce black bandit; and the storied albatross, with white and arching wing like an archangel's, his haughty beak curved like a scimeter.[27] Yes, a whole hour might be spent in telling about either the fishes or the birds.

Furthermore, there are exceptional phenomena, such as the peculiar phosphoric aspect of the water sometimes. I have been in a whaleboat at midnight when, having lost the ship, we would keep steering through the lonely night for her, while the sea that weltered by us would present the pallid look of the face of a corpse, and lit by its spectral gleam we men in the boat showed to each other like so many weather-beaten ghosts. Then to mark Leviathan come wallowing along, dashing the pale sea into sparkling cascades of fire, showering it all over him till the monster would look like Milton's Satan, riding the flame billows of the infernal world.[28] We might fill night after

[27] If this paragraph as Melville delivered it included more details than appear in the present version, he may well have drawn on the third sketch of "The Encantadas," which describes both the pelican and the penguin at some length and mentions both the man-of-war hawk and the *"storied"* albatross. In *Moby Dick,* ch. 42, note, he had previously told of "the first albatross I ever saw," with its "vast *archangel wings.*" Merrell Davis, "Melville's Midwestern Lecture Tour," p. 55, compares the phrasing of the Chicago *Press and Tribune* report of this passage ("the war hawk black pirate of the feathered races") with that of *Typee,* ch. 2: "That piratical-looking fellow, appropriately named the man-of-war's hawk, with his blood-red bill and raven plumage, would come sweeping round us in gradually diminishing circles. . . ." Melville later wrote a brief poem entitled "The Man-of-War Hawk."

[28] Compare ch. 38 of *Mardi* (based in turn on Bennett's *Narrative of a Whaling Voyage*), where Melville had previously described "The Sea on Fire": "Starting, we beheld the ocean of a *pallid* white color, corruscating all over with tiny golden sparkles. But the pervading hue of the water cast *a cadaverous gleam* upon the boat, so that *we looked to each other like ghosts.* . . . Suddenly, as we gazed, there shot high into the air a bushy jet of flashes, accompanied by the unmistakable deep breathing sound of *a sperm whale.* Soon, the sea all round us spouted in fountains of *fire;* and vast forms, emitting a glare from their flanks, and ever and anon raising their heads above water, and shaking off the sparkles, showed where an immense shoal of Cachalots had risen from below to sport in

night with that fertile theme, the whaling voyage, and tell of
the adventurous sailors, either on the blank face of the waters,[29] where often for months together their ship floats lonely
as the ark of Noah, or in their intercourse with the natives of
coasts reached by few or none but themselves.

The islands, too, are an endless theme; thick as the stars in
the Milky Way. No notion of their number can be gathered
from a glance at the map, where the ink of one is run into that
of another, blended together in a dark indistinctness. If not
innumerable they are certainly unnumbered, as the name bestowed upon their swarming clusters—Polynesia—not inaptly
hints.[30] The most noted of these are the Sandwich and Society
groups; the Friendly, Navigator, and Feejee clusters; the Pe-
lew, Ladrone, Mulgrave, Kingsmills, and Radack chains [31]—
but there are more than Briareus could number on all his finger
ends.[32]

The popular notion, from the early vague accounts, imagines

---

these phosphorescent billows. . . . Heretofore, I had beheld several ex-
hibitions of marine phosphorescence, both in the Atlantic and Pacific. But
nothing in comparison with what was seen that night" (italics added).
This parallel has been previously noted by Merrell Davis, "Melville's Midwestern Lecture Tour," p. 55.

The reference to "Milton's Satan" in the lecture recalls *Paradise Lost,* I,
221–224:

> "Forthwith upright he rears from off the Pool
> His mighty Stature; on each hand the flames
> Driv'n backward slope their pointing spires, and roll'd
> In billows, leave i' th' midst a horrid Vale."

Compare *Moby Dick,* ch. 86: "So in dreams, have I seen majestic Satan
thrusting forth his tormented colossal claw from the flame Baltic of Hell."

[29] "Face of the waters" echoes the phrasing of Genesis 1:2.

[30] Polynesia: i.e., "many islands." Melville is apparently applying the
term to the entire South Pacific; it is now customary to distinguish the
Polynesian islands from those of Micronesia and Melanesia, which lie
further westward.

[31] The wording of this sentence is that of the Baltimore *American.*
The only other account to include names of islands at this point in the
lecture is that of the Chicago *Daily Press and Tribune,* which reads as
follows: "The chief groups are the Sandwich, the Society, the Georgian,
the Phillipian [Philippine], the Ladrone, the Marquesas, the Caroline,
and the Friendly Isles."

[32] In Greek mythology Briareus was a hundred-handed giant who
fought with the Olympians against the Titans.

them to hold enameled plains, with groves of shadowing palms, watered by purling brooks and the country but little elevated. The reverse of this is true: bold rock-bound coasts—a beating surf—lofty and craggy cliffs, split here and there into deep inlets opening to the view deeper valleys parted by masses of emerald mountains sweeping seaward from an interior of lofty peaks.[33]

But, would you get the best water view of a Polynesian is-

[33] Melville here drew upon a passage in *Typee*, ch. 2: "Those who for the first time visit the South Seas, generally are surprised at the appearance of the islands when beheld from the sea. From the *vague accounts* we sometimes have of their beauty, many people are apt to picture . . . *enamelled* and softly swelling *plains*, shaded over with delicious *groves*, and *watered by purling brooks*, and *the* entire *country but little elevated* above the surrounding ocean. The reality is very different; *bold rock-bound coasts*, with *the surf beating* high against the *lofty cliffs*, and broken *here and there into deep inlets*, which *open to the view* thickly-wooded *valleys*, separated by the spurs of *mountains* clothed with tufted grass, and *sweeping down towards the sea from* an elevated and furrowed *interior*, form the principal features of these islands" (italics added). This parallel has been noted in Merrell Davis, "Melville's Midwestern Lecture Tour," p. 56, and Jay Leyda, ed., *The Portable Melville*, p. 581, note.

The present text here follows the wording of the Baltimore *American*. A sampling of other newspaper accounts of the same passage indicates similar phrasing; the parallels with *Typee*, although by no means as striking, are nevertheless apparent. The Boston *Daily Courier*, to take the longest of these other versions, reads as follows: "It is an erroneous idea to picture the islands of the Pacific as *low tracts, barely rising above the surface*, and reposing as it were in quiet beauty upon its bosom. There are a few coral islands of this character; but for the most part they present a *bold* shore of *rocky cliffs, here and there breaking away* and receding into beautiful *ravines*, further inland rising into lofty *mountain summits*, which stand as gigantic chimney stacks to give vent to internal fires of the earth, to whose force they owe their existence." The Chicago *Daily Press and Tribune* gives these words: "We are apt, in our imaginings of those distant shores, to picture *enameled* caves [*sic*] and *pearly* [*sic*] brooks, and valleys of sylvan sweetness. Yet their distinctive features are *lofty broken coasts*, and *deep* and abrupt *valleys*. Sublimity, rather than graceful beauty, is their marked natural characteristic." According to the Milwaukee *Daily Wisconsin*, Melville "said we were apt to draw high colors of them in our fancy flights, and to imagine them *low, smooth beds of verdure, just elevated above the level of the sea*.—Though this might be true, in some respects, of the coral isles, yet the most of them have *bold coasts*, towering *mountains, lofty cliffs with deep inlets*, and similar features. The group comprising the Polynesian Archipelago are the most striking in the world." (Italics added in these quotations.)

On the persistence in Melville's memory of his first vision of Polynesia, see James Baird, *Ishmael* (Baltimore, 1956), pp. 107ff.

land, select one with a natural breakwater of surf-beaten coral all around it, leaving within a smooth, circular canal, broad and deep, entrance to which is had through natural sea-gates. Lounging in a canoe, there is nothing more pleasant than to float along—especially where Boraborra and Tahaa, the glorious twins of the Society group, rear their lofty masses to the ever vernal heights, belted about by the same zone of reef—the reef itself being dotted with small islets perpetually thick and green with grass.

The virgin freshness of these unviolated wastes, the exemption of those far-off archipelagoes from the heat and dust of civilization, acts sometimes as the last provocative to those jaded tourists to whom even Europe has become hackneyed, and who look upon the Parthenon and the Pyramids with a yawn.[34]

Why don't the English yachters give up the prosy Mediterranean and sail out here? Any one who treats the natives fairly is just as safe as if he were on the Nile or Danube. But I am sorry to say we whites have a sad reputation among many of the Polynesians. The natives of these islands are naturally of a kindly and hospitable temper, but there has been planted among them an almost instinctive hate of the white man. They esteem us, with rare exceptions, such as *some* of the missionaries,[35] the most barbarous, treacherous, irreligious, and devilish creatures on the earth.[36] This may of course be a mere

[34] Compare Melville's reaction here with the account in his journal, 7 December 1857, of the English resident at Salonica who "had been *a day's shooting in the Vale of Tempe*—Ye Gods! whortleberrying on Olympus. . . ." The Parthenon and the Pyramids had both affected Melville himself profoundly, as not only the journal but also his later poetry reveals.

[35] Compare Melville's preface to *Typee,* where he had declared that the "glorious" missionary cause "has not always been served by the proceedings of some of its advocates." His animadversions on the less worthy missionaries in both *Typee* and *Omoo,* which had made his name notorious among certain church groups of the day, were recalled in the comment of the Yonkers *Examiner* that "of course" Melville "could not forbear making a splenetic allusion to the missionaries, concerning whom his feelings are well-known, and are too bitter to be impersonal."

[36] Melville's Swiftian language here was variously reported by the newspapers: "villainous," "bloodthirsty," "atrocious," and "diabolical" also appear in several accounts.

prejudice of these unlettered savages, for have not our traders always treated them with brotherly affection? Who has ever heard of a vessel sustaining the honor of a Christian flag and the spirit of the Christian Gospel by opening its batteries in indiscriminate massacre upon some poor little village on the seaside—splattering the torn bamboo huts with blood and brains of women and children, defenseless and innocent? [37]

New and strange islands are being continually discovered in the South Seas. And there are still others unknown and un-discovered, respecting which our charts are as guiltless as the maps of the world in Plato's time, when the Pillars of Hercules were the western verge of the orbit. There are many places where a man might make himself a sylvan retreat and for years, at least, live as much removed from the life of the great world as though its people dwelt upon another planet. This mantle of mystery long hid the Buccaneers, who plundered the Spanish commerce; and covered for years Christian, the mutineer of the *Bounty,* who, after a life of exile and immunity from European law, was found, bent with age, amid a thriving colony of half-breed children and grandchildren, whom his savage wives had reared for him amid ever-green woods, under ever-healthful skies, and through the plenty of perpetual

[37] Among other instances, Melville probably had in mind in this ironic passage the story of the attack on the Typees given in *Typee,* ch. 4. Under "Captain Porter, about the year 1814," he had written, "a considerable detachment of sailors and marines from the frigate *Essex*" and their native allies, having been repulsed by the Typees, "consoled themselves" on their march back to the sea "by setting fire to every house and temple in their route; and a long line of smoking ruins defaced the once-smiling bosom of the valley, and proclaimed to its pagan inhabitants the spirit that reigned in the breasts of Christian soldiers." The chapter goes on to dwell upon other misdeeds of white men and their consequent reputation among Polynesians. According to the Yonkers *Examiner's* report of the lecture, however, Melville was speaking "indirectly of the destruction of Malolo [Fiji Islands] by the U. S. Squadron, in 1840, placing it in the light of an atrocity [rather] than just a punishment. We would remind our readers that the *slight* offence of the natives consisted in killing two officers of the Squadron, in an outrageous manner. Nor was this the first crime; for a long time murder after murder had been committed and passed unnoticed, till affairs were at such a crisis as to render it unsafe for ships and crews. The prevention of further evil was one avowed object of the expedition. However severe the punishments may have been, the benefit is now being reaped in the totally different state of things."

harvests.[38] Indeed, it is no difficult thing for a company of mutineers to bury themselves in the interior of one of these little worlds, and live undiscovered by navigators, who at most scarcely leave the beach if perchance they should land for fruit or water. Such colonies are sometimes found.

Then, too, there are some reformers who, despairing of civilizing Europe or America according to their rule, have projected establishments in the Pacific where they hope to find a fitting place for the good time coming.[39] Shortly after the pub-

[38] Either Melville or the Baltimore reporter, whose phrasing is followed here, was inaccurate. Fletcher Christian was indeed the ringleader of the famous mutiny in 1789, when the commander of the *Bounty*, Lt. Bligh, and eighteen of the crew were cast adrift in an open boat. Christian and some of the mutineers, having first sailed to Tahiti, later founded the colony on Pitcairn Island to which Melville is referring (as previously in *Mardi*, ch. 1). But Christian himself is said to have effected a return to England, and the man "bent with age" who was found on the island was not he but rather John Adams, otherwise known as Alexander Smith (1760?–1829), also of the *Bounty*. When the American merchant captain Folger accidentally touched at the island in 1808 he encountered Adams there at the head of a group of some eight or nine native women and several children; the other Englishmen, according to Adams, had been murdered by the Tahitian men, who in turn had been killed by the women. In 1814 two British frigates visited the island, and in 1825 the British captain Frederick W. Beechey obtained a detailed narrative from Adams, given in Beechey's *Narrative of a Voyage to the Pacific* (1831).

[39] This and the following paragraph are comparable to Melville's slighting allusions to contemporary Utopias and Utopians in the concluding paragraphs of "Statues in Rome," which in turn recall previous animadversions in both *Pierre* and *The Confidence-Man*. For one reason or another the present passage irritated several newspaper reviewers, beginning with the Yonkers *Examiner's* caustic reporter. In his words, "Mr. Melville mentioned, with a feeling that did him credit, his friend the King of Cannibal Islands, or Marquesas, we are not sure which, and the King's great dislike to Fourierism and polygamy. We had supposed that his majesty and subjects were rather practically fond of both these institutions, but we may be mistaken." Later, as Merrell Davis has pointed out in "Melville's Midwestern Lecture Tour," p. 54, three of the midwestern reviewers also took exception to this passage. "The Milwaukee *Free Democrat* . . . would have preferred 'personal remiscenses [sic] . . . to such bombast as his asserted reply to the young Fourierite.'" The Rockford *Republican* disliked Melville's "gratuitous advice to Reformers not to think of locating in any of the Islands of the South Seas, which in general were inhabited by a very sensible people, particularly the Typee's [sic], the confidence of whose government—incautiously let out as a diplomatic secret—the lecturer fully enjoyed." The Rockford *Register* also disparaged his "generous advice to Mormons, Free Lovers, and other Reformers."

lication of "Typee," I myself was waited upon by a pale young man with poetic look, dulcet voice, and Armenian beard—a disciple of Fourier.[40] He asked for information as to the prospects of a select party of seventy or eighty Fourierites emigrating to some of the South Sea islands, more particularly to the valley of Typee in the Marquesas. I replied that my old friends the Typees are undoubtedly good fellows, with strong points for admiration, and that their king [41] is as faithful to his friend as to his bottle. These people have kind hearts and natural urbanity, and are gentlemen by nature; but they have their eccentricities, are quick to anger, and are eminently conservative—they would never tolerate any new-fangled notions of the social state. Sometimes they do not hesitate to put a human being out of the way without the benefit of a trial by jury. The kind way in which they treated my comrade and myself, I concluded, furnished little indication of how they would treat others, and hardly warranted the success of a larger expedition, who might be taken as invaders and possibly eaten.

A company of Free Lovers in Ohio has also proposed to go to the South Seas, and the Mormons of Salt Lake have likewise thought of these secluded islands upon which to increase and multiply—or this has been recommended to them, showing the drifting of imagination in that direction. So an acquaintance met in Italy, who had exhausted Jerusalem and Baalbec,[42] and, like the man in the play, looked into Vesuvius and found

[40] No corroborative evidence is known for the existence either of this "disciple of Fourier" or of the "acquaintance met in Italy" whom Melville brings into the succeeding paragraph. Lacking other references to such striking characters in Melville's correspondence or journals, one suspects that he invented them in an effort to enliven his lecture and so to satisfy the demand by criticis of "Statues in Rome" for "something more modern and personal." Perhaps the reporter for the New York *Evening Post* had such instances as these in mind when he wrote that Melville "related some 'yarns' that bordered upon the 'Munchausen,' though they were undoubtedly true"!

[41] Presumably Mehevi, who according to *Typee*, ch. 25, "had from the first taken me as it were under his royal protection, and . . . continued to entertain for me the warmest regard."

[42] Baalbec is a ruined city in Lebanon, visited by Rolfe in *Clarel*, I, xxi.

"nothing in it," after an hour or two in conversation with me about the South Seas, started for an Italian port to sail for Rio en route to the Pacific; I hope that he has steered clear of the cannibals! The islands are admittedly good asylums—provided the natives do not object. But I can imagine the peril that a few ship-loads of Free Lovers would be in, on touching the Polynesian Isles. As for the plan suggested not long since, of making a home for the Mormons on some large island in Polynesia, where they could rear their pest houses and be at peace with their "institutions," the natives will resist their encroachments as did the Staten Islanders that of Quarantine. If sensible men wish to appropriate to themselves an uninhabited isle, that is all right, but I do not know of a populated island in the hundred millions of square miles embraced in the South Seas where these "fillibusterers" [43] would not be imperatively and indignantly expelled by the natives.

While our visionaries have been looking to the South Seas as a sort of Elysium, the Polynesians themselves have not been without their dream, their ideal, their Utopia in the West. As Ponce de Leon hoped to find in Florida the fountain of perpetual youth, so the mystic Kamapiikai left the western shore of the island of Hawaii, where he suffered with his restless philosophy, hoping to find the joy-giving fountain and the people like to the gods. Thus he sailed after the sinking sun, and, like all who go to Paradise, has not yet returned to cheer mankind with his discoveries. [44]

[43] "Fillibusterers": i.e., insurrectionists.

[44] Only two of the five reporters who included references to this passage on "the mystic Kamapiikai" in their accounts of the lecture attempted to spell the unfamiliar name. The Baltimore *American's* version is "Kamapuhai"; the Boston *Journal* reads "Cama Pecai." Melville's allusion derives from a passage in William Ellis, *Narrative of a Tour through Hawaii, or Owhyhee* (London, 1827), pp. 399–401, called to my attention by Dr. Kenneth P. Emory of the Bernice P. Bishop Museum in Honolulu. According to Ellis, in the natives' account of "The Voyage of Kamapiikai" they state that Kamapiikai "(child running, or climbing, the sea,—from *kama*, a child, *pii*, to run or climb, and *kai*, the sea) was priest of a temple in Kohala, dedicated to Kanenuiakea. The exact period of their history when he lived, we have not been able to ascertain; but it is added, that the god appeared to him in a vision, and revealed to him the existence, situation.

Another strange quest was that of Alvaro Mendaña, a bold Spanish captain, who stirred up such enthusiasm among the courtly Dons and Donnas of his time that many of them joined his expedition, in which he was sure he would find the Phoenician Ophir of King Hiram and bring from it more than the treasure stores with which Solomon had beautified his temple. After months and months of voyaging with hope deferred, the mines of Mammon were not found, and the poor Captain, dying, was buried in the solitude of an unfathomed sea. His followers returned to Peru, strongly impressed with the truth of those words of the Hebrew king, "Vanity of vanities; all is vanity." A group of the isles was called Solomon's in commemoration of the event.[45]

---

and distance of *Tahiti,* and directed him to make a voyage thither. In obedience to the communication, he immediately prepared for the voyage, and, with about forty of his companions, set sail from Hawaii in four double canoes. After an absence of fifteen years, they returned, and gave a most flattering account of Haupokane, the country which they had visited. We know of no island in the neighbourhood called by this name, which appears to be a compound of *Haupo,* sometimes a lap, and *Kane,* one of their gods. Among other things, they described the *one rauena,* a peculiar kind of sandy beach, well stocked with shell-fish, &c. The country, they said, was inhabited by handsome people, whose property was abundant, and the fruits of the earth delicious and plentiful. There was also a stream or fountain, which was called the *wai ora roa,* (water of enduring life.)

"Kamapiikai made three subsequent voyages to the country he had discovered, accompanied by many of the Sandwich Islanders. From the fourth voyage they never returned, and were supposed to have perished at sea, or to have taken up their permanent residence at Tahiti. Many were induced to accompany this priest to the country he visited, for the purpose of bathing in the life-giving waters, in consequence of the marvellous change they were reported to produce in those who used them; for it was said, that however infirm, emaciated, or deformed they might be when they went into the water, they invariably came out young, strong and handsome." For additional information on Melville's rather limited knowledge of Hawaiian mythology I am further indebted to Dr. Emory and also to the late Dr. Ralph Linton of Yale University, Mr. W. C. McKern of the Milwaukee Public Museum, and Professor Chandler W. Rowe of Lawrence College.

[45] Alvaro de Mendaña de Neyra (1541–1595) was nephew of the Viceroy of Peru and discoverer in 1567 of the Solomon Islands—"which still remain incognita," Melville had remarked in *Moby Dick,* ch. 57, "though once high-ruffed Mendanna trod them. . . ." Admiral Burney's *History,* I, 287, states that "the islands of Mendana were not revisited by Europeans till two centuries after their discovery, though the appellation

There are two places in the world where men can most effectively disappear—the city of London [46] and the South Seas. In cruising through the Pacific one frequently meets white men living as permanent residents, and others hope to return there some day. Many of the sailors who are supposed to be lost are thus really alive on islands of this ocean, though others, of course, lie in graves upon land or else have been eaten by

---

of the *Salomon Islands* encouraged romantic ideas concerning the riches to be found there. Lopez Vaz says . . . that 'the discoverer of these islands, named them the *Isles of Salomon*, to the end that the Spaniards, supposing them to be those isles from whence Solomon fetched gold to adorn the temple at *Jerusalem*, might be the more desirous to go and inhabit the same' (*Hakluyt*, Vol. III. p. 802.).'' In his account of Mendaña's second voyage, an unsuccessful attempt to return to the islands twenty-eight years later, Burney, II, 180, notes that this expedition "has been entitled a Voyage for the Discovery of the *Salomon Islands*, which perhaps may be defended by the intention of the undertaking; but this title, when compared with the fact, has a whimsical appearance. In this second voyage, the *Salomon Islands* were sought for far beyond where report had placed their discovery; and the voyage having concluded without their being found, has afforded occasion to remark, that what Mendana discovered in his First Voyage, he lost in his Second."

Melville had long been fascinated with the exploits of Mendaña, and later, in *Clarel*, III, xxix, he was to refer to the Pacific as "old Mendanna's sea." He had used two extracts from "Figueroa, the chronicler of Mendanna's voyage," in ch. 25 of *Typee*, dealing with Mendaña's discovery of the Marquesas in 1595 (cf. ch. 1); in *White-Jacket*, ch. 76, he mentioned "the Spanish cavalier Mendanna, of Lima," who "made love to the lady Isabella, as they voyaged in quest of the Solomon Islands, the fabulous Ophir, the Grand Cyclades. . . ." Burney states that Mendaña's wife, Doña Isabel Berreto, embarked with him on the second voyage, succeeding to the command of the expedition after her husband's death at the island of Santa Cruz on 18 October 1595. Mendaña was not buried at sea, however, as Melville declared, for the body was taken into one of the ships which later was found stranded in the Philippines with "all her people dead" (Burney, II, 172). Doña Isabel married again and eventually settled in Mexico; others of the party returned to Lima, where the Viceroy declined to furnish ships and men for a continuation of Mendaña's enterprise.

The quotation "Vanity of vanities . . ." (Ecclesiastes 1:2) was a favorite with Melville (see *Moby Dick*, ed. Mansfield and Vincent, 1951, note 422.25, pp. 800–801).

[46] This mention of London recalls the concluding words of ch. 25 of *Israel Potter*, where in discussing Israel's fate Melville had written of "its remoteness from relief and its depth of obscurity—London, adversity, and the sea, three Armageddons, which, at one and the same time, slay and secrete their victims."

the fish of the sea. It was my fortune on one occasion, after five months of weary navigation out of sight of land, to go ashore upon a secluded island in search of fruit. The pensive natives lay upon a bank, gazing listlessly, hardly turning on their mats at our landing, for they had seen white men before. And there, in that remote island, among its sixty or seventy lazy inhabitants, we found an American, settled down for life and to all appearances fully *naturalized*.[47] He was scarcely imposing in his breech cloth and the scanty shreds of tappa which hung from his shoulders as signals of distress, which, it appeared to us, the assiduous dilligence of three wives—for the ill-clothed gentleman was blessed with that number—might have remedied. In conversation this virtuous exile from civilization manifested no ordinary intelligence. He stated that he had fulfilled the post of Professor of Moral Philosophy in some college in his own land whose name he wisely withheld; he was now, however, contented to lead a quiet and lazy life, apart from the walks of restless ambition.

The modes in which seamen disappear in the South Seas are

[47] Here again it is impossible to say whether Melville's colorful "yarn" is true, partly true, or wholly invented. The circumstance of "five months . . . out of sight of land," mentioned in several newspaper versions of the passage, at first recalls the opening chapter of *Typee*, where the *Dolly* (*Acushnet*), described as "six months out of sight of land" with her "fresh provisions" exhausted, had also landed in search of fruit; she, however, had headed for the Marquesas and landed not at "a secluded island" but at Nukuheva. During Melville's later service aboard the whaler *Charles and Henry*, on an extended cruise from November 1842 until the following May, at least one landing for fruit appears to have been made. This took place at Rurutu, "a lone island" in the Tubuai group, where a dying white man was encountered (*Omoo*, ch. 33; Leyda, *Log*, I, 156), but he does not fit the present description. If Melville's meeting with the "professor" is authentic it may also date from this same period, even though no such story appears among allusions to the cruise in either *Omoo* or the opening chapters of *Mardi*. It should also be noted that a single version of the anecdote, that given in the New York *Evening Express*, describes the "professor's" countenance as tattooed—"so disfigured that . . . he would never have shown his face on Broadway" (compare note 50 below); another, that of the Milwaukee *Daily Wisconsin*, says he had taught in "some Eastern Institution of learning," and "Herr Honeytown" in his letter to the Yonkers *Examiner* termed him "a real white skinned veritable professor of humanity, or *something else* from Princeton or Cambridge. Probably our friend Kikiriki."

various and singular. Some fall overboard, some are left on shore by unprincipled captains, some are killed in brawls, and so on. Some join that class of adventurers known as the "beach-combers," who infest the shores of the Pacific. This cognomen is derived from the fact that they hover upon the beaches and seem always upon the point of embarking or disembarking, being ready for anything—for a war in Peru, a whaling voyage, or to marry a Polynesian princess.[48] They were among the first in California in the gold times, and afforded subjects for strange newspaper stories. They were also the occasion, as much as anything, of the Vigilance Committee there.

I have met many an old sailor in the South Seas not sufficiently educated to write who could tell tales about these regions stranger far than any that have ever yet been written. "Typee" and "Omoo" give scarcely a full idea of them except, perhaps, that part which tells of the long captivity in the valley of Typee. Had I time I should particularly like to repeat a traditional Polynesian legend, peculiarly adapted to the ladies of my audience, for it is a love legend of Kamekamehaha, Tahiti, and Otaheite, that was told by a king of one of these islands, and which has much of the grace, strangeness, and audacity of the Grecian fables.[49]

[48] So with Melville's tattooed "Lem Hardy" in *Omoo*, chs. 7–8: an Englishman who had deserted a trading brig in the Marquesas, Hardy became the military leader of a native tribe; "three days after landing, the exquisitely tattooed hand of a princess was his."

[49] The wording and placement of this sentence are conjectural. The Milwaukee *Daily Wisconsin*, whose long account of the lecture appears to involve little rearrangement of material, includes the following sentence at this point: "Spoke of a manuscript tradition he had seen that was told by a King of one of those Islands. It had much of the grace, strangeness and audacity of the Grecian fables." The Yonkers *Examiner*, which did not summarize the lecture, noted however that among Melville's topics was "a love story, peculiarly adapted to ladies, which he would not tell," and "Herr Honeytown," in his letter to the same paper, mentioned "that legend so interesting to the 'ladies of my audience, for it is a love legend of Kamekamehaha, Tahiti, and Otaheite.' " In the absence of other evidence it has been assumed that all three references are to the same allusion, and that it occurred at this point in the lecture. The Milwaukee writer, it might be added, is not referring here to the legend of Kamapiikai previously introduced, for he had already devoted two sentences to that subject in an earlier paragraph.

Some of these strange characters I have met exhibit sure vouchers of their stories in the shape of tattooing upon their persons. Many of them present such a horrid fright that they will never be caught showing their faces on Broadway! [50] The custom of tattooing is prompted by religion, love of novelty, and various other causes. Many of the natives think it is necessary for their eternal welfare, and, unless a man submits to be tattooed, he is looked upon as damned. In their opinion I may now be in peril, for I stoutly resisted the importunities of the native artists to be naturalized by marks on my face as from a gridiron.[51]

Different islanders have a different style of tattooing, so that one can often tell from this to what island a native belongs. The tattooing of the New Zealander and the Tahitian are thus as different as some styles of painting differ. A New Zealander presents a horrifying picture, but some of the Marquesan natives have a pleasant appearance. I have seen among them as graceful a young girl's foot and as delicately-turned ankle as

[50] At this point in the lecture, if not earlier (cf. note 47 above), Melville apparently employed the old device of appealing to his audiences by introducing appropriate local allusions. At Milwaukee, for example, according to the *Daily Wisconsin*, his words were: "showing their faces—well at the table of the Newhall House"; i.e., at the stylish local hotel where his friend Cramer, the *Wisconsin's* editor, long maintained an apartment. (See Frances Stover, "Milwaukee's Famous Blind Editor," Milwaukee *Journal*, 6 May 1955, Part I, p. 18.) Merrell Davis, "Melville's Midwestern Lecture Tour," p. 56, note, suggests that Melville was thinking here of the tattooed "Lem Hardy" of *Omoo* (see note 48 above).

[51] Melville had similarly explained in his discussion of tattooing in *Typee*, ch. 30, that the practice was "connected with their religion; and it was evident . . . that they were resolved to make a convert of me." Ch. 8 of *Omoo* is also devoted to tattooing, a subject discussed by James Baird, *Ishmael*, pp. 113–116, as "the most impressive visual art which Melville encountered in the Pacific."

Of this section of the lecture the Yonkers *Examiner* observed sarcastically that Melville's "account of tattooing was fine, and corroborated in every particular by Lieut. Wilkes in his Narrative of the U.S. Exploring Expedition." J. H. Birss, who reprinted the *Examiner's* review in his "Herman Melville Lectures in Yonkers," *American Book Collector*, V (February 1934), 50–52, offered there the suggestion that Melville himself had cited Wilkes' volumes in the lecture (as previously in *Omoo* and *Moby Dick*); it appears more likely that the reviewer had simply made a shrewd guess in identifying one of Melville's literary sources.

those of the Grecian girls whose duplicate statues adorn the galleries of Europe. The men, too, have splendid figures, with symmetrical and columnar legs.

Tattooing is sometimes, like dress, an index of character, to be worn as an ornament which will never wear off, and which can not be pawned, lost, or stolen. Thus in the Georgian Isles the dandies wear stripes up and down their legs like pantaloons, and the dames have characters on their skins for jewelry —on their fingers, about their necks, and so on. Indeed, that style has many advantages for nuptial rings, since it can never be removed. Some of the robust islanders have tattooing of military insignia, others of eatables, and others of school-boy trinkets; and all reveal the character of the individual who wears them.

I would direct the gas to be turned down, and repeat in a whisper the mysterious rites of the "taboo," [52] but the relation would so far transcend any of Mrs. Radcliffe's stories in the element of the horrible that I would not willingly afflict any one with its needless recital.[53]

[52] Davis, "Melville's Midwestern Lecture Tour," p. 56, note, compares *Typee*, ch. 30, where Melville had stated that he "perceived every hour the effects of this all-controlling power, without in the least comprehending it." Davis finds some evidence in certain of the newspaper accounts for taking this passage as "representing the usual conclusion of the lecture" (p. 51), but the majority of the reports clearly indicate that, as in the present version, Melville ended with a survey of the future prospects of Polynesia and the possibility of annexing various islands to the United States.

[53] According to the Yonkers *Examiner,* Melville here "alluded to some legends he had plucked from the native lore, which would cause excellent Mrs. Radcliffe to shake in her stockings, and, told by the dim gas light, would force even the bravest heart to

'quake
And tremble like a leaf of Aspen green.' "

This quotation from *The Faerie Queene,* I, ix, 51, may well have occurred in the lecture itself; Melville's *Piazza Tales* had recently illustrated his fondness for Spenserian allusions. He had referred to "romantic Mrs. Radcliffe" in "The Apple-Tree Table" (1856), and to "her curdling romances" in his journal while in Jerusalem in 1857 (Horsford ed., p. 151); in *Billy Budd,* ch. 11, he was later to mention "that prime element of Radcliffian romance, *the mysterious.*" On Melville's interest in her writings see Newton Arvin, "Melville and the Gothic Novel," *New England Quarterly,* XXII (March 1949), 33–48.

By contrast, the modern progress in some of these islands is seen in the publication there of newspapers; but on close inspection I have often found them to be conducted by Americans, English, or French. I have recently met with a Honolulu paper, the Honolulu "Advertiser," which is a mark of the prosperity of the Sandwich Islands, being almost a counterpart of the London "Times" with its advertisements, arrivals and departures of vessels, and so on—and that, too, where not long since the inhabitants were cannibals. But now Americans and other foreigners are there, and lately a suggestion has been reported to abolish the Hawaiian language in their schools and exclude those children who speak it. I threw down the paper on reading this, exclaiming, "Are they to give up all that binds them together as a nation or race—their language? Then are they indeed blotted out as a people." So the result of civilization, at the Sandwich Islands and elsewhere, is found productive to the civilizers, destructive to the civilizees. It is said to be compensation—a very philosophical word; [54] but it appears to be very much on the principle of the old game, "You lose, I win": good philosophy for the winner.

The future prospects of Polynesia are uncertain and will only admit of fanciful speculation. [55] Projects have recently been set on foot for annexing Hawaii and the Georgian Islands to the United States, and meanwhile the whalemen of Nantucket and the Westward ho! of California are every day getting them more and more annexed. I shall close with the earnest wish that adventurers from our soil and from the lands of Europe will abstain from those brutal and cruel vices which disgust even savages with our manners, while they turn an earthly paradise

[54] As in *Pierre*, Bk. XX, i, Melville is clearly hitting at Emerson and other "amiable philosophers of either the 'Compensation,' or 'Optimist' school. They deny that any misery is in the world, except for the purpose of throwing the fine *povertiresque* element into its general picture." The portrait of Mark Winsome in *The Confidence-Man* is in a similar vein.

[55] "Their prospects are hopeless," Melville had written of the Tahitians in *Omoo*, ch. 49, holding that "like other uncivilized beings, brought into contact with Europeans, they must here remain stationary until utterly extinct."

into a pandemonium. As a philanthropist in general, and a friend to the Polynesians in particular, I hope that these Edens of the South Seas,[56] blessed with fertile soils and peopled with happy natives, many being yet uncontaminated by the contact of civilization, will long remain unspoiled in their simplicity, beauty, and purity. And as for annexation, I beg to offer up an earnest prayer—and I entreat all present and all Christians to join me in it—that the banns of that union should be forbidden until *we* have found for ourselves a civilization morally, mentally, and physically higher than one which has culminated in almshouses, prisons, and hospitals.

[56] Compare Rolfe's words in *Clarel*, III, xxix, as he reminisces of a youthful adventure (like Melville's in *Typee*):

> "Where Eden, isled, empurpled glows
> In old Mendanna's sea. . . ."

TRAVELING

Its Pleasures, Pains, and Profits

[In the absence of a manuscript of Melville's third lecture the present text is a reprinting, with minor emendations of spelling and punctuation, of the sole newspaper report: that in the Cambridge, Massachusetts, *Chronicle* of 25 February 1860. The *Chronicle's* summary obviously represents only a portion of the full lecture. The manuscript is unmentioned in correspondence of the Melville family later than a letter of 4 January 1860 from Melville's sister Augusta to Catherine Gansevoort ("I read it in M S. . . ."). The newspaper version was first reprinted, also with emendations, in J. H. Birss, " 'Travelling': A New Lecture by Herman Melville," *New England Quarterly,* VII (December 1934), 725–728.

There is some indication that Melville himself used a longer title than either "Travel," found in the heading of the *Chronicle's* report, or "Traveling." In Flushing, New York, where he delivered the same lecture on 7 November 1859, it was advertised under the full title given above (Birss, p. 727, note); the phrasing "Travel, its pains, pleasures and profits" was used by John C. Hoadley in a letter of 30 November 1859 when writing to a business associate in search of a lecture engagement for Melville, his brother-in-law. There was no newspaper publicity concerning the last reading of the lecture at South Danvers, Massachusetts, on 14 February 1860. For extracts from the letters of Hoadley and Augusta Melville see Leyda, *Log,* II, 609.]

I_N the isolated cluster of mountains called Greylock, there lies a deep valley named The Hopper,[1] which is a huge sort of verdant dungeon among the hills. Suppose a person should be born there, and know nothing of what lay beyond, and should after a time ascend the mountain, with what delight would

[1] In the opening sketch of *Piazza Tales* (1856), "The Piazza," of which this lecture is curiously reminiscent, Melville had described the view of Greylock from his home near Pittsfield, mentioning in particular "a hopper-like hollow." His journal entry for 26 February 1856 likens the Roman Coliseum to the "Hopper of Greylock" (see "Statues in Rome," note 27).

he view the landscape from the summit! The novel objects
spread out before him would bewilder and enchant him. Now
it is in this very kind of experience that the prime pleasure of
travel consists. Every man's home is in a certain sense a "Hopper," which however fair and sheltered, shuts him in from the
outer world. Books of travel do not satisfy; they only stimulate
the desire to see. To be a good traveler, and derive from travel
real enjoyment, there are several requisites. One must be
young, care-free, and gifted with geniality and imagination,[2]
for if without these last he may as well stay at home. Then, if
from the North, his first landing should be on a fine day, in a
tropical climate, with palm trees and gaily dressed natives in
view, and he will have the full pleasure of novelty. If without
the above qualities, and of a somewhat sour nature besides, he
might be set down even in Paradise and have no enjoyment,
for joy is for the joyous nature. To be a good lounger,—that is
essential, for the traveler can derive pleasure and instruction
from the long galleries of pictures, the magnificent squares, the
cathedrals, and other places that require leisurely survey, only
through this quality. The pleasure of leaving home, care-free,
with no concern but to enjoy, has also as a pendant the pleasure of coming back to the old hearthstone, the home to which,
however traveled, the heart still fondly turns, ignoring the
burden of its anxieties and cares.

One must not anticipate unalloyed pleasure. Pleasure, pain,
and profit are all to be received from travel. As Washington
Irving has remarked, the sea-voyage, with its excitements, its
discomforts, and its enforced self-discipline, is a good preparation for foreign travel.[3] The minute discomforts, the afflictions
of Egypt and Italy, in the shape of fleas and other insects, we

---

[2] Geniality was a quality that Melville continued to celebrate in such
later prose pieces as his Burgundy Club sketches, written after the completion of *Clarel;* as for imagination, he had noted at the back of his Mediterranean journal (Horsford ed., p. 268): *"More imagination* wanted *at* Rome
than at home to appreciate the place."

[3] "To an American visiting Europe," Irving had observed in *The
Sketch-Book* ("The Voyage"), "the long voyage he has to make is an excellent preparative."

will pass over lightly, though they by no means pass lightly over the traveler. A great grievance from first to last is the passport. You soon learn by official demands, what becomes to you an adage,—Open passport, open purse; and its endless crosses at the close of your travels remind you of the crosses it has cost you all the way through. The persecutions and extortions of guides, not only the rough and robber-like, but those who combine the most finished politeness with the most delicate knavery, are another serious drawback on your pleasure, though when we think of the thousand times worse extortions practised on the immigrants here, we acknowledge Europe does not hold all the rogues. There is one infallible method of escape from this annoyance: full pockets.[4] Pay the rascals, laugh at them, and escape. Honest and humane men are also to be found, but not in an overwhelming majority.

For the profit of travel: in the first place, you get rid of a *few* prejudices. The native of Norway who goes to Naples finds the climate so delicious as almost to counterbalance the miseries of government. The Spanish matador, who devoutly believes in the proverb, "Cruel as a Turk," goes to Turkey, sees that people are kind to all animals; sees docile horses, never balky, gentle, obedient, exceedingly intelligent, yet *never beaten;* [5] and comes home to his bull-fights with a very differ-

---

[4] To N. P. Willis, Melville had written on 14 December 1849: "I very much doubt whether Gabriel enters the portals of Heaven without a fee to Peter the porter—so impossible is it to travel without money" (*Log*, I, 347). In his copy of Vol. VIII of Francis J. Child's *English and Scottish Ballads* (8 vols., Boston, 1854–1857), acquired in September 1859 (now in the Harvard College Library), Melville marked a passage of "George Barnwell" which may well have been in his mind here:

> "For without money, George,
> A man is but a beast:
> But bringing money, thou shalt be
> Always my welcome guest. . . ."

[5] This passage anticipates lines spoken by Ungar in Melville's *Clarel,* IV, ix:

> "As cruel as a Turk: Whence came
> That proverb old as the crusades?
> From Anglo-Saxons. What are they?
> Let the horse answer, and blockades
> Of medicine in civil fray!"

ent impression of his own humanity. The stock-broker goes to Thessalonica and finds infidels more honest than Christians; the teetotaller finds a country in France where all drink and no one gets drunk; the prejudiced against color finds several hundred millions of people of all shades of color, and all degrees of intellect, rank, and social worth, generals, judges, priests and kings, and learns to give up his foolish prejudice.

Travel liberalizes us also in minor points. Our notions of dress become much modified, and comfort is studied far more than formerly. The beard also, of late years, from our traveled experience, is admitted to its rightful degree of favor.[6] In the adornment of our houses, frescoes have taken the place of dead white. God is liberal of color; so should man be.

Travel to a large and generous nature is as a new birth. Its legitimate tendency is to teach profound personal humility, while it enlarges the sphere of comprehensive benevolence till it includes the whole human race.

Among minor benefits is that of seeing for one's self all striking natural or artificial objects, for every individual sees differently according to his idiosyncrasies.[7] One may perhaps ac-

---

Melville's own feeling toward horses has already been observed (see "Statues in Rome," note 35).

[6] Melville's partiality to his "own brown beard" is expressed in *White-Jacket* (1850), ch. 85: "The Great Massacre of the Beards." Hawthorne, seeing Melville in Liverpool in 1856, noted in his journal that "as he wears his beard and moustache, and so needs no dressing-case—nothing but a tooth-brush—I do not know a more independent personage. He learned his travelling habits by drifting about, all over the South Sea, with no other clothes or equipage than a red flannel shirt and a pair of duck trowsers. Yet we seldom see men of less criticizable manners than he." The comment, from Hawthorne's *English Note-books*, is quoted in *Log*, II, 531.

[7] "But in gazing at such scenes" as that of the breaching whale, Melville had written in *Moby Dick*, ch. 86, "it is all in all what mood you are in; if in the Dantean, the devils will occur to you; if in that of Isaiah, the archangels." Nature, he added in *Pierre*, Bk. XXIV, iv, supplies an alphabet whereby "each man reads his own peculiar lesson according to his own peculiar mind and mood." So in "The Piazza" the young Marianna confesses to the narrator her weariness of a view which had once greatly delighted her. Answering his question as to what has changed, she replies: " 'I don't know,' while a tear fell; 'but it is not the view, it is Marianna.' "

quire the justest of all views by reading and comparing all
writers of travels. Great men do this, and yet yearn to travel.
Richter longed to behold the sea. Schiller thought so earnestly
of travel that it filled his dreams with sights of other lands.
Dr. Johnson had the same longing, with exaggerated ideas of
the distinction to be reflected from it. It is important to be
something of a linguist to travel to advantage; at least to speak
French fluently. In the Levant, where all nations congregate,
unpretending people speak half a dozen languages, and a person who thought himself well educated at home is often
abashed at his ignorance there.

It is proposed to have steam communication direct between
New York and some Mediterranean port. Then the traveler
would enter the old world by the main portal, instead of as
now, through a side door.

England, France, the Mediterranean,—it is needless to
dwell on their attractions. But as travel indicates change and
novelty, and change and novelty are often essential to healthy
life, let a narrower range not deter us. A trip to Florida will
open a large field of pleasant and instructive enjoyment. Go
even to Nahant, if you can go no farther—*that* is travel. To an
invalid it is travel, that is, change, to go to other rooms in the
house.[8] The sight of novel objects, the acquirement of novel
ideas, the breaking up of old prejudices, the enlargement of
heart and mind,—are the proper fruit of rightly undertaken
travel.

Ch. 99 of *Moby Dick,* "The Doubloon," also well illustrates Melville's
point.

[8] Melville may well have been drawing on recent experience here, his
own health having given cause for concern to himself and his family ever
since the completion of *Pierre* (1852). The correspondence of his relatives
and friends in 1858 and 1859 frequently mentions his recurrent illness.
"Herman Melville is not well," wrote his neighbor Sarah Morewood on
21 November 1859 (*Log,* II, 609), "—do not call him moody, he is ill."

APPENDIX

1. Melville's Notebook of Lecture Engagements

Melville recorded his lecture engagements and fees in a small notebook, 4⅞ by 7⅛ inches, which is now in the Harvard College Library (MS Am 188, No. 376). On the front cover of the notebook, which is bound in blue cardboard, is a paper label bearing the notation "Lecture Engagements 1857–8–9–1860." Inside the front cover are two brief memoranda: "Herald stops Jan. 7ᵗʰ 1854" and "Brown owes me 75 cts."

The facsimiles which follow reproduce seven of the eight pages of the notebook, the eighth being without entries.

PAGE 1. "T. D. S." is unidentified. On 14 September 1850 Melville bought his Pittsfield farm, Arrowhead, from Dr. John Brewster. The other notations refer to the lecture season of 1857–58.

PAGES 2 AND 3. The entries record tentative lecture engagements for 1857–58.

PAGE 4. The first address is that of Richard Tobias Greene, the "Toby" of Melville's *Typee*. Melville's relationship to Archibald T. Cochran of Louisville has not been established.

PAGE 5. Concerning Charles Wells of Cincinnati, see Chapter 2, note 28.

PAGE 6. Melville's lecture engagements and fees, 1857–58. A printed transcription with omissions supplied and errors corrected faces the facsimile of the original.

PAGE 7. Melville's lecture engagements and fees, 1858–59, 1859–60.

Lectures - 1857-8-9, 1860

R R R 2050. May 1st 1857. For five years. Worcester

Brigstock's Note (1500) is dated Sept. 1st 1850.

at Boston after Concord lec	15. 00
few days after	9. 00
Before going to Montreal	19. 00
at N. H. on leaving	19. 00

1 00
5 0
3 0
2 4 0

2
1857

8 ✗ Cleveland   Night of Sunday.
                         Jan 11th R
                              Fixed

✗9 Detroit — Early part of January. 12th ✗
                    Jan 12th Fixed

6
✗ Auburn   First week in Jan. (Fixed)
                    Jan 5th

     Wilmington   End of Mason Last week
     ~~Jan. 10th 1st week of July~~
       ~~January 15th~~

1858
✗ Ithaca   First week in January Jan 7th
   ~~Syracuse~~   (Fixed)

✗ 11 Rochester   — Feb 18th (~~Fixed~~)
                         Fixed

       ~~Detroit~~

       ~~Rockford~~   About middle of Jan 5 no.

Jan 22? ?
   Clarksville – Tenn.   Middle or later part of
                            January.

3

3 Boston Mercantile Library — Nothing before or after

X Shackopy. — Nothing after dec. 2ᵈ (Fixed)

5 Newton near Newington Institute — Middle or latter part of December Dec. 30ᵗʰ Fixed
~~About the new life. Beginning of January.~~

12
4 New Bedford — Last of may to be sent.
~~of Dec. 9ᵗʰ ?~~
1858 Feby 23ʳᵈ Fixed ~~~~

10
X Charlestown — ~~After Thursday~~ a late in the season Feb. 10ᵗʰ
Fixed

Xᵃ Concord (N. H.) November ~~Fate~~ 24ᵗʰ
Fixed

X¹ Lawrence November 23ᵈ
Fixed

4 Montreal Dec. 10ᵗʰ

Malden ~~Dec. 28ᵗʰ~~ ?

Call on A. D. Lawson 70 State St.
after 1ˢᵗ Jan — see note

4 - Toby's address -

166 Water St - Sandusky - Ohio -
"Cosmopolitan Art Association"
his brother-in-law connected
with it named Derby (C. L.)

Archibald S. Cochran
Jefferson St - between 7th & 8th
streets - south side - ~~Cincinnati~~
Louisville, Ky.

(376)

Feby 2d. Cincinnati ? Charles Wells

Lectures   1858 - $9

6

Nov 23ʳᵈ	Lawrence —	—
" 24ᵗʰ	Concord	30.00
Decʳ 2ᵈ	Boston	40.00
" 10ᵗʰ	Montreal	50.00
" 30ᵗʰ	Saratoga	—
30ᵗʰ	New Haven	50.00
Janʳ 5ᵗʰ	Auburn	40.00 1859
" 7ᵗʰ	Ithaca	50.00
" 11ᵗʰ	Cleveland	50.00
12ᵗʰ	Detroit	50.00
22ᵈ	Clarksville	75.00 1858
	Chillicothe ~~Louisville~~	40.00
	Cincinnati	50.00
Felʸ 10	Charlestown	20.00
Felʸ 23	Rochester	50.00
" 23ᵈ	New Bedford	50.00
	Malden	645.00
Travelling Expenses —		221.30
		423.70

LECTURES 1857-8

[A corrected transcript of Page 6 of the notebook]

Nov 23d	Lawrence	....	
" 24th	Concord	30.00	
Decr 2d	Boston	40.00	
" 10th	Montreal	50.00	
" 30th [21]	Saratoga	....	
" 30th	New Haven	50.00	
Jan 5th	Auburn	40.00	1858
" 7th	Ithaca	50.00	
" 11th	Cleveland	50.00	
" 12th	Detroit	50.00	
" 22d	Clarksville	75.00	1858
[Feb 3]	Chillicothe	40.00	
[Feb 2]	Cincinnati	50.00	
Feby 10	Charlestown	20.00	
Feby 23 [18]	Rochester	50.00	
" 23d	New Bedford	50.00	
		....	
		645.00	
		....	
Travelling Expenses		221.30	
		....	
		423.70	

Dec 6th	Yonkers N.Y.	30 00
14th	Pittsfield Mass	50.00
Jan 31st	Boston 1859	50.00
Feby 7th	New York	55.00
8th	Baltimore Md	100.00
24th	Chicago	50.00
25th	Milwaukee	50 00
29th	Rockford Ill	50.00
March 2d	Quincy Ill	23.50
March 18	Lynn Mass - 2 lec.	60.00
		518.50

	1859-60	
Nov 7th	Flushing L.I.	30.00
Feby 14th	Danvers - Mass	25.00
21st	Cambridgeport Mass	55.00

2. Melville's Memoranda of Travel Expenses 1857-58

Kept with the notebook of lecture engagements are Melville's memoranda of travel expenses during his first lecture season, 1857–58, jotted mostly in pencil on separate and dissimilar sheets of paper. The entries on these sheets as arranged in sequence are transcribed here substantially as Melville wrote them, although the difficulties of his handwriting have not always been solved beyond possible question. Little editorial apparatus has seemed appropriate or necessary. A few canceled words of no importance have been silently omitted; careted insertions have been included without comment; some expansions and explanations have been sparingly added in square brackets when the convenience of the reader appeared to demand them.

Fare from Boston to Montreal	$9.
Apples	3
Dinner	42
R.R. Guide	15
Lodging & Breakft at Rut[land]	1.
Dinner, Lodge, & Breakft at R[ouse's] P[oint]	1.50
Telegraph fm R. P. to M[ontreal]	35
Carri[a]ge fm F[?] to Steamer	35
Fare fr. Mont. to Sar[atoga Springs]	7.50
Supper at Essex Junct[ion, Vt.]	14
2 lodges & 3 meals at R[utland?]	2.50
Post. Stamp (Mama)	1.
Presents for Uncle, (Tobacco & pipes, 12.)	3.25
Fare from Saratoga & Augusta's [Melville's sister]	2.20
6 Fares to & from Saratoga Spgs (Lecture)	2.40
Coffee & Blacking	67
Candy	10
Fare fr. Sar[atoga Springs] to Albany	1.40
D[itt]o to Springfield	2.80
Bill at Do	1.25
Fare to N. Haven	1.75
(Lizzie took—	1.50

Gratuity to Servt	25	
Dinner at Albany	37½	
Tea on R.R.	18	
Books—	6.62	
Rubbers	80	[$48.48½]

EXPENCES New Haven to New York

[$2.00 added below]	$	
N. York to Albany	$2.	
Albany to Auburn	3.50	
Supper at Albany	50	
Lodge & Break. at L[ittle] Falls	65	
(Expences at Auburn hotel paid by [Young Men's] Ass[ociation])		
Omnibus at Auburn	12	
Aub to Syracuse	65	
Syracus to Binghampton	2.25	
Bing. to Owego	.65	
Owego to Ithaca	1.20	
Lodge at Bing.	50	
Supper at Syracus	35	
Break. at Owego	50	
Buss at Syracuse	10	
Hack, Buffalo	25	
Cane "	37	
Bill at Ithaca	2.50	
Washing "	50	
Ithaca to Owego	1.20	
Lodge at Owego	50	
Owego to Hornersville [Hornell, N. Y.?]	2.65	
Horn'r. to Buffalo	2.50	
Break. at Hornersville	10	
Bill at Buffalo (Ale)	4.37	
Buss Do	25	
Tobacco	6	
Buffalo to Cleveland	5.	
Dinner on R.R.	12	
Buss at Cleveland	25	
Bill at "	1.50	
Buss "	25	
Cleveland to Detroit	4.50	

Carried Over $39.84

Dinner & Tea on R.R.	.60
Bill at Detroit	2.
Detroit to Toledo	2.
Toledo to Evansville (450 miles)	12.
Supper & Lodge at Do	1.
Dinner at Lafayette	.40
Tobacco	. 5
Buss at Do	.25
" " Greencastle (Mud to the hub)	.25
" " "	.25
Lodge & Break at "	.75
Dinner at Terra Haute	.50
Buss at Vincennes	.25
" " "	.25
Supper " " (Ale)	. 5
Lodge & Break at "	1.
Buss at Evansville	.25
Bill at "	2.50
Evansville to Smithland (River)	3.
Bill at — " (damned rascal)	1.50
From Smithland to Clarksville	5.
To Nashville	1.
Hat "	5.
Neckerchief	2.
Hair cut	.25
Break & Dinner at Nashville	1.
Nash. to Clarksville	2.50
Bill at Do (landlord fat & honest)	2.50
Washing Do (40 cts ovechge)	1.
Porter (Nut Brown Stout, but stout black)	25
	$89.19

Carried Over	89.19
Clarksville to Paducah	$5.
Dinner & Supper at Do (1st Day)	1.
Cigar (Dismal Sunday night)	5
" at Owego (N.Y.)	5
Lodge. Break. & Dinner at Paducah (2d Day)	1.50
Bath (Buffalo)	.37
From Paducah to Louisville ([Steamer] U[nited] S[tates])	8.

Boot black (boat)	10
Car from Portland to Louisville	10
Solace—(Anderson's)	10
Bill at Louisville	1.25
From Louisville to Cincinnati	2.50
Cigar & Candy	.20
Theatre at Cincinnati ["Mazeppa; or, The Wild Horses of Tartary," and "Karmel, the Scout; or, The Rebel of the Jerseys," at the National Theatre]	.50
Telegraph to Chil[l]icothe	1.
	$110.91

Tobacco—Toll—	.10
Bill at Cincinnati } $4—.75—5.50. }	10.25
3 Newspapers	15
From Cincin. to Chil[l]- icothe	2.90
Buss at Cincin.	25
" " Chillicothe	15
Bill at Do	1.50
Fare from Chill. to Co- lum[bus?]	2.50
[*Note transposed fig- ures:*]	110.19
	$127.99
[*Error for*	$128.71]

Carried over—	$127.99
Breakfast (Stage)	40
Dinner (Zanesville)	25
Bridge Toll (Wheeling)	10
Bill at Wheeling	1.
Baggage Master	10
Breakfast (R.R)	2
Police Gazette	5
Dinner Pittsburgh	75
Cigar Do	5
Ale Do	10
Supper Do	35
Breakfast (Harrisburgh)	10

Dinner Philad[elphia]	18
Supper (boat)	50
Omnibus N[ew] Y[ork]	6
Cars 3d Av. Sunday	10
Baggage Master (Pittsburgh)	10
	$132.20
[*Error for*	$132.92]

New-York to Boston	5.
Circleville (Ohio) to New York.	18.65
	$155.85
[*Error for*	$156.57]

Recd from Lectures	$355
Travelling Expences &c	155.85
On Hand—New York—	214.50
	$370.35

[*Carried forward*]	155.85
Dinner—	$ .27
Supper	.10
Hack	50
Lodging	1.

[*Not added in:*]		
George	30.00	
Gaiters	2.00	
(add ex NH to NY)		2.00
	,	$159.72
[*Error for*		$160.44]

Cane	.37	
Hat	5.00	
Neckerchief	2.00	
	7.37	7.37
		$152.35
[*Error for*		$152.07]
[*Grand total, corrected:*		$200.55½]

Index

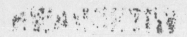